MW00850270

Homeschooling Quick Start

Homeschooling Quick Start

What You Need to Know

SUSANNE GIBBS

OPEN UNIVERSE
Chicago

To find out more about Open Universe and Carus Books, visit our website at www.carusbooks.com.

Copyright © 2024 by Carus Books

All rights reserved. No part of this publication may be reproduced, stored in a retrieval system, or transmitted, in any form or by any means, electronic, mechanical, photocopying, recording, or otherwise, without the prior written permission of the publisher, Carus Books, 315 Fifth Street, Peru, Illinois 61354.

Printed and bound in the United States of America. Printed on acid-free paper.

Homeschooling Quick Start: What You Need to Know

ISBN: 978-1-63770-053-2

This book is also available as an e-book (978-1-63770-054-9).

Library of Congress Control Number: 2023942049

Contents

How to Use This Book

I have known families who were faced with a sudden crisis and had to learn enough to begin homeschooling from scratch within a week. They went on to homeschool without a hitch. It is possible!

I have designed this book so that it can help you do that, if necessary. But if you want to take a few weeks, or months, or a whole year, to consider your options, this book will offer you everything you need to know. Don't rush if you don't have to.

One aim of this book is to give you the information you need *fast*. The chapters do not build on each other which means that you can begin by skipping immediately to the chapter that is most urgent for you. Let's say you want to know about the state laws you have to comply with (there are no federal laws regulating homeschooling), you can go directly to Chapter 2.

If you have unpleasant memories of your own school days, with some subjects, say math or science, or literature, and have a bad feeling about your own ability to teach these subjects, you can go straight to Chapters 9, 10, or 6—the chapters on Math, Science, and Literature.

As you think about your ability to teach, remember that many professional schoolteachers are not experts on the subjects they teach. They follow a curriculum and learn the subject while teaching it; you can do the same.

You can find a curriculum for any subject online, and even for free. With the help of the curriculum choices I list in this book, you can do this within a few minutes if necessary. Part of what this book does is to give you vital information, but it also lists books and websites that will give you more detailed information, including many free resources. I have personally used or thoroughly vetted all these sources, except in rare cases where I mention that fact.

This book also gives you some juicy morsels you won't find anywhere else, recollections and insights I gained from homeschooling my own kids, talking with hundreds of other homeschooling parents and students, and thinking and talking with educators about homeschooling, over more than two decades.

This book naturally reflects my own Christian worldview, yet it will be useful for non-Christian homeschoolers who're looking for a practical guide. I have known Muslim, atheist, and agnostic homeschoolers and can testify to the common essence of homeschooling which works for everyone regardless of their worldview.

1

Why Homeschool?

A friend of mine wanted to start homeschooling her daughter mid-year because there was much bullying going on at school. Dealing with this situation was creating enormous stress for the family.

This was a very real and immediate problem that needed to be addressed quickly. I helped her choose a teaching philosophy, pointed her toward basic curriculum choices, and within less than a week, she was set.

The intensity of the school situation helped move their family forward in making choices and acting on behalf of their daughter. They were able to begin homeschooling within the week. And I was super excited for them. This example shows how quickly you can begin to homeschool your child. It is also a great illustration of parents taking responsibility and action to ensure their child's education is on the best track possible.

Knowing Your Reasons for Homeschooling

When I look back and think about all my friends who were and still are homeschooling their children, I realize that every one of them had a firm reason or two why they chose this kind of education for their children. These reasons might have changed from time to time, but they helped keep the momentum going.

The day will come when you or someone else will question your decision. How will you stay motivated and continue to believe that you made the right decision? How are you going to combat these 'arrows' of doubt when they come your way?

Having one or more solid reasons worked out ahead of time is what will get you through these struggles. Some people print them out and hang them up as a reminder.

Some Common Reasons for Homeschooling

1. Parents (or Guardians) Are Responsible for Their Children's Education

Right at the top is the reason that probably caused you to think about homeschooling in the first place. You feel responsible for your child's education and want to make sure it's done properly. (When I say 'parents', I always include guardians or other parent-like figures.)

a. Parents actively choose the type of school, either public, private, or homeschool.

b. If public or private school is chosen, parents know and support their child's principal and teacher and understand the basic morality that is being taught in the classroom.

c. Parents have a good feel for the atmosphere in the classroom.

d. If parents find big problems with the morality or atmosphere of the classroom, the child should attend a different school. (I'm not talking about small issues like tattling or gossiping, but content of sexual nature, bullying, or extremist political indoctrination.)

e. If homeschool is chosen, parents personally choose the curriculum and teachers.

f. Each year parents evaluate and re-evaluate the school choice for their child to see if changes need to be made.

It's difficult to know what exactly is taught in the classroom of any school. But homeschooling is not always possible for everyone. So, if you're thinking about homeschooling in the future and have kids in school right now, become involved in your children's school so that you can inform yourself about what's going on.

2. SHORT-TERM AND LONG-TERM HOMESCHOOLING

Are your reasons for homeschooling addressing short term issues or are they more long-term? Short-term reasons can be helpful if you are just wanting to check it out or have an urgent life change, such as illness, sports, or travel, that makes short term-homeschooling a viable option.

3. SAFETY CONCERNS

Are you concerned for your children's safety, after yet another shooting in the news? A safe environment is by far the most important prerequisite for any setting that involves children, be it school, home, or anywhere else.

4. MORAL INSTRUCTION

The NCES did a study in 2019 documenting the reasons paremts choose to homeschool. Around 75 percent of parents expressed the desire to provide moral instruction for their children. That makes sense if you take a deeper look at the underlying reason for safety problems.

5. I DON'T LIKE THE SCHOOLS AROUND ME

Another reason you may choose to homeschool could be that you're dissatisfied with your local public or private schools. In that same study, almost three fourths of homeschooling parents list this dissatisfaction as one of their reasons to homeschool.

6. FAMILY, RELIGION, NON-TRADITIONAL PHILOSOPHIES

Almost three quarters of the parents also list the desire to focus on life as a family as one of their reasons to homeschool.

Almost 60 percent choose to homeschool for religious reasons, and nearly 55 percent of the parents want to use non-traditional teaching philosophies to educate their children.

7. SPECIAL NEEDS

Many families choose to homeschool because their child needs special attention and a unique learning environment, and they feel that the best way to accomplish this is the home.

Perhaps your child has a diagnosis that makes it more convenient to keep her at home.

Despite all the exhaustion that accompanies family life, I encourage you to consider homeschooling your special needs child for the following reasons:

a. The home is the safest and most comfortable location for your child. Being in a school setting for many hours, and very likely with other children on the spectrum, may not be ideal since so many events take place outside your control and knowledge.

b. You will know instantly if there is any change in behavior or other area in your child's life.

c. You can adjust the level of education to your child's specific needs instead of relying on the classroom setting of varying levels of special education levels.

d. You can be in tune with your child's therapist and practice assignments with more precision since your child is with you for most of the day every day.

If it's too difficult to homeschool right now, a school environment may be the best option for a period of time, and you can assess the situation again in a year or two.

8. TRIP SCHOOLING

Some parents have the opportunity to travel frequently, and they choose to take their kids on these trips and do 'trip schooling'. This is a wonderful opportunity to teach children about the world with all its fascination and its problems.

9. JOBS AND SPECIAL INTERESTS

One of my favorite reasons to homeschool teenagers is that the flexibility of their school schedule makes it possible for them to pursue interests and jobs which they would otherwise not be able to do.

Allowing our children to work for pay (within reason) is invaluable and teaches a wealth of life skills that cannot be learned in any school setting.

Homeschool Statistics Are in Your Favor

Here are some encouraging statistics regarding homeschooled kids. Studies done by the National Home Education Research Institute (NHERI) show that, on average, homeschooled students perform better than their public-school peers on standardized tests with the mean score at least in the eightieth percentile.

A different part of that study revealed the statistical relationship between the level of education of the homeschooling parent and the academic achievement of their homeschooled children: children whose parents did not have college education out-performed their public-school peers. (These are homeschooling parents without a college education who might not seem qualified in the eyes of the state, and sometimes not in their own eyes, either.)

Also, homeschooled children whose parents (either one or both) have a teaching certificate do not perform better than children whose parents do not have a teaching certificate. As a matter of fact, the research showed a slight advantage on the side of the children whose parents were not teacher-certified.

Your Reasons Help Create Momentum

Are you finding some of these reasons compelling? Which of these resonate with you the most? Thinking about the reasons why we choose to homeschool will put us on the right track to create momentum.

Starting on the homeschool journey is very exciting. And depending on the number, age, and disposition of your children, it can be smooth sailing for a long time, or it can be a bit rocky at times. Initial momentum will aid in allowing you time to plan for possible hiccup days.

Your Reasons Help Create a Vision

As you move forward, these reasons will also help you create a vision and goal to aim for which, again, will keep you focused and confident about homeschooling. Jot down one or more reasons that resonate with you. or underline them above.

Perhaps you have different reasons that I didn't mention; write them down as a reminder. Simply jot down some key words that will trigger your memory when you re-read it. It does not have to look pretty or amount to an essay. When you find yourself wondering why you started homeschooling in the first place and whether to continue, it'll be there to jog your memory.

Am I Qualified to Educate My Children?

Before digging into being qualified or not, let's think about what education is actually supposed to accomplish. Then we can make a decision about being qualified.

Education has several definitions, most of them mentioning the teaching of skills and information. However, in my opinion, a definition like that leaves out the most important points.

I like Charlotte Mason's ideas about education. She was focused on the child, and not so much on the input. I am paraphrasing some of her points:

- Education is the act of nourishing our students with ideas and relationships.

- The exposure to ideas creates a natural curiosity about a variety of subjects in our kids.

- Education is training up a person to live a purposeful life.

- Character training plays a vital part in education.

- Education is best achieved in the home.

If you're like me, you're sighing with relief that there is no mention of math tests and essays on this list. My guess is that you are already doing most of the things on this list.

Reading aloud, playing outside, and going on field trips take care of the first two points. And teaching your child proper behavior and giving him chores to do is taking care of points three and four. In other words, you are already educating your child.

Of course, there's more than reading aloud, field trips, and chores, but my point is that you are already doing many things, and probably without folllowing a teachers' manual. So what you will do when starting to homeschool is to continue on the path you're already on.

How Do I Know that I'm Qualified to Teach My Child?

Whenever my kids and I were out and about during 'normal school hours', people frequently asked them why they were not in school. When my kids answered that they were homeschooled, I prepared myself for a negative comment or snarky remark. But to my surprise, no one ever made one.

I know that was not always so, but the last two decades have seen a dramatic rise in the number of homeschooling families, and the general public has become noticeably more open and receptive to it. In my experience, people were curious and even complimented me on choosing to homeschool.

One thing that I frequently heard was that many parents wish they could do it but didn't feel they had what it takes. Either they felt unqualified, or they couldn't imagine pulling their kids away from their friends. Most of them were worried about the implications it has if they mess up, and they expressed fear of taking charge of the whole ginormous process of education.

I totally get it. It's very intimidating when I think about what's at stake. And then I go down a rabbit hole and imagine ruining my kids' future. So, what's a good answer to this seeming dilemma?

You Are Qualified

Think back to the day when you brought your baby home after she was born. Or maybe you adopted a young child, so remember the day your new family member came home.

After only a few short weeks or months, you knew your child better than anyone else did. Even if you hired a daycare provider or baby-sitter, there was no one who knew your child better than you did. There is a unique bond between parent and child.

My guess is that you read books to make sure your baby grew and developed normally. You supplied age-appropriate toys, and enjoyed spending time watching her start moving around and making sounds that could be words, then start walking, saying more words, and becoming more and more independent.

If you adopt an older child, it adds another layer of complexity, but in the end, you are the final authority over your child and know what is best. This knowledge you have of your child continues past the age of five, which is the age where parents have been led to think they no longer know what's best for their child.

If You're a Parent, You're a Teacher

I remember distinctly that time when I switched my view on education as a 'formal process that I observe as a bystander' to 'a normal part of family life with me as an integral part'. It was like a light bulb turning on, and it gave me a feeling of excitement that it is possible for me to play an active role in my children's education.

The fun, but challenging part for me was to grow into and feel comfortable with my role as parent and teacher. I found that it's easier to grow into this role when starting homeschooling in the preschool years compared to starting with an eighth grader.

But it can be accomplished at any school age, it just takes a little more time, effort, and above all, patience. Believe it or not, if you're a parent, you're already a teacher. You have been from the day you brought your child home.

Surround yourself with loving and supportive people, which is a topic I will address in a later chapter. And if you're a praying person, pray every day. Pray for wisdom, patience, understanding, and grace.

When I Start Feeling Unqualified

Here's my list of points to consider when I start feeling unqualified as a teacher:

My Reasons for Homeschooling

Usually, I go to my list of reasons for why I'm homeschooling in the first place. This is why it's helpful to have these nearby.

It's either me or someone else—who doesn't know my child

I remind myself that my spouse and I are the only qualified people on this planet to make decisions regarding our child's education because we know our child better than anyone else does. And our kids belong to my spouse and me, not to any other person or institution.

If I want my kids to think in a way that reflects my family's values, I need to take care of it myself

If I give them over to someone else, I will have to accept the fact that they will think by someone else's standard. Someone has to make the choice of what my kids learn, so it may as well be me.

Homeschooling is far more efficient than school classrooms.

If I mess up, my chances of being able to adjust quickly are higher.

I make sure I hang out with other homeschool families who have successfully graduated one or more students.

Watching them helps me feel at ease.

I make sure I listen to podcasts and read blogs that build me up.

I try to always have several encouraging books placed around the house, so it is inviting for me to pick one up and start reading.

To a certain extent, feeling inadequate is not a bad thing.

It keeps me striving for better and deeper knowledge and pushes me to keep going forward even if I feel tired and ready to give up.

I spend time in prayer asking for much needed wisdom.

Help Is Just Around the Corner

Okay, so I want to teach my kids, but what do I teach them? This is what most moms and dads are nervous about.

If you can read, you're equipped to find exactly what you need to teach your kids. The curriculum market is filled with 'open and go' teaching materials. All you need to bring to the table is an atmosphere of curiosity and a space for learning. There are thousands of helpful materials out there, many of them free, and I list many of them throughout this book.

In other chapters of this book, I walk you through the process of choosing the right level and content of teaching materials. Once you start looking at all the curriculum options, you will be amazed how easy teaching becomes. Many subjects can also be outsourced, such as with a tutor, or a co-op, or online. There is something for everyone.

You may tell yourself you're not an expert in some of the subjects you'll have to teach your kids. Remember that many public or private schoolteachers are also not experts in the subjects they teach! They 'follow the curriculum'. You can do the same as they do. I will point you to a wide range of materials which will cover what you need to know in each subject.

Homeschooling Is Not for Every Family at All Times

While I'm a strong proponent of homeschooling, I do not believe it works for everyone at all times and in every situation. There is a season for everything. So, perhaps you are reading this book, and won't homeschool for years to come. The point is: you, the parent, are in charge of your child's education, one way or another. Make a decision and go for it. You can always change your mind next year.

2

Your State's Laws on Homeschooling

Homeschooling is absolutely legal in all fifty states. Each state, however, has different laws regulating homeschooling. Some states are much more heavily regulated than others.

I'm not a lawyer, and what I say is not legal advice, but a broad summary of steps that are necessary in most states to start homeschooling.

On your laptop or phone, visit the homepage of the Homeschool Legal Defense Association at www.hslda.org. In the menu bar at the top, hover over 'legal', then choose 'state homeschool laws'. This will open an interactive map.

If you click on the name of your state, you'll find a brief summary of your state's laws and the requirements you must fulfill when homeschooling. It will take only about a minute or two to read it but will give you a good idea of what you need to know.

Starting to Homeschool a Kindergartener

Depending on your state's laws, you may have to

1. send a letter of intent, and

2. an outline of your plan of study, and

3. some other required information, to your local school board,

4. or (in some states) you may not have to do any correspondence.

Homeschooling a Child Currently Enrolled in School

1. You will need to send an official letter of withdrawal to the school and

2. depending on your state law, you may need to send a letter of intent to the school board,

3. an outline of your plan of studies to the school board, and other required information to your school board or superintendent before you can legally start homeschooling.

You do not need the state's permission to homeschool. In some states, you need to let the school board know that you are planning on homeschooling, while `in other states, you don't even have to let anyone know. Be careful to comply with the law but don't do anything you don't have to.

If you're withdrawing your child because of an extremely stressful situation at school, contact HSLDA and ask for their advice on whether you could start homeschooling as soon as these letters are sent, or whether you should wait a few days. (If you need to get legal counsel, you will have to purchase a membership, which I will discuss later in this chapter.

HSLDA recommends that you send any correspondence via certified mail, requesting a return receipt. Keep the receipt with your records.

There may be some items to be taken care of with the school, for example, returning books, laptops, or other school property.

Deadlines

There are usually deadlines by which the paperwork must be received. Try to stick with these deadlines which are usually reasonable.

People sometimes do get in trouble by sending their required papers late, so it's best to simply send everything off in one packet right at the end of your school year (if you follow the traditional school schedule which ends sometime in late May).

I usually sent off the previous school year's assessment reports, and following school year's information all at once. That meant that I had to have the following year's curriculum already chosen and laid out by May.

Laws about Special Education

All fifty states allow homeschooling your special needs child. But again, every state has different options and regulations for this circumstance.

First of all, you'll have to read up on your state laws and find out how to begin homeschooling, which we already talked about. All the same rules apply for special education.

Next, and depending on whether your special needs child has been established at a public school with an Individualized Education Plan (IEP) or not, you might have to make some more decisions and fill out some more paperwork after withdrawing your child from school.

If your child is enrolled in school and is being taught using an IEP, some states allow for several options:

1. staying part time enrolled in public school and begin home-schooling with help of the education team that you have been working with, or

2. terminating the IEP and creating your own program with help of a different special education team that helps you get started.

3. Some states have no requirements in addition to the existing homeschool law, and will still allow you to receive special needs services.

I highly recommend that you refer to the HSLDA website for more detailed information. They have a team of consultants you can contact, and you can find great support and suggestions (you'll need a paid membership).

I will also address special education in a different part of this book, so stay tuned if you are interested.

Homeschool Legal Organizations

Making any curriculum purchases or plans for your homeschool will somewhat depend on the type of regulation in your state. Once you familiarize yourself with your state's homeschool law, I recommend joining a legal organization such as HSLDA (Homeschool Legal Defense Association), or Heritage Defense for at least a few years.

If you go to their websites, you will find a great amount of valuable information regarding your homeschooling and parenting rights. Members have 27/4 access to lawyers who are tirelessly at work advising and defending homeschool families for the cost of somewhere between $150–$200 per year.

If you choose not to join right away, the HSLDA website has excellent, free information about your state law, and what it means. Joining gives you more access to information, and the benefit of calling an HSLDA attorney, who specializes in your state's law, whenever you have questions.

Both, HSLDA and Heritage Defense support Christian pro-life policies. In my opinion, these are the two organizations that supply the best and most supportive legal information available on the Internet regarding home education.

Don't Share Too Much Information

Something I learned, through years of correspondence with my school board: don't give out more info than is absolutely needed so you don't make life harder on future homeschoolers.

If people working for the school board get used to compliant homeschool parents, they will keep pushing for more information, even if it's not legally required.

Also, if you're required to correspond with your district's school board, keep copies of every page you include.

And again, send your letter using certified mail and keep the receipt for the school year together with the copies of your correspondence. In case there is ever a dispute, you will have these on hand for reference.

Who Makes Sure I Don't Mess Up?

Over the years, I have been confronted with many versions of the question, 'Who makes sure that my children learn anything and don't watch PBS all day?'

I agree wholeheartedly that homeschooling families should have a system of accountability. The question is, who is responsible for this? And this is where opinions diverge. State or parents?

Before finding an answer, here are a few facts to consider.

1. Statistically speaking, homeschool parents show tremendous interest and initiative to be active in the community and in homeschool groups or co-ops, which leads me to think that naturally, these parents understand the need for accountability. So, if there are accountability problems, they usually self-correct.

The horror stories that come to mind when we think of homeschooling gone wrong are in the vast minority, and there are at least as many such stories taking place in the public or private schools.

2. Academically, the children of public schools are not outperforming their homeschooled peers, and universities nowadays seek out homeschool graduates because they come with purpose of studying.

3. In addition to academics, people like to talk about domestic violence. There is no statistical evidence that suggests that homeschooled children are at higher risk in any area of domestic abuse.

4. But let's say people demand that the state be the accountability partner. If state regulations were indeed effectively raising the standard of homeschool education, you should be able to see evidence that high regulation states have higher academic outcomes than low regulation states.

    But there is no evidence that homeschooled students from states with low homeschool regulations underperform compared to their peers from moderately or highly regulated states.

    If parents choose to homeschool, they usually know and understand the task they are undertaking and are willing to pay a premium since their tax dollars will continue to go toward public schools, and on top of that, they will be spending money on curriculum.

A Natural Accountability System

I am not in favor of a state-regulated system to keep homeschool parents accountable, but I do believe there needs to be a natural way of keeping a high standard for homeschooling. Here is how I think that homeschool families should be held accountable:

1. Join a homeschool group.

Even just getting together with other homeschool families once a week or twice a month is enough to get you out and about and interact with others. Chances are that you feel encouraged, inspired, and curious about what everyone else is doing. You will be far more likely to have a high standard with your own homeschool if you frequently get exposed to other homeschool families.

2. Be visible and involved in the community.

This counteracts isolation and helps your kids get used to social etiquette.

3. Be in frequent communication with spouse or other family members about progress and issues you are facing.

4. Attend a homeschool conference.

You will be refreshed, encouraged, and inspired to continue homeschooling your child. It's truly amazing to see the number of other homeschool families and the huge amount of homeschool material and resources that's available.

5. Listen to homeschooling podcasts to see how other parents do it.

6. And yes, do follow your state's homeschool law.

World News on Homeschooling

THE UN AND HOMESCHOOLING IN THE US

The notion that parents need to be certified and qualified by an outside source, like the state, is a slippery slope and eventually leads to complete surrender, first, of parental responsibilities, and then of parental rights altogether.

A current issue at the United Nations level is a treaty called the Convention of the Rights of the Child (CRC) which was signed by Secretary of State Madeline Albright in 1995 but never actually ratified by the US Senate.

According to the Homeschool Legal Defense Association, as of 2020, this treaty has been ratified by every UN member except the US.

One of the main points of this treaty is regarding governmental decisions in the "best interest of the child." Commonly in the US, the definition of "best interest of the child" referred to cases in which the judge had to make decisions on behalf of children who were abused or neglected.

But the definition of "best interest of the child" in this treaty includes parental choices of any kind, attacking the ability of parents to make any choice on their child's behalf, including homeschooling.

Here's the problem with the treaty that makes this a current issue: The treaty has been signed by the Secretary of State and the only step left is ratification by two thirds of the senate. Ratification would open the door to UN laws and statutes possibly overruling US federal and state laws.

If the UN decides that you or I are not acting in the "best interest of the child," US law will not protect us. As of now, the treaty is not ratified, but it could happen at any time, depending on who the current senators are. Remember this next time you vote.

The State Wants to Educate Our Kids

And now you might be asking yourself what the UN and being qualified to teach have to do with each other. Here is the connection: it's the slippery slope of being told and finally believing that parents are unqualified to teach their children that led to giving up the right to do so in the first place.

The result of surrendering our children to the state is further surrender of issues surrounding our children, such as their development, their nutrition, and their beliefs.

By default, any state wants control of the children, because they are the future.

It Only Takes One Generation

If only one generation has lost its connection to their roots in history, the following generation has little hope of ever returning to them. All you have to do is remember what you learned in school or ask your parents and grandparents what they learned and compare the 'drift' of the classroom to today's 'drift' in Congress.

The direction of the US government is clear: more control of the classroom is the goal. The way to fix this is to break free of the system and start afresh.

Today, it has become rather obvious that schools are not producing citizens who value high personal responsibility, but rather low personal responsibility, which usually goes hand in hand with political and religious convictions.

If we value the freedom to homeschool, and would like to retain it, we have the responsibility to raise the next generation to value this freedom by educating them in such a way that they gain a clear vision of what is at stake.

Checklist Questions

1. What is my state's homeschool law (visit www.hslda.org)?

2. Do I need to withdraw my child from school?

3. What is the paperwork I need to send off?

4. What are the deadlines?

5. Do I have special requirements?

6. Do I know of any useful groups I can join?

7. Do I want to join a legal organization such as HSLDA?

8. How can I set myself up for accountability?

9. Who can be my accountability partner?

3

What's Your Teaching Philosophy?

You can think of a teaching philosophy—or 'educational philosophy'—as the general framework in which your homeschool will function. It sets the atmosphere in your home, and you should absolutely love it. If you find yourself struggling with the 'feel' of your homeschool atmosphere and the general flow of your day, the problem might be with your teaching philosophy.

Your teaching philosophy guides your subject choice and helps you decide how you start your day, how many subjects are taught in a day, and how much time to spend on each subject. In other words, choosing a philosophy that fits with your family's personality is super helpful and will save you lots of time and brain power.

Homeschool Flavors

Sonya Schafer from Simply Charlotte Mason calls the various teaching philosophies "flavors," which is a great description because it emphasizes the uniqueness and 'learning taste' of each family. Depending on your personality, planning style, your children's learning preferences, or your budget, and your season as a family, you may change your taste over time and change from one philosophy to another.

If you're just now beginning your homeschool journey and are new to these ideas, you might not exactly know which 'flavor' you enjoy most. That's perfectly okay and normal. At one point or another, every homeschool parent and teacher has been there. Try several of them out for a few weeks and see which is the best fit.

Most likely, you'll enjoy several methods for different subjects, and even blend them. Give yourself time to explore. In later chapters I will guide you through how you choose your best fit and 'custom design' your plan of study from a list of curriculum publishers.

It's hard to pinpoint the exact number of different teaching philosophies in existence, so I will just mention the five that are most commonly known. All five have plenty of helpful guides and instructional materials (listed below).

1. TRADITIONAL

The traditional teaching philosophy is what most of us think of when we hear the word 'school' with its very structured style and schedule. This may include the cute set-up of the classroom with chairs and tables. This approach is completely teacher-led, and the materials include scripted lesson plans and a schedule of how many days a week you should teach each subject.

The teacher leads the class and gives assignments. There are textbooks, workbooks, and worksheets that the students fill out. Your student is required to sit still for periods of time and receive instruction. Students can also read the textbooks independently, so it's important to choose a good textbook.

Usually, the subjects in the traditional approach are what you would already be familiar with if you went to almost any school: math, science, language arts, composition, social studies, foreign language, PE, fine arts, and electives.

While this is what many of us grew up with in a school setting, it can be difficult to maintain in our homes, especially if you're teaching multiple kids in different grades. Let's say you have three children, each of them in a different grade. There are simply not enough hours in the day to instruct each of your kids in their own level of every subject. You would have to outsource some subjects and teach your student's independent learning skills, so you can spend time with each individually.

But then again, for some families with one or two students, this way of structuring their day may be exactly what they are looking for, and this style may even make them more comfortable when they start out as brand-new homeschool parents.

2. CLASSICAL OR CLASSICAL CHRISTIAN

This method is called classical—or classical-Christian if the content is distinctly Christian—because it focuses on the Greek way of logical and empirical thinking, as well as on the Latin and Greek languages and western literature. In this approach, you will find subjects like Logic and Rhetoric.

Classical education may feel a little bit like the traditional approach since it is teacher-led, and the student will be required to sit still for periods of time and receive instruction. Usually, there is a textbook with the lesson, and either the teacher teaches the lesson, or the student reads it independently.

However, the goal and content of this education philosophy are distinctly different from a typical traditional curriculum. A catch phrase in this philosophy is 'truth, goodness, and beauty', as students are taught how to recognize these concepts in the real world. In addition, students are taught how to think, and by default, how to learn, through a specific method of asking questions—the Socratic Method.

It goes all the way back to the ancient Greeks, who categorized areas of learning and knowledge into the Trivium (Grammar, Logic, Rhetoric) and the Quadrivium (Arithmetic, Music, Geometry, and Astronomy). The Trivium, which is a pre-requisite to the Quadrivium, is the foundation of classical education in grades K–12, while the quadrivium is the continuation in college level learning. The Trivium and the Quadrivium are also referred to as a Liberal Arts Education.

The ancient Greeks may or may not have educated their students in a specific order of the three parts of the Trivium, but in the 1940s, Dorothy Sayers introduced the idea that schools can use the three parts as three phases, starting with Grammar, followed by Logic, and then Rhetoric.

Each of these phases follows the ability of the child to absorb and process information. The Grammar Phase, Kindergarten through fifth or sixth grade, focuses on utilizing the immense ability to memorize and learn language vocabulary and grammar rules, Latin being one of those languages.

Sixth to ninth or tenth grade is called the Logic Phase. All subjects taught during this phase employ the student's desire at this age to argue—to defend opinions or behaviors in a logical way with solid reasoning. Logic is one of the subjects in this phase.

The third and last phase is called the Rhetoric Phase and focuses on the ability to communicate the acquired knowledge well, with Rhetoric being one of the subjects.

So much more can be said about this teaching philosophy, which is among my personal favorites, but what I have said here is a good starting point for your own research.

Generally speaking, classical curricula are rigorous and require a love for reading (or listening to) the classic literature of human history. However, if you like this idea but are rather intimidated by it, remember that you can always slow down—definitely one of the greatest advantages of homeschooling—and still enjoy the benefits of this style of education.

3. CHARLOTTE MASON

This philosophy is named after an early twentieth-century teacher who founded a school in Ambleside, England, a beautiful spot away from the city. Her desire was for children to grow up with the beauty of nature surrounding them. Charlotte Mason defines education as having four pillars: education is an atmosphere, education is a discipline, education is a life, education is a science of relations.

Her teaching style is based on living books, living ideas and a large variety of subjects with short lessons to capture the attention of the students. Extensive amounts of time are designated to be spent outdoors. You'll find unique subjects such as Nature Study, Handicrafts, Swedish Drill, and Narration.

The Charlotte Mason educator will spend much time reading aloud from 'living books'—meaning books written by first-hand-account experts—and engage the reader through these books' descriptive language and narrative style.

Charlotte Mason's idea was to allow the students to discover truths and conclusions on their own. The teacher's job is to be a facilitator, guide, and provider of a rich environment for the learning experience, while making sure not to interfere too much in the student's learning and discovery.

The number of subjects covered over the school year can seem intimidating, but not every subject is taught every day. Short lessons and a feast of subjects allow the student to gain a wide variety of knowledge and experience. Subjects include math, science, narration, nature study, handicrafts, literature, poetry, art and composer study, folk song study, several foreign languages, PE (Swedish drill), composition, and more.

4. UNSCHOOLING (INTEREST-LED BY STUDENT)

The name might sound a bit misleading. We are not talking about skipping school all day. Rather, the name stems from the idea to step away from the teacher-led traditional school model and move toward a student-interest-led model.

In his book *How Children Learn*, John Holt observed that children remember information far better when they are allowed active engagement than simply being told that same information in a classroom, so there is heavy emphasis on hands-on learning and handicrafts. A high priority is to allow the students to explore and discover things on their own.

Many 'Unschoolers' spend a lot of time outdoors, and there's usually no schedule in the traditional sense. The challenge is that you as the teacher must be ready for changing interests and find new materials quickly, which might be difficult over time. There are curriculum publishers that help with that. Many moms and dads enjoy this approach for a season or so, especially in the early years; on the other hand, some families thrive with this approach and use it for many years.

In case you're wondering, the Montessori and Waldorf methods would fit best into this category, but they do share some aspects with the Charlotte Mason method.

Dr. Maria Montessori invented a philosophy originally designed for special-needs children in Italy. Many of her newly invented techniques included manipulatives and hands-on learning tools. Soon after implementing these brand-new ideas in her classrooms, she found them to be very useful for teaching all children, regardless of their learning abilities. The student explores and guides himself through the materials that are offered. Learning is a by-product of interacting with real-world objects. Originally, this method was developed for the classroom setting with a wide age-range of children, but it can be adapted and included in a home-school setting.

The Waldorf method was named after a cigarette factory in Stuttgart, Germany, where the first Waldorf school was opened. With a strong emphasis on the arts, this method is based on experiencing learning through dancing, singing, drawing, gardening, and other activities.

Rudolf Steiner, the inventor of this method, was invited to speak at the factory about the need for social and political renewal, just after World War I had come to an end. The director of the factory was so impressed, he asked Steiner to become the pedagogical director for the factory workers' children. Steiner developed a way of teaching that was not forced upon the student but took the students' abilities and interests into account.

He coined the philosophical term 'anthroposophy', which means that humans have intellectual access to the spiritual world by developing certain senses. The Waldorf method aids in fostering these senses. Like Montessori, the Waldorf method allows the student to guide himself through activities and learn through exploration.

The ideas of both, Montessori and Waldorf, have left a mark on all existing teaching philosophies. Manipulatives, arts, and movement are more common nowadays than they used to be a hundred years ago.

5. UNIT STUDIES

Think of a great children's book, say *Make Way for Ducklings* by Robert McCloskey. Now imagine reading this book and using it as the backbone of your school subjects. Math could, depending on the age of your student, include adding or subtracting ducks, counting duck feet, wings, or beaks.

History might be about Boston at the time of the War for Independence, such as the Boston Tea Party and Paul Revere's midnight ride. Geography may include Massachusetts, Boston, and surrounding states and waters. Science may cover birds, rivers and ponds, and duck habitation.

Instead of a book, a unit study can also focus on a specific topic that guides your subject content. An example of this would be 'Attentiveness'. All your subjects focus on the topic of attentiveness such as listening to some music or a story very carefully and noticing details. You could learn about the ear, and how it functions. The possibilities are endless.

There are numerous unit studies available either for purchase or for free online, so if this appeals to you, you can jump right in. This is generally geared toward eighth grade and below, so if you have kids in this age range, you might enjoy this approach.

The unit study approach usually has a weekly schedule, so you know ahead of time how many weeks it will take you to finish. This makes it a great tool if you want to take a short break from your normal school routine.

Some families use unit studies as their primary way of learning, while others use it to change things up a bit. This approach can be a stand-alone teaching philosophy or be adapted to fit into other philosophies.

Unit studies can easily be adapted to your needs. For example, you can skip the math part if you have a different math curriculum. Or you can just read the book (if you're using one) and choose only the activities that fit into your schedule. Your imagination is the limit.

How to Choose?

You may be wondering how to choose which approach is right for your family. If this is new information to you, the important thing to remember is that all these approaches have been demonstrated to work. There is no right or wrong approach. It is all about which style comes naturally to you and your family.

This is not a monumental decision, so don't panic. None of these decisions are set in stone. You can switch to a different one whenever you choose. You'll probably want to try out different methods to see which one is the best fit for you.

1. WHEN CHOOSING A PHILOSOPHY, THINK OF YOURSELF

You may be tempted to consider what would appeal to your children before you think of yourself. The term 'learning style' has had some traction, so as teachers, we may be tempted to over-analyze our kids and forget about ourselves.

But, unless you outsource most subjects, you will be the one doing the teaching. And if you want to help your student learn, you should probably have some grasp on the topic yourself. So, having materials that appeal to you is a great benefit.

In the long run, your kids will be just fine with most of what's out there. It's really more about you and how you envision your family's interaction. You're the one who needs to stay motivated, and if you are positive and excited about your day and what you will be learning, your kids will follow.

The irony is that children are many times very different from their parents, so let's say you are a very structured parent with a spontaneous, fly-by-the-seat-of-your-pants child, or vice versa. You might be wondering how that will play out. From my own experience, and from what I have seen among many other homeschooling families, you do what suits your personal style best, and your child will adapt.

So, choose your teaching philosophy based on what appeals to you, and your children will follow your lead.

2. MIX AND MATCH

If you're like most homeschool families, you'll tend to lean toward one homeschool 'flavor', but then you'll find that as you use the materials, other methods will fit in. My family started out with the classical Christian method, but over the years I found Charlotte Mason's approach very inviting. So, I added a few read-aloud books and nature study into our school day.

That meant I had to remove something else to allow time and space for this new addition. So, I removed spelling and vocabulary from our schedule. After doing that and feeling guilty about it, I noticed that these subjects were automatically covered in the way the reading aloud was done in the Charlotte Mason method, and in the end, it was not a loss but a gain since everything became more streamlined.

3. Do You Love It? Think about Monday Morning.

Choose a teaching philosophy that gets you excited and makes you look forward to starting your day on Monday morning. This choice is important mainly because it will set you up for long-term success. If you choose a philosophy because your friend absolutely loves it, but you don't like it that much, you're setting yourself up for failure.

It's true for me, and it's probably true for you, as well. If I looked forward to the day, I knew I was on the right track. But if I dreaded the day, I knew I needed to change something. So, have the Monday Morning Mindset, and adopt a philosophy that doesn't create anxiety in you when Sunday evening arrives, and you're thinking about Monday morning.

4. Your Kids

Finally, you may be wondering whether your kids play any part in this choice at all. The answer is yes. However, your kids are not the driving force, but the 'tweaking' and 'slight adjustment making'. Choose your philosophy based on your own liking, then select the corresponding curriculum with yourself and your child in mind.

There are so many curricula on the market, you will be able to find one that satisfies both your and your student's interests. You will most likely purchase some materials that you use only a few times, and then abandon. That is not unusual, so don't beat yourself up over it. If you're on a tight budget, you can re-sell these materials on various platforms. Or you can hold on to them if you have more students in the pipeline.

Researching Homeschool Philosophies

Below, I list several websites for you to check out. Most of them sell their own materials, and some of them sell from a variety of publishers. Seeing the large number of subjects and curricula can be overwhelming. Welcome to the world of homeschooling! There is an amazing abundance of good-quality materials. Remember, we're only looking at philosophies for now, not specific curriculum. Each website will explain its educational approach in a unique way, and it will give you a better idea of each philosophy. This checklist should help with that.

1. Visit the websites (listed below).

2. Find the 'About' or 'About Us' tab.

3. Don't look at the subjects and curricula quite yet (unless you absolutely can't help yourself).

4. Find any other menu-options on the website that look interesting.

5. Add the websites to your favorites if you like what you see.

Let a few hours or days go by. Then go back to your favorites and follow the next checklist. By now you're probably getting used to the large quantity of homeschool materials available. The truth is, the best way to figure out your own homeschool philosophy is to see it in action, so let's take a look at some curriculum options. To make it more digestible, do these things:

1. Read over the 'About' or 'About Us' again.

2. Now, the curriculum: For now, stick with these four subjects:

   Math   Language Arts   Science   Science

3. Either: Pick a grade level and subject and click on it.
   Or: pick a grade level and choose the curriculum package.

4. Scroll through the options.

5. Download free sample pages.

6. Add what you like to your favorites.

Most of these resources have free samples you can download and even try out.

Traditional

- Time 4 Learning, www.time4learning.com. In the search bar, type in "traditional homeschool philosophy" and hit Enter.
- Abeka (Christian content): www.abeka.com

Classical Christian

I have no experience with secular classical curricula, so I am listing only the ones I have used.

- Veritas Press
  www.veritaspress.com
- Logos Press
  www.logospress.com
- Classical Academic Press
  www.classicalacademicpress.com
- Classical Conversations
  www.classicalconversations.com
- Memoria Press
  www.memoriapress.com

Books about Classical Christian Education:

- *The Lost Tools of Learning* by Dorothy L. Sayers
- *The Well-Trained Mind* by Susan Wise Bauer
- *Rethinking School* by Susan Wise Bauer
- *The Well-Educated Mind* by Susan Wise Bauer

Charlotte Mason

- Ambleside Online
  www.amblesideonline.com
- Simply Charlotte Mason
  www.simplycm.com
- My Father's World
  www.mfwbooks.com
- Master Books
  www.masterbooks.com

Books about the Charlotte Mason Philosophy

- *Planning your Charlotte Mason Education* by Sonya Schafer
- *Laying down the Rails* by Sonya Schafer

- *A Charlotte Mason Education* by Catherine Levison

- *A Philosophy of Education*, Volume 6, by Charlotte Mason

- *For the Children's Sake* by Susan Schaeffer Macaulay. She recalls her experiences growing up in Europe and tells of her Charlotte Mason journey.

- *When Children Love to Learn* by Elaine Cooper. An anthology of helpful essays on Charlotte Mason's teaching methods for today's homeschool teachers.

Unschooling

I have never personally been an Unschooler but have met several families that adhere to this philosophy. I find it very appealing in the elementary school years. There is no curriculum in the traditional sense, so these websites will just list philosophies and ideas.

- Happiness Is Here
  www.happinessishereblog.com

- Unschool Rules
  www.unschoolrules.com

- General Information
  www.rainbowresource.com
  and enter 'unschooling' in the search bar.

Book about Unschooling:
- *Unschooled*, Kerry McDonald

Unit Studies
- Literature-based
  www.fiveinarow.com

- Amanda Bennett
  www.unitstudy.com

- Beautiful Feet Books
  www.bfbooks.com

- Konos
  www.konos.com

Other Quality Publishers

The following publishers do not fit into one or two categories but share aspects of three or more.

- Traditional, Unit Study, and Charlotte Mason
  www.sonlight.com

- Classical, Charlotte Mason, Unit Study
  www.tapestryofgrace.com

- Hands on curriculum from Timberdoodle
  www.timberdoodle.com

4

Choosing Which Subjects to Teach

What subjects shall I teach? Choosing the subjects is one of my favorite tasks because I can use my child's unique gifts and interests to guide me and at the same time add my own twist.

On page 35 there's a list of subjects to give you an idea of possible choices. Some of them are familiar to most people such as math and composition. Then there are a few subjects that might seem unusual at first glance, like Nature Study and Rhetoric.

Detailed advice on how to teach these subjects is given in the relevant chapters. However, if you need to get started quickly and don't have much time to think about the deeper motivation for choosing each subject, I'm adding a short-cut which you can find below. Once you get started and are gaining experience in home-schooling your child over the next school year, you can decide which subjects you would like to add.

When you're ready to read about each subject, go to the chapter that interests you most and start reading there. You can then jump around from subject to subject. This information is meant to help you be intentional about each subject, so take your time as you read through it.

Ask yourself the following questions to help you decide which subjects to teach:

1. ARE THERE SPECIFIC SUBJECTS THAT ARE REQUIRED BY MY STATE'S HOMESCHOOL LAW?

If your state requires Math, History (or 'Social Studies'), Composition (or 'Language Study'), and Science, start with these subjects, then move to question two. If your state has no requirements, these four areas are still a good place to start. Choose a subject from each of these areas, and you have your core subjects.

2. Which Subjects Are Important to Me?

You have many options within the state's requirements. There are a number of different ways, for example, to meet the requirement for 'social studies'. Geography, history, economics all fall into this category. Choose based on your own and your student's interests. If you're not sure, pick something that looks interesting for now and try it out. You can adjust over the years if you want to change direction.

While you should, of course, consider your student's interests and personality, don't forget to instruct your student in what makes you unique as a parent and as a family. For instance, if you have a certain ethnic background, learn the language, history, literature, culinary arts, or traditions of your culture. I tried to always incorporate something German into our subjects. Think about your strengths and interests so you can create a list of subjects you can sustain in the long term. Your student will adapt and follow your lead.

3. Is this necessary for what we're trying to accomplish?

This depends on your family's goals. There may be short-term goals and long-term goals. Both of them are important to keep in mind. If you are like me, you will research the subjects you want to choose, and then stumble upon one or more that look so amazing and have such great reviews; so, you begin to add more and more to your list. It is easy to overload yourself with materials that look all so fantastic and fun that it is extra important to remind ourselves and ask this question: is this absolutely necessary?

Every time you pull out your wallet or get ready to click "BUY," you should ask how this will aid in furthering your end goal. A good visual is a target with a couple of descriptions in the center and ten or twelve circles around it, each representing a school year. What words could you use to describe the progress you are making toward the final, center result? If the item(s) in the cart don't fit this requirement 100%, resist buying it for now. You can always get it later.

4. WHICH SUBJECTS DO I FEEL COMFORTABLE TEACHING, AND WHICH ONES WOULD I RATHER OUTSOURCE?

This question is easier to answer after you have already spent some time looking at the curriculum choices. Some subjects are easier taught than you might expect. And some are worth paying a little extra for so you can have a break and not have to worry about preparing a lesson. There is a multitude of options for every comfort level of teaching. Below, I will outline a list of available teaching choices depending on your comfort level of teaching.

5. AS THE STUDENT GETS OLDER

Is this in line with the student's plans and interests after high school? (Community college, four-year-college, gap year, apprenticeship, etc.)

SKILL BASED VERSUS CONTENT BASED SUBJECTS

Skill-based subjects are completely dependent on maturity and the ability or skill of the student. These include math, writing, spelling, some sciences with pre-requisites (Physics or Chemistry), and reading. Content-based subjects are less founded on maturity and skill level but guided by interest and oral understanding. In this category you will find history, literature, some elementary level sciences (botany, astronomy, zoology), geography, poetry, art, or PE.

These latter subjects are ideal for combining all your children and aim your teaching toward the oldest child. The younger children will catch on and learn what they are able to understand. Plus, you will probably cover this material again before they graduate high school, so everyone is served well.

Teaching Choices

1. COMPLETELY PARENT-LED

You teach every single subject with the help of curriculum materials. Depending on the subject, this is the most time-consuming and demanding, but also exciting as parent and child discover knowledge together. The good news is that there are countless open-and-go curricula available, which means you have minimum preparation, and maximum flexibility. The older your student is, the more you should think ahead, and be ready to guide her when needed. At the same time, the older student should be allowed increasing independence and leadership in the high school years which takes pressure off the parent.

2. COMPLETELY ONLINE AND SUPERVISED BY A PARENT

Live and Self-Paced

The student completes all her classes online and the parent supervises the assignments and progress. The involvement of the parent varies, epending on the subject and the student. Sometimes, online classes require minimal involvement from the parent. You may ask from time to time how things are going and if your student is on top of all assignments. But sometimes, an online class can be frustrating and overwhelming for the student, and the parent needs to be in tune with the student's judgement of how things are going. Before choosing an online class, you can preview sample lessons to see if this is a good fit.

There are two main types of online instruction, live and self-paced. During live classes, a teacher teaches the lessons online on specific days at specific times, the student watches in real-time, and interacts with a live classroom. The student has deadlines, uploads her assignments, and the teacher grades the work. This is a virtual version of traditional school with a teacher and a classroom. These are generally pricey, but considering the fact that you are not having to drive anywhere and wait for your student to finish, this may be worthwhile. You can also use this time to work with a different child or prepare a meal.

Self-Paced classes consist of uploaded videos, games, and assignments that are available for the student to complete in his own time. There are no deadlines, but usually you have a calendar year (twelve months) to complete the course work. The assignments and tests are multiple choice, grades are available to download, and at the end of the school year there is usually a grade sheet to be downloaded for your reference. These are not as pricey as the live classes but can still be expensive.

Many times, the online lessons are available for the parent to view which is very helpful if the student has questions that are not answered in the lesson. You can better help your student find the answer if you yourself understand the question. There's a large number of online classes available for all agas and subjects. I will list several of my favorites for you to get started.

— Sidebar: Core Subjects and Enrichment Subjects —

There are two layers of subjects, core subjects and enrichment subjects (interest-led subjects or electives). The core subjects are the spine of your education. These will be your priority and should be taught most days of the week. If your child applies for admission to college or applies for a job, these are the subjects that will be decisive. The interest-led subjects are additional subjects that you choose to teach, but they are not top priority. You should focus on them several days per week.

There is a lot of wiggle room, and there are numerous subjects not listed here. But here's the big picture.

Core Subjects

LANGUAGE ARTS (ENGLISH) IS THE LARGEST CATEGORY

- Phonics
- Journal Time
- Reading Aloud
- Reading Individually
- Literature (Aloud or individually)
- Dictation
- Handwriting
- Copy Work
- Spelling
- Grammar
- Composition
- Vocabulary
- Literature

SCIENCE IS THE SECOND-BIGGEST CATEGORY

Most of the different science subjects are broadly familiar by name to everyone:

- Astronomy
- Biology
- Botany
- Chemistry
- Entomology
- Geology
- Meteorology
- Paleontology
- Physics

- Zoology
- Earth Science

THEOLOGY

- Bible (This is a core subject for my family, but not necessarily for everyone.)

OTHER CORE SUBJECTS

- Logic
- History/Social Studies
- Math
- Math Drills
- Foreign Language (Spanish, German, Latin, Greek, any of them, any grade level)

Enrichment Subjects

- Poetry
- Shakespeare
- Public Speaking
- Debate
- Memory Work
- Nature Study
- Health
- Rhetoric
- Economics
- Geography
- PE
- Music/Music Appreciation/Composer Study
- Art/Art Appreciation/Artist Study
- Handicraft
- Coding
- Typing
- Life Skills
- Home Economics

This is a long list and includes every grade level K–12. Not every subject on this list will be taught every year, or even every grade level. Many are one-year subjects like

- Logic
- Rhetoric
- Economics
- Public Speaking
- or Home Economics

3. PARTLY PARENT-LED, PARTLY ONLINE

You teach some subjects, and some subjects are taught online. This is what I have usually chosen in the past. Self-paced classes are perfect for a very flexible schedule, but if you like a predictable and consistent schedule, you can assign your student to work on the self-paced class at a specific time. Or perhaps a live class is right for your family because there is live interaction, and it feels more like traditional schooling than computer work. With the live class, you will have to schedule your day around the meeting time while the self-paced class can be done any time you choose.

4. HIRE A TUTOR

If you know a person or place that has tutors, this is very helpful if you are struggling with teaching a subject to a highly emotional child. Or even just if no one is emotional until the very moment this subject is on the schedule. Sometimes you can go to a tutoring center. Community colleges usually have something like this, but if your child is not old enough to go there, maybe you can find a student to come to your house and tutor once or twice a week. Having a third-party help with certain subjects gives you room to breathe, while you are still choosing the curriculum for your child.

5. CO-OP / GROUP ACTIVITIES

The parents are still supervising and grading, but the co-op teacher leads the core subjects in a classroom setting, usually once a week at the co-op meeting. The rest of the week will be spent on doing the assignments and working through the curriculum, which is chosen by the co-op. Joining a co-op can be extremely beneficial for both, parent and child, as you will find likeminded people and a community that helps you stay motivated. If you have a co-op in your area, it is definitely worth checking out and visiting. I may even be worth driving a good distance to participate. That is what our family did for a while, and it was absolutely worth the travel time.

The other option is to join a homeschool group. If the name does not specifically say "co-op," it usually means that it is a little less structured than a co-op. There's a wide range of homeschool groups, and some are more structured than others. Some groups supplement a few classes with group activities. Field trips and P.E. are often accomplished this way, but some others that could be taught this way are art, science experiments, or book clubs. Depending on what group members are interested in leading, your options are as numerous as there are leaders. If you are not part of a co-op, I recommend finding a group that meets frequently to do activities together. I cannot emphasize enough the importance of fellowship with other homeschoolers on a regular basis.

In the end you will find that each school year is different, and you will likely change from year to year what and how you will out-source. You may hire a tutor one year, and do a self-paced math class the next, while teaching all the other subjects yourself. I have taught math to one of my children one year, and the next year decided to use and online program for the same child. This kept things fresh, and I was able to spend this time with one of my other students. Re-evaluating your children's learning progress at the end of each term or semester will be useful in determining whether you need to make any changes. Again, this is a good time to remind ourselves to think long-term, and not to give up if your student is struggling in an area.

Find a Group

I already mentioned it above, but it is worth repeating that joining a homeschool group or co-op that meets anywhere from weekly to monthly is a huge benefit and will keep you motivated and excited to educate your child. Over the years, my family has been part of several groups, and while the dynamics and goals of each group were different, I would have struggled continuing to homeschool had I not had the friendship and encouragement of the home-school families that were part of these groups. One group we were part of met weekly for several hours for P.E. and projects. About once every six to eight weeks we went on a field trip together, and at the end of the school year there was a big party and usually a trip to a theme park. We had Christmas showcases and campouts, potluck, picnics, and hiking trips. Several parents shared the leadership role for these activities. Some of our favorite homeschool memories and closest friendships were formed in that group.

Short Cut Curriculum Choices

Grades K–2

LANGUAGE ARTS

- Primary Arts of Language (Institute for Excellence in Writing, www.iew.com), AND/OR

- Pathway Readers (www.pathwayreaders.com),
- Reading Aloud
- Independent reading and conversations (for ideas, see pages 48–50, and 60)

MATH (Choose one item on the list)

- Saxon Math (www.christianbook.com), or
- Horizons Math (www.aop.com), or
- Math-U-See (www.store.demmelearning.com), or
- CTC Math (online only, www.ctcmath.com)

SOCIAL STUDIES

HISTORY

- Historical Fiction (for ideas see chapter 11), AND
- *The Mystery of History* (www.themysteryofhistory.com), or
- Veritas Press History courses (self-paced online or parent led, www.veritaspress.com)

GEOGRAPHY Choose one item on the list)

- *Visits to . . .* series by Simply Charlotte Mason (www.simplycm.com), or
- *Legends and Leagues* by Veritas Press (www.veritaspress.com)

SCIENCE Choose one item on the list)

Distinctly Christian content
- Sonlight Science Curriculum (www.sonlight.com), or
- *Exploring Creation* (www.apologia.com), or
- *Discovering Design* (www.bereanbuilders.com)

Non-religious content
- Book Shark at (www.bookshark.com)

Grades 3–5
LANGUAGE ARTS

Composition (Choose one item on the list)
- *Teaching Writing: Structure and Style* by the Institute of Excellence in Writing (www.iew.com), or
  Structure and Style for Students (Level A) (www.iew.com)

Spelling

- *Phonetic Zoo* (www.iew.com)

Grammar/Vocabulary

- Fix-It Grammar (www.iew.com)

Reading

- Reading Aloud, and/or
- Audio Books, and
- Independent reading and conversations (with or without curriculum, for ideas, see page 60)
- *Teaching the Classics* (guidance to conversations and asking questions, www.centerforlit.com)

MATH (Choose one item on the list)

- Saxon Math (www.christianbook.com), or
- *Horizons Math* (www.aop.com), or
- *Math-U-See* (www.store.demmelearning.com), or
- CTC Math (online only, www.ctcmath.com)

SOCIAL STUDIES

HISTORY

- Historical Fiction (for ideas, see chapter 11), and
- *The Mystery of History* (www.themysteryofhistory.com), or
- Veritas Press History (self-paced online or parent-led, www.veritaspress.com)

GEOGRAPHY Choose one item on the list)

- *Visits to . . .* series by Simply Charlotte Mason (www.simplycm.com), or
- *Legends and Leagues* by Veritas Press (www.veritaspress.com)

SCIENCE Choose one item on the list)

Distinctly Christian content

- Sonlight Science Curriculum (www.sonlight.com), or
- *Exploring Creation* (www.apologia.com), or
- *Discovering Design* (www.bereanbuilders.com)

Non-religious content

- Book Shark (www.bookshark.com)

Grades 6–8

LANGUAGE ARTS

Composition (Choose one item on the list)
- *Teaching Writing: Structure and Style* by the Institute of Excellence in Writing (www.iew.com), or
- *Structure and Style for Students* (Level B) (www.iew.com)

Spelling
- *Phonetic Zoo* (www.iew.com)

Grammar/Vocabulary
- Fix-It Grammar (www.iew.com)

Literature
- *Omnibus by Veritas Press (www.veritaspress.com)* If you choose classical education: starting in seventh grade, this curriculum is three classes in one: history, literature, and theology. If you complete all assignments, each level of *Omnibus* is worth three high school credits. There are six levels, grades 7–12.
  Or you may choose no curriculum at all:
  DIY curriculum: choose several books and read them together or independently. Then have conversations about them. For ideas, see chapters five and six.
- Continue reading aloud.
- *Teaching the Classics* (for ideas to conversations and questions to ask, www.centerforlit.com)

MATH (Choose one item on the list)
- Saxon Math (www.christianbook.com), or
- *Math-U-See* (www.store.demmelearning.com), or
- *Thinkwell* Math Courses (online only, www.thinkwellhomeschool.com), or
- CTC Math (online only, www.ctcmath.com)

SOCIAL STUDIES

HISTORY
- Historical Fiction (for ideas see chapter 11), and
- *The Mystery of History (www.themysteryofhistory.com)*, or
- Veritas Press History (self-paced online or parent-led, www.veritaspress.com)

GEOGRAPHY (Choose one item on the list)
- *Visits to . . .* series by Simply Charlotte Mason (www.simplycm.com)

SCIENCE Choose one item on the list)

Distinctly Christian content
- *Exploring Creation* (www.apologia.com), or
- *Discovering Design* (www.bereanbuilders.com)

Non-religious content:
- Book Shark at (www.bookshark.com)

Grades 9–12

LANGUAGE ARTS

Composition (Choose one item on the list)
- *Teaching Writing: Structure and Style* by the Institute of Excellence in Writing (www.iew.com), or
- *Structure and Style for Students* (Level C) (www.iew.com)

Grammar/Vocabulary
Fix-It Grammar (www.iew.com)

Literature Choose one item on the list)
- *Omnibus* by Veritas Press (www.veritaspress.com) If you choose classical education: starting in seventh grade, this curriculum is three classes in one: history, literature, and theology. If you complete all assignments, each level of *Omnibus* is worth three high school credits. There are six levels, grades 7–12.
  Or you may choose no curriculum at all:
- DIY curriculum: choose several books and read them together or independently. Then have conversations about them. For ideas, see chapters five and six.
- Continue reading aloud.
  Teaching the Classics (for ideas to conversations and questions to ask, www.centerforlit.com)
  Structure and Style for Students (Level C)

MATH (Choose one item on the list)
- Saxon Math (www.christianbook.com), or
- Math-U-See (www.store.demmelearning.com), or

- Thinkwell Math classes (online only, www.thinkwellhomeschoool.com), or
- CTC Math (online only, www.ctcmath.com)

SOCIAL STUDIES

HISTORY
- Historical Fiction (for ideas, see chapter 11), AND
- The Mystery of History (www.themysteryofhistory.com), or

GEOGRAPHY
- Visits to . . . series by Simply Charlotte Mason (www.simplycm.com)

Electives (Christian content)
- Exploring Economics by Ray Notgrass (www.shop.notgrass.com), or Exploring Government by Ray Notgrass (www.shop.notgrass.com)

SCIENCE (Choose one item on the list)

Distinctly Christian content
- Exploring Creation (www.apologia.com), or
- Discovering Design (www.bereanbuilders.com), or

Non-religious
- Shark (www.bookshark.com)
- Thinkwell Science Courses (online only, www.thinkwellhomeschool.com)

5

Getting Hooked on Reading

My oldest son was in second grade. He was able to sound out simple words and knew all his sight words, but he showed absolutely no interest in reading anything outside of school assignments.

Because I myself had been an early reader, I had always assumed that reading would come easily to my children. But now it seemed as if the other kids in my son's class were zipping through book after book, while my son was stuck. I was starting to worry.

One morning in late fall during his second-grade year, he woke up with several swollen scratches on his face. Poison ivy. I sent him to school anyway, because this was not the first time he'd had poison ivy. He usually recovered without problems. However, his teacher called me around 8:30 A.M. and told me I needed to pick him up because she was worried he would develop a severe reaction.

So, I loaded my other kids into the car and picked him up. Since our morning was now completely jumbled up, I decided to take them to the library. We spent a few hours there, and this is the day when we encountered Henry and Mudge, Mr. Putter and Tabby, and Poppleton, books by Cynthia Rylant.

We checked out about ten of these, and on the way home, my son had finished two of them. At home he finished all the books within the week and moved on to *Boxcar Children*.

Looking back, I have to smile at the fact that the reason he fell in love with reading was poison ivy. And a worried second grade teacher.

Why the Rush?

If our child does not read fluently by age six or seven, we begin to worry. I'm not really sure who invented this age of fluency, but it is there. Many times, schoolteachers don't help with this, either, and add to the worry by agreeing that the child should, indeed, be a fluent reader by now.

But there's really no rush. So many things have to be developmentally lined up in the child, and if I can just take a deep breath and allow my child to develop at her own rate, that would lower my stress level significantly.

Ears and Eyes

There are two important elements in learning to read: ears and eyes. First, very young children learn to read using their ears. As they get older, they learn to read using their eyes.

The first element is taught by frequently reading aloud to your child, starting in infancy. The second, more complex, element is taught by using a systematic approach to reading letters and sounding out letter combinations and words, and finally comprehending whole sentences.

If you have a child who's still learning to read fluently (regardless of age), the three focal points should be reading aloud, reading along, and phonics lessons. Reading aloud and reading along (where the child follows along in the book) can be done simultaneously.

Early Reading Lessons—Phonics

Phonics is a method of instructing students in matching letters to their sound. This includes individual letters at first, and, once these are mastered, moves on to combinations of letters, called phonemes. Most curricula on the market today employ this method.

The phonics method is by far the most efficient approach to teach children (and adults if English is not their native language) reading. There has been much debate about this over the past century, but the evidence has accumulated: teaching reading without phonics is not effective and has a likelihood of leading to reading deficiencies.

RULE #1: KEEP LESSONS SHORT

For a kindergartener or first grader, the phonics lesson should cover around ten or fifteen minutes a day. It should feel more like a game than a lesson. If you are consistent with this, you will be amazed how much ground you cover.

As your student progresses, add a few minutes of reading from a fluency reader which is many times included in a curriculum if you purchase one.

Then spend some time reading aloud to your child. Frequently, I let my child read along, and whenever I got to a word that I knew he could read or sound out, I stopped and let him help me. This reinforced the words he was familiar with, introduced new words, and created immediate pleasure.

How do I know when to start on fluency readers?

During the early reading phase, your student will sound out individual three-letter words, and slowly move up to longer, more complex words. As the reading knowledge base grows, sentences are formed with these words.

As soon as your student is not easily frustrated by sounding out words and putting sounds and words together comes easy, you can add a fluency reader to make things a little more exciting.

These readers have advantages and disadvantages. The advantages are that they enforce fluency and expose the student to the concept of reading something meaningful with her eyes. The disadvantage is that, since the vocabulary is so limited, it can be tricky to find some with captivating content.

Sight Words

In my experience, it's a great idea to write some 'sight words' on index cards (one word per card) and practice these every day as part of the phonics lesson.

VOCABULARY PRACTICE

Vocabulary practice is not necessarily included in a reading curriculum if you plan on purchasing one. But there are different strategies to make up your own. You can simply take any book you're reading aloud and write ten words on a whiteboard that you think will be helpful for your student to know before reading aloud.

READING COMPREHENSION

Reading comprehension can be assessed by asking a few open-ended questions. Who was the good guy? Who was the bad guy? These are the most basic questions and kids know the answer quickly if they paid attention (if there is a good and a bad guy in the story, that is).

Who was funny? What did he do that was funny? Why did he get in trouble? What was the weather like? Was there a sad part? Was there a dangerous situation? What made it dangerous? You get the idea. Use your student as your guide and ask questions you know she likes to talk about.

Language Arts Lesson Guides

This subject of Language Arts is so extensive, I was very grateful when I found materials to help me with this subject because I was terrified that I would accidentally neglect to teach one of the language art topics. Investing in a phonics curriculum helped me with the frequence of lessons, the sequence of words to learn, and the curriculum materials usually included fluency readers.

Some language arts skills should be covered daily, while others only need to be taught one, two, or three times a week. As a rule of thumb, your student should read and write something every day, plus one other language arts skill.

With the help of the curriculum, and some consistency and effort, my kids have turned out to be proficient readers and writers, witty in their use of language.

Create a Love for Reading

As I instruct my student in reading, I keep my mind on the big picture: I want to create an atmosphere that promotes a love for reading and turns my child into a life-long reader. I will come back to this in the section about teaching literature.

EARLY READING

Read Alongs: books you can read together and have your child read along

- *Little Bear* books by Else Homelund Minarik
- *Frog and Toad* books by Arnold Lobel
- *Henry and Mudge* by Cynthia Rylant
- *Annie and Snowball* by Cynthia Rylant
- *Poppleton* by Cynthia Rylant
- *Mr. Putter and Tabby* by Cynthia Rylant
- *Mercy Watson* by Kate DiCamillo
- *Billy and Blaze* by C.W. Anderson

- *Magic Treehouse* by Mary Pope Osborne
- *Boxcar Children* by Gertrude Chandler Warner

Phonics Curricula

- *Primary Arts of Language* (PAL) by the Institute for Excellence in Writing is my personal, all-time favorite reading and writing curriculum. PAL uses poetry memorization to teach patterns and sounds of language, and to make it enjoyable for the student. I used this program with my youngest when it had just been published for the first time, and I was amazed at the progress my daughter made and the fun that we both had. Check out the videos on the IEW website to help you decide if this is for you. You can find all the materials at www.iew.com.

- *All About Spelling* and *All About Reading* by All About Learning Press is an intuitive system of learning phonics and spelling by using letter tiles of phonograms to build words. Also included are some sight words for each lesson, so there is no need for you to make index cards; the work is all done. The fluency readers are among the best I have seen. They start with just a page, then eventually get longer. You can find these materials at www.allaboutlearningpress.com.

- *Phonics Museum* by Veritas Press www.veritaspress.com. This is a complete phonics program which follows the Classical Christian method. It is available as an app as well.

- *Reading Eggs* www.readingeggs.com is an online game that's fun to play as reinforcement. I'm not a fan of using only online tools, especially at a young age. But I am also realistic and know that many kids play on devices. They may as well play a game that teaches reading.

- *Sing, Spell, Read, and Write* www.songsthatteachus.com is another program I used as a supplement to change things up a bit. It is based on songs, and the first-grade level teaches phonics using the image of a Ferris wheel which has all the vowels arranged in a circle going up the wheel and then again going down.

PATHWAY READERS

My favorite early reading books are published by Pathway Readers. Each book is filled with fun stories written to gain fluency and has a language workbook companion if you're interested in that. There is a companion for each reader and a language workbook called *Climbing to Good English*.

- *First Steps*
- *Days Go By*
- *More Days Go By*
- *Busy Times*
- *More Busy Times*

  Companions to each of the previous books
- *Climbing to Good English* series (Pathway Readers language program)

  These are relatively inexpensive and make a good stand-alone reading and phonics programs for the elementary school years (at this point around $65 for the whole set). The setting of the stories is Amish country with Christian values. My children loved to re-read every story multiple times. Find these at www.pathwayreaders.com.
- *Bob Books* by Bobby Lynn Maslen. A popular early reader set. The first book only uses four different letters to create a story by using mat, sat, and at. These short little books teach fluency and confidence. Bear with the stories, as they are extremely limited in their content, but effective in teaching phonetic recognition. There are five levels of these sets available on Amazon.

The Benefits of Reading Aloud

Reading aloud impacts speech and language development profoundly, even during pregnancy. The Proceedings of the National Academy of Sciences of the United States of America (PNAS) found a strong correlation between sounds that the fetus heard during pregnancy and the brain activity after birth when exposed to these sounds.

Babies were able to recognize speech in various forms, and the more they had been exposed to during pregnancy, the more active their brains were.

'Speech features', or sounds of speech and language patterns, are the foundation of learning to speak, and later, to read and comprehend. Infants benefit when they are being read to even during pregnancy, but this positive impact of the spoken word increases as kids get older.

Reading and Vocabulary

Our vocabulary and language development have a huge impact on our ability to read, write, and comprehend for the sake of learning. Much of our knowledge and communication during the school years and as working adults is acquired in reading and writing. How can we make sure our children are prepared for this task?

"Research shows that reading aloud is the single most important thing to help your child prepare for reading and learning" and "the number of words that a child knows on entering kindergarten is a key predictor of his or her future success." (Dr. John Hutton, pediatrician and clinical researcher at the Cincinnati Children's Hospital Reading and Literacy Discovery Center).

The reason that reading aloud is so important is that many words do not lend themselves to being easily used in a conversation with a very young child.

As parents, we tend to speak to our children at a level that communicates in the quickest and easiest way. Books, on the other hand, don't have this problem. The author can use much more sophisticated language, and the reader will usually wonder and figure out the meaning of the word.

Correct Pronunciation Effectively Increases Active Vocabulary

Pronunciation may not be an obvious learning step, but it is not always clear how a word is pronounced correctly by reading it yourself without first hearing it spoken. I know this because English is not my native language, so I have had some interesting experiences from reading English books and trying to apply my freshly acquired vocabulary in conversation.

When people stared at me with confused looks, I quickly realized that my new word did not sound the way I had imagined. Not knowing the correct pronunciation of a word makes me hesitate to use it after so many embarrassing moments.

It's very likely that when we read aloud to our kids, we try to pronounce words correctly. And if we do not know how to pronounce it, we probably make light of it by trying out various options and ask our phones (at least that's what I do) or simply tell our kids, 'Sorry, I have no clue how to say this word'.

Understanding the meaning and pronunciation of a word increases the likelihood of our using that word in conversation.

The Hawzes, the Snawzes, and Pastie

My oldest son read *When Hitler Stole Pink Rabbit* by Judith Kerr as a fifth grader. I had bought him this book because, growing up, I had read the German version in fifth grade and remembered it as a wonderful introduction to that period in German history. Well, my son encountered the words 'Sozis' (pronounced zoh-tsees) and 'Nazis' (pronounced nah-tsees). The Sozis referred to the Socialists and the Nazis to the National-Socialists.

I asked him one day where in the book he was and whom he encountered so far. He looked at me with a confused expression on his face and told me about the 'hawzes' and the 'snawzes'. Now it was my turn to look confused, and I asked him to bring me the book and show me the words. We quickly sorted out the confusion and had a good laugh.

A similar thing happened to my daughter who read the name 'Patsy' as 'Pastie', which reminded her of pastries. Except, in her case, I did not find out in time to correct her. Several years later, we were reading the same book aloud as a family. When I pronounced the name Patsy correctly, my daughter had no idea whom I was talking about. This is when her mistake came out, and to this day we laugh about the Pastie mix up.

Repetition Builds Brain Pathways

'Read it again!!' How many times have we read a book to a toddler, only to hear these words? There's usually so much passion and excitement behind this request; how can you say no to that? The funny thing is that these toddlers know what's good for them. What they find entertaining is actually a crucial part of vocabulary building: repetition.

If anyone wants to learn anything, regardless of skill or age, repetition is the way to do it. Performing the same task repeatedly stimulates the brain again and again in similar fashions.

This repeated brain activity is responsible for creating paths of least resistance so that the task can be done quicker and with less effort than before. The more repetition there is, the easier and quicker it is for the brain to follow this path until it becomes involuntary.

RAISING SPIDERMAN

If I spend time reading aloud to my child, she will gain experience and a taste for the kind of content I choose to read to her. If I continuously choose quality literature with deep content, she will adapt her taste buds to this diet and learn to prefer this over other types of literature.

It's the same philosophy as that which is used in training people to recognize counterfeit money. They never handle it, but only real money, so their spidey-sense is alerted when they encounter counterfeit bills or coins.

Similar to the counterfeit money detectives, our children will develop their own spidey-sense for the kinds of book that are worth reading. That doesn't mean that you only read Plutarch or Shakespeare to your kids, but these should definitely be on the list. One day, your child will appreciate being a Literature Spiderman.

Learning from the Masters

Each field of study has their master that everyone who wants to be anyone in that field needs to study. For example, every good writer studies Shakespeare, just like every good musician studies Mozart. Every artist studies DaVinci or Rembrandt.

In the same way, if we feed our children a variety of books written by the masters of literature, they will develop a taste for them. Later on, as young adults and even as adults with their own families, they will have this inner compass to guide them in choosing literature.

They will experiment, try new genres and 'weird books', but ultimately, their regular diet will most likely consist of what you would call a good book.

Read Aloud Above Your Student's Reading Level

Andrew Pudewa recommends reading aloud from books with a higher reading level than the child would normally read to himself. The reading level is determined by the level of vocabulary and complexity of the sentences.

A book that the child reads alone should be at or below the reading level of the child, at least when he is reading for information and doing research. That way you are making sure that your student gets exposed to some new vocabulary, while at the same time not getting frustrated with difficult words when reading alone.

As your child improves and gets more comfortable with fluency, you can increase the difficulty of read-alone books as you and your child see fit.

Set Yourself Up for Success

Parents are highly motivated to set their kids up for future success. Realizing the importance of reading aloud is an important step in the right direction. But like so many things, this task of frequently reading to our kids is easier said than done.

The solution? We must put an intentional plan in place that becomes part of our everyday life. This plan should be realistic and natural to your daily lifestyle. Plus, it becomes easier if you actually look forward to it.

Set yourself up for success by putting a basket of several books in an easily accessible place so it is inviting and effortless to pick one up and start reading aloud. Or use a Kindle or other tablet if you prefer.

If you find yourself dreading these fifteen minutes of reading aloud, you may have the wrong book. Choose a different one.

Many times, listening to audio books is a great option. This is an easy go-to if you find yourself not enjoying reading aloud. Be sure to choose a variety of books, but the rest is up to you.

If needed, you can give your children something to do with their hands. I usually have Thinking Putty, play dough, pencils and paper, or even a simple (very simple) activity like geoboards or lacing cards.

I have also many times read aloud during snack time. Whatever you need to do to make your read aloud sessions successful, have it ready ahead of time so you can simply sit down and start without scrambling last minute to find supplies.

Short Reading Sessions Add Up Over Time

Ten to fifteen minutes is what we're aiming for. If you want to do more, great. If not, that's okay. If we consistently spend ten to fifteen minutes, think of how much this adds up to.

If you read aloud for ten minutes each day five times a week, you will have read forty-three hours over the span of a year. For seven days a week, it adds up to almost sixty-one hours. That's a significant amount, and only ten minutes each time.

Not only will everyone's vocabulary benefit, but the common experience and relationships among siblings and parents will grow.

⸻ Sidebar: The Reading Wars ⸻

For a century and a half, there has been passionate disagreement about which method is most effective in teaching reading: on the one hand, there is a method using the Whole Language (Whole Word or Look-Say) approach, and on the other hand a method called Phonics. This disagreement has been so divisive, it is often referred to as The Reading Wars.

The Phonics method has been around for as long as people have been learning to read. It teaches students to associate letters, and combinations of letters, with sounds. Thus, a child can figure out how to pronounce a word by 'sounding out' what it should sound like. For almost two centuries, children in the colonies and the early United States, were successfully taught to read and spell using the Phonics method with the New England Primer, first published in 1690. That is, until the arrival of a new philosophy.

HORACE MANN AND JOHN DEWEY

In the mid-1800s, Horace Mann, sometimes known as the Father of American Education, first introduced the Whole Language approach. A strong proponent of teaching whole word recognition, he discouraged the method of sounding out words arguing that it distracts from comprehending what is being read. This new method was to teach reading by teaching children entire words without first introducing the individual letter sounds to them.

In the 1920s, John Dewey's 'progressive' education theory embraced this approach and pushed it further along, making it the dominant method of reading instruction in the U.S. Whole Language won a decisive victory over Phonics, and within the next several decades, the country saw a decrease in reading competency.

RUDOLF FLESCH AND JEANNE CHALL

A major breakthrough came in 1955 with Rudolf Flesch's amazing book, *Why Johnny Can't Read*. Flesch thoroughly investigated the history of teaching reading and concluded: "The teaching of reading—all over the United States—is totally wrong and flies in the face of all logic and common sense."

Flesch's book stirred up tremendous controversy. Educational establishments condemned both author and book, calling him "Devil in the Flesch" (*Time Magazine*). Flesch's book became a popular best seller, and numerous parents turned to Phonics to help their children become competent readers. Few establishment educators agreed with Flesch, and years passed. All the while, the American education system continued producing students with increasingly poor reading skills.

In 1967 Jeanne S. Chall, founder of the Harvard Reading Laboratory, published *Learning to Read: The Great Debate*, in which she argued for what turned out to be Flesch's fundamental conclusions. Opinion among educational theorists shifted toward Phonics, but the mass of schoolteachers, principals, and colleges of education were little affected.

THE NATIONAL READING PANEL

Finally, an extensive study done in the year 2000 by the National Reading Panel conclusively showed the overwhelming success rate that Phonics instruction provides. The Panel distinguished five areas of instruction, all of which work together in training to be a proficient reader: phonemic awareness, phonics, fluency, vocabulary, and comprehension.

This study revealed that explicit instruction in all five areas is necessary to teach children to read proficiently. Teaching Phonics creates the basis for word recognition with fluency as a result. Vocabulary and comprehension are taught explicitly through reading aloud and various programs that are designed for this purpose.

Phonics is a vital ingredient for maximizing favorable reading outcomes. There are of course other important factors involved in teaching reading, which this book treats in Chapter 5. There are also several different variations in methods of teaching Phonics, which you can pursue, if you wish, by reading some of the works listed in the Bibliography.

The Results Are In—But . . .

After all these years, the Phonics method had clearly won the scientific war, but it did not accomplish the expected clear-cut change in the way reading is taught in schools. Despite studies and success stories, many public and even private schools still do not teach explicit Phonics effectively in the early grades.

WHY IS THIS CHANGE SO DIFFICULT TO MAKE?

Making changes takes effort and strong reasons why it is necessary to make these changes. In the American education system, both effort and reasons quickly fizzled out mainly because it is difficult to give up one's old ways. Part of the explanation is that people forget the details of how they learned to read. Then, as adults, they make the assumption that learning to read is like learning to talk, and that learning to talk comes naturally, therefore learning to read should come naturally.

In fact, the opposite is the case. Watching infants develop, you can easily witness their desire to talk while their desire to read, unless encouraged by adults, does not follow those same patterns. The earliest stories in human history were handed down through oral narratives. The idea of reading and writing was eventually discovered but was still mainly limited to specially educated scribes.

It wasn't until the printing press was invented in the mid-1400s that reading became more widely spread across Europe. Along with the Protestant Reformation during the mid to late 1500s, reading books and pamphlets became an integral part of people's lives. Scientists, thinkers, and philosophers started publishing their works in printed books and over the next several hundred years, the reading community grew more than ever.

I am proud to be related to one of the inventors of the printing press. Believe it or not, Gutenberg had rivals. If you google Laurens Coster (or Laurentius Costerus, as the Dutch call him), you can read his story. My mother's maiden name is Costerus and, yes, she is a descendant of this inventor. It's pretty amazing to stand in front of his statue in Haarlem, Netherlands, and know that we are related.

The bottom line is that reading would not have taken off in Europe had there not been a way to print in great quantities with content that people wanted to read. Gutenberg became famous because he printed the Bible. Of course, it wasn't until Martin Luther translated it into German that the common person could understand it. This opened the door to mass literacy in Europe, which eventually spread to other parts of the world.

Learning to read takes work and determination. The point of teaching this skill in the first place is so our children can use it throughout their lives. It just so happens that reading and writing anything in the English language is a bit trickier than many other European languages. When Horace Mann returned from Prussia, he likely did not stop to think that there is a huge difference in learning to read and write the German language compared to English. Reading German does not require the same amount of "sounding out" as the English language. If you know how to say the German alphabet, you can read most German words with some exceptions here and there. Not so with the English language!

English is an enormous conglomerate of various languages that have left some bizarre (not bazaar) signs (not sines) of their presence (not presents). Think about these words: though, tough, thorough, through, trough. If your brain isn't twisted by now, good job!

Horace Mann discounted the vast number of rules that you must learn before you can make sense of 75 percent of written English words, and that is only reading, not even spelling yet.

BALANCED LITERACY

So, after the National Reading Panel conducted its thoroughly documented study in 2000, things did somewhat change in the American education system. Phonics was accepted as the way to teach reading, but the undercurrent of the Whole Language approach was so strong that Phonics did not stay in its pure form very long. Instead, a compromise called 'Balanced Literacy' was invented.

This sounds like a good approach at first, but when you look into it, it continues to emphasize whole-word recognition over Phonics. Students continue to have trouble sounding out simple words because they are never taught Phonics past its simplest rules, and now there is much guessing involved in order to read a simple sentence from a classic novel.

Educators are increasingly aware of this battle, but the school system is so large and rigid, it's difficult to make changes. The leading education authorities are now battling to bring colleges of education, and ultimately the elementary and high school teachers in the public schools, into conformity with the scientific findings. This is an enormous undertaking.

Will they succeed? Don't hold your breath.

READ ALOUD SUGGESTIONS

On the following list you will find my favorite books we have read over the years. These are classics and never get boring. You can read them again and again, and your kids will love them every time.

My children have fond memories of each one of these books and will read them even in adulthood. Reading aloud continues to build vocabulary, relationships, and great enjoyment as a family, no matter how old your child is.

Infant to High School Book Lists

- *Honey for a Child's Heart* by Gladys Hunt. An entire book written about the best books you can read to your children ages birth to twelve.

- Book Recommendations by IEW. A great list of books to read aloud or alone.
  https://iew.com/sites/default/files/page/fileattachment/IEW_Book_Recommendations.pdf

- *Before Five in a Row, More Before Five in a Row,* and *Five in a Row* www.fiveinarow.com.

- *Read Aloud Revival.* Sarah Mackenzie has a passion for reading aloud, and her website is full of amazing content from books lists to book clubs.
  www.readaloudrevival.com

- Sonlight Curriculum has some great suggestions regarding books for young children ages three and older.
  www.sonlight.com

- Dr. Hutton, Cincinnati Children's Hospital Pediatrician and researcher has a book list at www.readaloud.org

- *My Book House.* A collection of great literature for all ages in a collection. It has been described as a liberal arts education in one book collection.

SOME OF MY FAVORITE READ ALOUD STORIES

Infants and Toddlers
- *Good Night, Moon* by Margaret Wise Brown
- *The Very Hungry Caterpillar* by Eric Carle
- *Brown Bear, Brown Bear, What Do You See?* by Eric Carle
- Dr. Suess Books
- Mother Goose Stories

Preschool to Second Grade Read Aloud and Read Along Suggestions
- *Blueberries for Sal* by Robert McCloskey
- *Caps for Sale* by Esphyr Slobodkina
- *Bread and Jam for Frances* by Russel Hoban
- *Curious George* by H.A. Rey
- *Corduroy* by Don Freeman
- *Billy and Blaze* by C.W. Anderson

- *Doctor DeSoto* by William Steig
- *Frog and Toad* by Arnold Lobel
- *Little Bear* by Else Homelund Minarik
- *Miss Nelson is Missing!* by Harry Allard
- *The Little Engine that Could* by Watty Piper
- *Stone Soup* by Marcia Brown

Grade Three and Up

- *Pinocchio* by Carlo Collodi (Puffin Classics)
- *The Castle in the Attic* by Elizabet Winthrop
- *The Battle for the Castle* by Elizabeth Winthrop
- The *Penderwicks* series by Jeanne Birdsall
- *The Wingfeather Saga* by Andrew Peterson
- *The Green Ember* series by S.D. Smith
- *The Prydain Chronicles* by Lloyd Alexander
- *The Chronicles of Narnia* by C.S. Lewis
- The *Little House* series by Laura Ingalls Wilder
- *The Wonderful Wizard of Oz* by L. Frank Baum
- *Alice's Adventures in Wonderland* by Lewis Carroll
- *Alice through the Looking Glass* by Lewis Carroll
- *The Secret Garden* by Frances Hodgson Burnett
- *The Vanderbeekers of 141st Street* by Karina Yan Glaser
- *Childhood of Famous Americans* series by various authors
- Books from the Historical Fiction Book List in the History Chapter

Morning Time

A very practical and enjoyable way to make reading aloud happen in your homeschool is to put it in a block that is specifically intended for reading together. This could be called Morning Time or Morning Basket if it's in the morning, or, if it is later in the day, Story Time, Story Hour, Reading Hour, or whatever you like. You can add any subject into this time during which all your students will be combined. But if you simply like to accomplish your reading aloud during this time, choose your books, gather your kids, set a timer, and have fun.

One thing that pleasantly surprised me when I started Morning Time with my children is how many subjects you can cover during this time—simply by reading aloud. Science, history, literature, geography, and pretty much anything that has a reading component. Even math can be addressed by reading books like *Mathematicians are People Too: Stories from the Lives of Great Mathematicians* by Luetta Reimer.

This idea of reading aloud to your students, regardless of what you're reading to them, fits any educational philosophy. It can be done as a stand-alone block that is just for fun, or it can include reading content from other subjects. You can choose the books, or your student can choose. This can be counted as school credit, or you can count it as extra-curricular content—activities that are done for fun and not necessarily for school credit.

Several wonderful open-and-go resources for this read-aloud family time are available with a wide selection of fun and educational choices, including copy-work, art, memory work, all based upon the book or topic you chose. After reading aloud, you can pick which activities you like to do, and simply follow the provided plans. Or you can stick with only reading aloud and call it a day.

Here are a few of my favorite resources:

Charlotte Mason Style Morning Time Plans:

- Awaken to Delight www.awakentodelight.com
- Morning Time Plans at www.pambarnhill.com
  Find them under 'Shop', Older episodes of the Homeschool Better Together podcast.
- Cindy Rollins's Resources for Morning Time
  The New Mason Jar Podcast
  The Literary Life Podcast www.morningtimeformoms.com

Resources for Choosing Books:

- Read Aloud Revival www.readaloudrevival.com
- Literature and history selections from
  www.veritaspress.com
  www.sonlight.com
  www.bookshark.com
  www.masterbooks.com
- Simply Charlotte Mason's Bookfinder
  www.simplycharlottemason.com,
  in the menu, click on Account and choose CM Organizer

6

Literature

"Pleeeeeease! One more chapter!" All my kids were in agreement that we should keep reading aloud. The problem was, once again, the schedule. I had given us twenty minutes for reading aloud, and we were pushing the limit. What do I do? The book we were reading was an adaptation of Virgil's *Aeneid*. How could I refuse?

I decided that this excitement for reading a classic piece of literature does not present itself every day. This was one of those uncommon but vital 'teachable moments'. So, despite the schedule issues, I gave in. We spent another fifteen minutes or so reading the next chapter. And yes, they still wanted to keep going. But I asked them a few questions that intrigued them, so we transitioned to a conversation that was almost as much fun as reading aloud.

The extra time reading aloud made the conversation more interesting because we had more to talk about since we had covered more ground. And each of my kids was eager to give their opinion on the topic of interference of the Greek Gods and the wisdom (or folly) on the choices that Aeneas made along the way.

The ages of my kids were at that time upper elementary, middle, and high school. My high schooler was supposed to read the 'real thing' (not an adaptation) a little later that school year, so this prepared him for that task. His younger siblings were enjoying the story and conversations so much, it didn't even feel like school.

This scenario is exactly what I wanted to achieve when my husband and I decided to homeschool our kids. And I bet you, too, share this sentiment. We want our kids to enjoy the learning process and not feel as if they're being forced to learn.

The Goal and Our Mindset

During my early homeschool years, I felt a huge burden that I needed to somehow expose my kids to every book and every idea possible. But that created a lot of stress in me and made this subject not as enjoyable as it could have been. I had been homeschooling for quite some time before it occurred to me that my goal in teaching literature was really quite simple.

My goal was to enjoy stories and learn from people of the past. That's it. It doesn't mean that I have to read every book out there. And it doesn't mean that I have to have deep conversations about every detail that presents itself. It simply means that we read some of the suggested books that appeal to us and talk about them.

Reading stories from the past gives us glimpses of what life was like, what people enjoyed, and what challenges they faced. We get insights into science, inventions, and worldview. After enjoying stories, we might even venture out into some of the heavier, more academic content.

It felt as if a burden had been lifted from my shoulders. With this new mindset of enjoying stories and learning from the people from the past, my approach changed. I felt more freedom in choosing from the books that my curriculum recommended.

I even substituted some books because I found a few books that were a better fit for my family. For example, I added a few books by Goethe and Lessing (English translations) and omitted a few books from the curriculum. I did this because I wanted my kids to know a few works from some German poets and thinkers.

Younger Kids Need Stories

Teaching literature will look different for a younger child compared to a high schooler. You can jump right into reading Heidi, or an adaptation of the *Odyssey*. Stories are the easiest way to introduce our young children to great literature.

Read aloud every day from any quality book, and you are well on your way to teaching literature. Conversations about these books are going to be much more fun if everyone enjoys the story, including the teacher. So, feel free to pick a book you can see yourself getting into.

Later in this chapter I will give you some good conversation starters. All you need is the book (your choice of print, audio, or e-book) and a few questions. There is no quiz at the end, just a conversation.

TILLING THE GROUND FOR A GOOD LITERATURE SESSION WITH AN OLDER CHILD

Yes, older children need stories, too, so we shouldn't stop reading these with our older kids. But starting in around seventh grade and up, there should be some sprinkling in of some more advanced works of literature. Before jumping into these new waters, however, there should be some ground-tilling.

If I told my children, 'Please read the first five pages of Plutarch's *Parallel Lives*' without adequately preparing them, I wonder how they would have responded. Probably by ignoring my request and hoping I would forget about it. I know how I would respond. To quote my youngest daughter, "No, thank you. I'll pass."

A few things should happen to prepare for the encounters with the great minds and heroes of the past and present. We should create an atmosphere in which we learn from that person. Next, there should be a basic understanding of the times and circumstances that we will be talking about. And finally, we need to create relevancy in our students' minds.

Creating a Workshop Atmosphere

Have you ever been to a workshop? The kind, where they have coffee and snacks set up and you can bring your plate and drink into the room? How does that affect the atmosphere?

It creates a relaxing mood. Conversation usually comes easier when you have something to nibble on. This helps take the pressure off, because seeing everyone eat makes us equals in a sense, which is a great foundation for deep conversations.

It also creates anticipation. It's like getting ready to watch a movie in the theater and getting popcorn and drinks before finding your seat.

Now, imagine doing this at home. How many kids would refuse a yummy snack in connection with reading or listening. If you have a reluctant student who is not interested in listening to these books, food is usually a successful solution. But even with eager listeners or readers, food improves sense perception,

Understanding the Times and Circumstances

When I prepare my kids to start reading a literary work, I usually spend some time reading a short biography and a few childhood stories if there are any, to break the ice. Stories about the childhood of an author usually help kids identify with him or her. Usually, my curriculum provides this. If not, I check the Internet.

After that, I try to address, as efficiently as possible, a bit of the historical setting if it wasn't already mentioned in the biography. This is like building a rough frame that will be added onto over the years. For this reason, it makes sense to read a cluster of books that were written in a similar timeframe.

My favorite tool for this step is historical fiction because it gives a glimpse of how life was, and how people interacted and talked.

Finally, we read a short summary, which, again, is usually provided by my curriculum. Usually, the summary is written in a way that gives just enough but not too much information so as to not ruin suspenseful moments.

This combination usually piques the interest of my students, and they want to find out for themselves what the author wrote. Even though many times, the book does not seem directly related to the times and circumstances in which the author was living in, there is always a connection in some way.

Fictional works usually reflect some current issue that the author addresses in a very creative and imaginary manner. Non-fictional works are usually more direct and address the issue by pondering and explaining which can seem tedious. But exactly this is what will give us insight into the times and circumstances.

Creating Relevancy

It is crucial to make this person, whom you are learning about and reading from, relevant in your own eyes and in your child's eyes. That means we need to figure out what made them relevant in their own time and see how it affects us today. What did they accomplish, and what effect did this have on history?

To find information about this, I read from several sources: my teacher guide, a well-written children's history book, and from a quick Internet search. This gives me a good overview of the future impact the author's book had on people.

Depending on the maturity of my student and the complexity of the situation, I read a few highlights aloud to my students, and sometimes I let them read these sources by themselves. Having some familiarity with the author and his/her motivation of writing the book we are about to read gives us a good foundation for understanding the content of the book.

The beauty about books is that they can be read and re-read. I can go back and double check if I forgot something. It's really very convenient if you think about it that way. Books are simply a carefully selected accumulation of thoughts that the author had in his or her lifetime. You never have to ask them to repeat what they said, but simply re-read the sentence.

They were just people like you and me who took time to write their thoughts down. With a bit of imagination, reading their books can be like sitting down to coffee with them and listening to them speak.

BABY STEPS

Remember that the easiest way to establish openness to reading what's considered 'difficult' by some is by taking baby steps over a long period of time. You don't have to start with Plato or Milton. You also don't have to read great quantities in one sitting, but take one paragraph at a time.

There's no rush to get through every book in the library because there will always be more. Imagine we had our kids read every good book while they're still in school. What would they read for fun as adults?

THE GREAT BOOKS

Some of you may be familiar with the late Mortimer Adler, an American philosopher, author, and teacher. His focus was literature and the great ideas that have been addressed and contemplated by philosophers, scientists, statesmen, and theologians. Adler and Robert Hutchins worked together and compiled a fifty-four-volume collection called "The Great Books of the Western World" and published by Encyclopaedia Britannica.

Together, these two men coined the phrase "The Great Conversation," which connects all the thinkers, philosophers, scientists, statesmen, and theologians who have ever written about the ideas and answers to the questions that touch the human heart and mind at the deepest level. All of these authors are participating in one long conversation spanning thousands of years.

I do want to mention that Adler and Hutchins have had to take some heat because they excluded books that clearly could have been added. They also focused on the western world, and did not include eastern works (Confucius, etc.).

The criticism can be harsh in our current culture, which likes to have everything just so and reminds me a little of Goldilocks. I am generally not bothered by excluding certain authors because I'm glad these two men came up with a list to begin with.

Also, in their defense, you must draw the line somewhere, and just because certain books are not included doesn't mean we cannot enjoy them. Plus, since I live in the US, I live in the western world, and it will be a good idea to study the works that led us to this point in history. The eastern works are interesting, too, so you can add them yourself to your personal collection of great books.

There are a number of books not on that list that in my opinion qualify, so I have a shelf full of them. John Bunyan's "Pilgrim's Progress" is among these, and so is "The Cost of Discipleship" by Dietrich Bonhoeffer.

The point is that Adler and Hutchins paved the way and got a movement going that brought these books back into the life of today's readers. Regardless of the disagreements, these two men did extensive research and went above and beyond anything I could ever do, so I greatly appreciate their legacy.

The Goal of Teaching Literature

TIMELESS IDEAS

Do you sometimes ask yourself, 'What kind of world are my kids growing up in?' It's certainly a different world than twenty or even ten years ago. Our culture has changed much in the last decade. But if you look at the overarching ideas that are dominating the headlines, they are not new.

One of the goals of teaching literature is to read and understand the timeless ideas and their consequences that people have thought of and dealt with since the beginning of history. Much of the knowledge we take for granted today, such as microscopic germs, atomic theory, and electricity, has only been around for less than two hundred years.

However, many ideas and theories about society, government, education, entertainment, or the ongoing search for a formula that explains everything have been around for thousands of years. People wrote these things down, and we can learn from them directly and see how they dealt with them.

Reading these books directly is by far superior that reading what other people wrote about them. The ideas that great books contain are timeless. How did Mark Twain put it? "The great books are the books that everyone wishes he had read, but no one wants to read."

Learn to Ask Good Questions

Before jumping into heavy literature, we need to train our kids how to think and ask good questions. Some books are lighter reading, and some are a bit intimidating and somewhat difficult to comprehend. That's why it's better to start doing this at an early age, even with your kindergartener, carefully selecting the books of course.

If we start early, our kids will get accustomed to asking questions and finding little gems in the book we are reading. A great resource that helped me get started was *Teaching the Classics* by Adam Andrews.

YOU DO NOT HAVE TO HAVE A CURRICULUM

My discussions were guided by the curriculum, but since then I have learned that you don't need to go and spend a bunch of money on this. If you're equipped with the right questions and mindset, you should be able to have some great conversations without using a discussion and answer guide.

I did not feel equipped, and without reading the suggestions and teacher notes, I would have been lost. So, it was money well spent. If you feel like I did, purchasing or borrowing a curriculum is a good idea. It will be your friend when you are stuck.

Open Ended Questions

Whether you own a curriculum or you just make it up as you go, the following open-ended questions are helpful for both approaches. They make great questions to add into your curriculum if you so choose, or they will make great conversation starters with no curriculum and not much preparation on your part.

These questions will work best for stories and not so much for non-fiction.

1. Should he/she have done this?

2. How is X like/different from Y?

3. Who was ———— in this story? (Fill in the blank with character traits like brave, fearful, or loyal.)

4. What other story does this one remind you of?

5. What is something that you don't want to forget?

I found these on the *Read Aloud Revival* Podcast by Sarah Mackenzie. Her "Five Questions Guide" is available at
    www.readaloudrevival.com.
Search for episode #196 and scroll down until you see the box that says, "Get your free 5 questions guide." If you listen to the episode, you will hear more details about it.

The answers to these questions are not clear cut and allow for differences in opinions. They also cannot be answered with either yes or no, which is the idea behind open-ended questions.

Disagreement Is Okay

You may be unsure about how to handle answers that you disagree with. I frequently made the mistake of voicing my opinion when I disagreed with my children. That is not necessarily a good idea.

They are on a journey, and while I am already an adult, they are not. There's still much growing and maturing going on in their brains, so sometimes it's best to let a disagreement rest. The relationship is more important than being right or wrong.

Instead, ask questions if you disagree and be curious how your child arrived at his conclusion. This is a far more valuable conversation than preaching at him (which I have definitely done before) and trying to convince him to change his mind.

DIFFICULT BOOKS: ONE EASY READ FOR EACH DIFFICULT BOOK

I usually read several books side by side, and I found a good rule to follow regarding the right balance of books was this: for each book with heavy content choose a book with lighter content to read alongside. For example, an assigned book was *The Peloponnesian War* by Thucydides, quite the heavy reading, literally and figuratively. The book we own is over three inches thick.

But alongside, I read to them *The Incorrigible Children of Ashton Place* by Mayrose Wood. After that, we usually read something from the Bible, then a US history section, and worked on memory selections. So, in all, we covered broad ground, but it was not overly exhausting for the brain.

Independent reading for lower elementary age:

The following book series familiarize children with timeless, classic literature, wonderful stories, a variety of ideas, and famous characters. Being familiar with these stories and characters allows you to introduce the original text at a later time without having to figure out what is going on. It helped me and my children to enjoy the original works of Charles Dickens and Shakespeare because we already know the basic storyline.

- *Great Illustrated Classics.* My kids devoured these books as second through sixth graders. The sentence structure and vocabulary are less complicated while the basic plot remains. Every other page has an appealing illustration of a scene from the opposite page. My children enjoyed looking at these simple yet reflective drawings which slowed their reading and helped the content stick.

  Reading fluently is the goal, but reading too fast makes us miss details. These illustrations review what just happened and help process details of the plot. There's a large number to choose from, so look at them online or check several out at the library and choose whichever seems most appealing.

- *The Great Classics for Children.* These are similar to the Great Illustrated Classics but are a bit shorter and have more illustrations. My children absolutely loved the illustrations. These, too, will slow their reading speed down and make them want to study each drawing. If you are like me and can't decide between the Great Illustrated Classics and the Great Classics for Children, you can provide a mixture of these. I have different stories from each set, and both were equally enjoyable for my kids. Again, they are available on Amazon or at your library.

- *Saddleback's Illustrated Classics.* These comic-style story books are a collection of classic literature adapted for children using the Dale-Chall vocabulary formula. Chall, as you may remember, refers to the same Jeanne Chall who founded the Harvard Reading Laboratory. She and Edgar Dale created a readability formula to assess the difficulty level of a text based on vocabulary usage.

  Their word base extends to 3,000 words which are familiar to an average fourth grader (readabilityformulas.com).

These words are the basis of Saddleback's Illustrated Classics. Included are helpful steps to guide the teacher in facilitating reading and comprehension.

These books are for fun, for a reluctant reader, or to allow various students on different reading levels to enjoy the same classic, with younger kids reading the graphic version, and the older kids perhaps reading the original. You can find them on Amazon or at your library.

- *Fairy Books of Many Colors.* Fairy Tales by Andrew Lang (you can get the whole set for a low price on Kindle).
- The Bible. *Genesis, Exodus, 1 and 2 Samuel*, the *Gospels*, and *Acts* are great to read to young kids.
- *Gilgamesh Trilogy* by Ludmila Zeman
- *Winnie the Pooh* by A.A. Milne
- *Pilgrim's Progress* by John Bunyon
- *American Tall Tales* by Mary Pope Osborne or other versions
- *Aesop's Fables*
- Various *Poems* by Robert Louis Stevenson
- *The Chronicles of Narnia* by C.S. Lewis
- *The Hobbit* by J.R.R. Tolkien
- *The Prydain Chronicles* by Lloyd Alexander
- *My Bookhouse* Set by Olive Beaupre Miller
- *Little House* series by Laura Ingalls Wilder
- *The Secret Garden* by Frances Hodgson Burnett
- *The Green Ember* series by S.D. Smith
- *Alice's Adventures in Wonderland* by Lewis Carroll

Middle and Highschool Kids

- *The Lord of the Rings* by J.R.R. Tolkien
- *The Wingfeather Saga* by Andrew Peterson
- *Gulliver's Travels* by Jonathan Swift
- *Frankenstein* by Mary Shelley
- *Anne of Green Gables* Series by Lucy Maud Montgomery
- *Little Women* by Louisa May Alcott
- *Little Men* by Louisa May Alcott

- *Little Britches* by Ralph Moody*Emma* by Jane Austen
- *Pride and Prejudice* by Jane Austen
- Shakespeare Plays. More information later in this chapter.
- *A Midsummer Night's Dream*
- *Hamlet*
- *Comedy of Errors*
- *Julius Caesar*
- *The Three Musketeers* by Alexandre Dumas
- *Robin Hood* by Roger Lanclyn Green
- *The Swiss Family Robinson* by Johann Wyss
- *Black Beauty* by Anna Sewell
- *Heidi* by Johanna Spyri

Book Recommendations for Seventh Grade and Up

- *How to Read a Book* by Mortimer J. Adler
  Find Mortimer Adler's reading list at
  www.ThinkingAsLeverage.wordpress.com.
  It's in the book list tab.

- *Histories* by Herodotus of Halicarnassus. If you're interested in ancient Persian and Greek history, this is a surprisingly easy read, if you get a good translation. We enjoyed *The Landmark Herodotus*, translated by Andrea L. Purvis.

- *The Theban Plays* trilogy (*Oedipus the King*, *Oedipus at Colonus*, and *Antigone*). The translations published by either Penguin Classics or Puffin Classics are good.

- *Parallel Lives* by Plutarch, a Greek writer who lived in the Roman Empire. He wrote biographies of famous Romans and famous Greeks and compared them to each other. It's a bit amusing that he always concluded the Greek characters were better than their Roman counterparts.

  Many translations keep the length of the original sentences. So, get ready to begin reading one sentence, and by the end you can't remember the beginning as it stretches over many lines. Keep at it, you'll get used to it. Plus, each of these lives of famous people is only a few pages long. You can stretch your reading out over several days. One page a day is a good start.

- *The Odyssey* by Homer is another great choice. The Penguin Classics version is a good read aloud for fourth grade and up. *The Hippocratic Oath* by Hippocrates. This is very short but leads to great conversation.

Middle Ages Great Books List

- *The Divine Comedy* by Dante Alighieri
- *Confessions* by Augustine of Hippo
- *Paradise Lost* by John Milton
- *Canterbury Tales* by Geoffrey Chaucer
- *Shakespeare's Plays*
- *Don Quixote* by Miguel de Cervantes

Modern Times Great Books List

- *Robinson Crusoe* by Daniel Defoe
- *The Communist Manifesto* by Karl Marx and Friedrich Engels
- *Democracy in America* by Alexis de Tocqueville
- *The Road to Serfdom* by F.A. Hayek
- *Federalist Papers* by James Madison, John Jay, and Alexander Hamilton
- *Animal Farm* by George Orwell
- *A Tale of Two Cities* by Charles Dickens

Pick any book from this list to start out, then, as you familiarize yourself with a few curricula, you may find different books you want to read. And once you have read a few, you will see that it becomes easier and more natural to pick and choose.

Adam Andrews writes that "you can plan a Literary Education of your own by keeping these questions and answers in mind:

> Which Great Books should you read?
> The ones that interest you.
> How many Great Books should you read?
> The next one.
> How fast should you read them?
> As slowly as necessary. There are no deadlines in real education."

SHOULD I GIVE READING ASSIGNMENTS?

There are legitimate reasons to assign or not to assign reading books to your students. On the con side: Having an assignment immediately switches your brain to a different function level. If you have a chore, you'd rather not do it. If you have to read a book, you'd probably rather not do it.

On the pro side, some books are like vitamins. We should read them, whether we feel like it or not. And once we have, we can honestly give an opinion. I would never have chosen any of the books I was assigned as a high schooler, however, now I am glad that I read them.

What's more, there is value in having our kids encounter certain books and ideas by themselves. It is like learning to walk without holding mom or dad's hands. They need some alone time with these ideas and concepts that are presented in the books they read.

My solution is to use a hybrid version of not assigning specific books by having them choose from a selection, and assigning a Great Book that is difficult, yet has a vitamin status.

WHICH BOOKS ARE VITAMINS?

Here is the sixty-four-thousand-dollar question: which books are vitamins? This is up to you. For my family, I have chosen the Bible, *Pilgrim's Progress,* and a few other books that I assigned my children to read. For each family, this will look different. If you are not sure what to choose (like me a long time ago), read through the book list and see if you find a book that you deem necessary reading.

You have to start somewhere, so research a little and enjoy reading your chosen book aloud. This is the best way to enjoy books with Vitamin status.

Books Shape Our Thinking

When I had to read Kant, Schiller, Goethe, or Freud for my high school literature class, I did not think they were very interesting and only read them because I had to. Looking back, of course, I know I should have put more effort into it.

But as I look back now, I realize that as I was reading these books, an interesting thing happened to me even if I did not realize it then. I was exposed to ideas that, without reading these books, I would never have thought about on my own. These books shaped my thinking, and my worldview.

I agreed with them on some things and disagreed on others, but without reading them I would have not known to have an opinion on these ideas I encountered.

And this is exactly why I have tried to be very intentional with my children's exposure to books. It matters now more than ever to be intentional about introducing them to ideas that they will eventually encounter as young adults but will probably not ever have thought about unless I give them a head start.

The great works of literature are filled with ideas, questions, and answers, all of which contribute to our way of thinking. The ideas speak for themselves, and our kids will recognize them easier and with more understanding the more they are exposed to them.

There are no new ideas in today's world that have not been thought of before. The difference is merely the degree to which the idea is expressed. Smart phones were not around five hundred years ago, but certainly the idea of communicating efficiently and quickly existed. Entertainment, one of the most widely used functions of a smart phone, is not new, either. While our access to entertainment and communication has changed from "delayed" to "instant," the concepts are the same.

WORLDVIEW IN LITERATURE

My worldview is the way I look at the world around me and the basic understanding I have of it. This is my foundation of thinking and has huge implications as to how I interpret ideas and respond to them. How do I decide whether I agree with Karl Marx, or with Jean Jacques Rousseau?

The ideas in these books are similar enough, but what do I do with them? Unless I understand the basic assumptions of these men (owning stuff is bad and leads to evil and hatred), and unless I understand what my basic assumption (worldview) regarding owning stuff is, I cannot decide whether I agree with them or not.

Reading and discussing great literature gives me a good opportunity to examine my basic assumptions and foundation of my values. The ideas that are found in the great books have been dealt with for thousands of years, and today's western culture generally does not look at them through a lens of solid reasoning, but through a lens of imaginary thinking.

We almost feel sorry for these people because they lived so long ago. It is easy to lose perspective because the lives these people lived are so far removed from our own lives, it is difficult to see past the differences.

CONNECTING THE GENERATIONS

A big problem is that many of the Millennials and younger generations have never heard of many of the thinkers of the past who have paved the way for certain ideologies to be part of our everyday thinking. The trouble is that if we lose the foundation and history of certain ideologies, we are without accountability.

Perhaps you remember the first *Jurassic Park* movie in which Dr. Malcolm said, "It didn't require any discipline to attain it. You read what others had done and you took the next step. You didn't earn the knowledge for yourselves, so you don't take any responsibility for it."

Scary things can happen when I believe things without understanding why. "I do things just because that's how I do it." Most of the time, this is not a good reason to do anything. History shows that the loudest ideas many times win, whether they are just or unjust.

People blindly follow the loud leader and don't think twice about the basic reasons why. Those who see the problems and speak up face injustice or worse, risk their and their family's livelihood.

READING BOOKS HELPS EQUIP US WITH DISCERNMENT

If I want my children to grow up to be able to continue what I have taught them, I must equip them with the fundamental knowledge of why I believe what I believe so they are capable of using discernment and making informed decisions.

This can feel like a battle, and I want to equip my children specifically for challenges that they will one day have to face without my help. So, as I choose my homeschool content and curriculum, I need to make sure I choose materials that help me accomplish that goal.

They will one day have to tune out countless noises which are surrounding them from every side. Social media, internet, friends, movies. How do you choose what is ok and what to avoid?

One thing is clear: We cannot escape the impact that our worldview has on our lives because it governs our decision making. It influences us in the smallest detail that we may not even recognize. Reading from the great works of literature allows us to be a "fly on the wall" and observe conditions of a different time period with different settings than our own, but from an outside perspective.

It is exactly that aspect that allows learning to occur. Looking from an outside perspective gives us a unique angle that makes problems and ideas simply jump off the page. It is such a privilege that we can read what people before us experienced and the conclusions they drew.

How do I choose which great book to read?

I had no clue which books to choose when I started homeschooling, but book lists got me going. The choice of books might depend on a few things: your interest in a specific era in history, or in certain authors or particular stories. You can look up Adler's and Hutchins's great books list and start there.

When my student or I had trouble understanding what we read, I found adaptations for younger readers, or summaries of the work. Many of the great books are not easy, and I had to read many adaptations and summaries when I first started. But once we got used to the ideas, we gained confidence.

Even if we didn't understand every word (most people don't), we still got the big picture. What makes these books great is the fact that you read them and re-read them, and still have not figured it all out.

How do I instill a desire in my student to love the great books?

The tricky part is, how do I teach my child to care about these great works when she clearly doesn't see the point of this? The answer is, I don't have to. The books speak for themselves. All I have to do is read them, and then talk about them.

Sooner or later, the rest will happen automatically. I can read them aloud, or I can read them myself, and share some things with my child.

Some kids enjoy reading more than others, so you can try out a few ideas. Challenge her to read a few pages by herself. Don't ask questions just yet but see if she wants to talk about it. If you meet with resistance, either have her read just one page, or share the reading by reading aloud.

Start reading and see how far you get before your or your student's brain is done. Note the amount of reading you were able to do and shoot for this same amount next time. Slowly, over weeks or months, you can stretch the time.

Celebrate

When you finish a book, have a celebration. Go out for ice cream or pizza. Everyone will feel proud of having finished a difficult book. There is no better way than to finish your book expedition with great food.

SHAKESPEARE

Why bother with Shakespeare? Regardless of the nature of the man, whether it was him or another bard by the same name, the impact he had on the English language is profound. Although we do not speak in the same manner anymore, many of the ideas, idioms, and flowery language remain.

Reading Shakespeare means learning about the cradle of modern English with many of its characteristics.

In addition, Shakespeare's plots address the ideas and deepest emotional state of human existence. Betrayal, dishonor, jealousy, fear, regret, despair, love, misunderstandings, practical jokes, humor, every aspect of human behavior and thought is addressed.

Usually, his plays are so complex that most of these themes show up in any one play. This fact makes his plays so enjoyable and creates plenty of topics for great conversations.

Also, Shakespeare's works should be listened to and watched, not only read. Nobody prefers reading the movie script of Captain America over watching the movie. To aid with understanding some of the words, I purchased either graphic novels, or a version of the script that is easy to read (large print with or without illustrations).

Here is how we studied *Julius Caesar*. We were studying the Roman Empire in history, so it made sense to pair it with this play. I added Shakespeare twice a week to our Morning Time.

The first few minutes, I read aloud from Charles and Mary Lamb's "Shakespeare for Children," which gives a great narration of the plot. Then we moved on to memorizing the "Friends, Romans, countrymen, lend me your ears" speech, each time a few more lines.

When we had finished reading aloud after a week or two, we started listening to an act of the play on the Arkangel cd's during our Morning Time twice a week, while reading along in large print scripts. Sometimes we only worked on memorizing.

When we were finished, we watched the movie with Charlton Heston. You can imagine how my kids reacted when we got the speech. Yup, you guessed it. They recited it right along with Mark Antony. It took us about two months from beginning to end before we were done.

Well, technically we were done. My kids loved Shakespeare so much that many times we kept going and moved on to the next play that appealed to us. It is hard to say no to Shakespeare!

Books and CDs

- *How to Teach Your Children Shakespeare* by Ken Ludwig
- *Tales from Shakespeare* by Charles and Mary Lamb
- *Beautiful Stories from Shakespeare* by Edith Nesbith (free on librivox.org)
- *The Shakespeare Stealer* by Gary Blackwood
- *The Bard of Avon: The Story of William Shakespeare* by Diane Stanley and Peter Vennema
- *Hamlet.* The Comic Book Shakespeare
- *Hamlet.* Saddleback Illustrated Classics
- *A Midsummer Night's Dream* by Saddleback Classics
- *The Merchant of Venice* by Saddleback Classics
- *The Tempest.* The Graphic Novel: Original Text
- *Romeo and Juliet.* The Graphic Novel: Original Text
- *Macbeth.* The Graphic Novel: Original Text
- *Julius Caesar* (Shakespeare Graphics) This is for younger readers and not the original text.
- *Folger Shakespeare Library*, original text with helpful notes and summaries

CDs

- Arkangel. Professional, full-cast dramatized version of Shakespeare's plays.
- Folger Shakespeare Library. A different full-cast, dramatized version of Shakespeare's plays.

Literature curriculum choices

- Ambleside Online. Free Charlotte Mason lesson plans, Grades K–12, Christian Content, www.amblesideonline.com.

- Sonlight Curriculum. Literature-based curriculum; covers history, Bible, and literature in one class. Grades K–12. Christian content, www.sonlight.com.

- *Book Shark.* Literature-based curriculum. History and literature combined. Grades K–12. Secular content www.bookshark.com.

- *Teaching the Classics* by Missy and Adam Andrews. Literary analysis made easy. Live-online classes available Grades 1–12. Secular but Christian-friendly, www.conterfotlit.com.

- *Omnibus.* History, literature, and theology in one class. Heavy on reading assignments but can be slowed down. Self-paced and live-online classes available. Grades 7–12. Christian content. www.veritaspress com.

- *Highschool Literature* courses by Master Books. From the website: "With this rich curriculum, your homeschool student will amply develop their critical thinking abilities, communication skills, and knowledge of literary classics— learning from a strong biblical worldview! Provides thorough college-prep coverage of literature and literary analysis." Grades 9–12. Christian worldview. www.masterbooks.com

Free resources

Books, study guides, synopses, etc., www.bibliomania.com

Free books in the public domain, www.gutenberg.org

Free audiobooks in the public domain, www.librivox.org

More links for free curriculum and lessons, www.amyswandering.com

7

Writing and Composition

"Learning to write' can refer to two very different skills. First, it can mean learning how to form letters and connect them into words. Then, it can mean using our ability to form letters, words, and sentences to compose something we have chosen to describe, such as a story or an essay.

The first learning we can call 'handwriting'; the second we can call 'composition'.

Although these are two different skills, in practice the first one usually leads fairly gradually into the second one. So we're covering both of these skills in this one chapter. If you've begun homeschooling a child who has already learned handwriting in school, you can now skip ahead a few pages to the heading "Composition."

Handwriting only refers to the physical aspect of the writing procedure, not the content. Later, when this first step is mastered, the student moves on to composition, which focuses on the content of the writing.

What that means is that, as the student gets older and improves in his skills, the writing lesson changes. Learning to write, both the letter formation and then the composition, takes hard work and diligence. It requires a tremendous interaction of different parts of the brain. Each child will have a different speed with which they move forward, but as long as they are making progress, even if it is slow, it is adequate.

Looking at the poor writing and composition skills of students in the United States, this subject is not being taught effectively in most schools, partly because it's difficult to teach every student well in a large classroom. But more importantly, many times the foundation of good writing is lacking.

How to Begin with an Early Writing Lesson

My youngest daughter was my first officially homeschooled kindergarten student. Her older siblings had attended a school, and I had experienced early writing lessons from the perspective of a mom.

But now I was the teacher. Gulp.

I knew that before my daughter was ready to begin writing letters, we had to exercise those little fingers. She loved to play the piano, so she was off to a good start.

I also found some great exercise books called *Get Ready for the Code*. These cute little workbooks are filled with fun and easy exercises (for Pre-K and K) to strengthen your student's fingers and practice fine motor control. The lessons are short and quickly finished, but really help improve hand-eye coordination and build fine motor muscles.

After preparing the little fingers and building up hand-eye coordination, it's time to move on to actual writing. The curriculum I have chosen for my students is, for the most part, that of Andrew Pudewa and the Institute of Excellence in Writing (IEW).

The approach that IEW takes is that of imitation learning. First, the student learns to write letters and words (a form of imitation). Once this skill is mastered, copy work of complete sentences is added to the list, which is another form of imitation.

Copy Work

As the name implies, you will choose a passage for your student to copy from. Again, the skill of letter formation must be mastered before copy work is assigned, but as soon as that has been accomplished, you can jump right in.

At this stage, copy work is perfect as a writing assignment. Don't worry about assigning essays or reports yet. Start with copying short sentences. As your student becomes more and more comfortable with this, you can assign longer passages to copy.

Andrew Pudewa emphasizes the importance of imitation as part of becoming a proficient writer. The reasoning is very similar to that of learning any other handiwork skill: you first learn by observing closely what your teacher does.

You then copy the techniques and style, and once you feel comfortable with the process, you make it your own and add your personal touch.

Copying a few sentences written by great authors might seem trivial but is foundational in learning and improving writing skills. This exercise shows firsthand the usage of words, expressions, and patterns of language. It's like learning to talk all over again, but slower because you can't write as fast as you think.

The approach of using copy work as writing assignments is also in line with the Charlotte Mason approach. Copying off great authors' language teaches the student about the use of the written word more effectively than a lecture ever could.

So, as soon as your student can copy a few short sentences, you can sprinkle into her copy work short passages from any of E.B. White's books (*The Trumpet of the Swan* for example) or C.S. Lewis's *Chronicles of Narnia*.

Before my daughter got to the point of copying off several sentences, she had to work her way up. I used several books that were designed for this very purpose. They were filled with short sentences about animals or other interesting topics.

After each section there followed a step-by-step guide on how to draw animals, trees, houses, and other objects. Illustrating is a fun addition to copy work.

A Daily or Weekly Journal

A great habit to start during the early writing phase is a notebook journal in which your student, with your help, writes one or two sentences each day and illustrates what she wrote.

Before my daughter was able to write words, she would tell me what to write and I wrote is in the journal. She then illustrated, again with my help.

You can find the primer notebook journals in many stores. The nice part about these notebooks is that they have lines only on the bottom half of each page, and the top half is blank. Your student can draw anything that goes with the sentence he wrote.

Some days, instead of a journal entry about our daily life, my daughter copied from the books I described above, so her journal is a mixture of personal entries and copied sentences. We absolutely love looking through these early journals now. They are adorable and bring back great memories.

Print or Cursive?

Most books are written in print, not cursive, so in order to learn to read, it's more effective to teach letter formation as printed letters rather than cursive letters. My kids learned to read print before they learned to read cursive, so they learned to write print before they learned to write cursive. But it was a fast transition.

Once your student can read and write every letter of the alphabet in print, it's time to start to teach her cursive. Why cursive?

The cursive technique promotes fluency in writing while at the same time making it easier for the student to write legibly and evenly. Printed letters are individually formed, and each of them must be put just right to make it look good. With cursive, there is an easier transition from letter to letter that eliminates this problem.

At the same time, cursive looks beautiful, even if it is not mastered well. So, learning to write in cursive instills in the student a sense of order and beauty. Fluency, evenly spaced-out writing, order, and beauty are the reasons to teach cursive to your children.

And when they are at the high-school stage, they will morph this into their own writing style. But having learned cursive will never leave them, because it will always be part of their "morphed" style. Cursive is the secret ingredient to beautiful handwriting.

Personally, I never used a cursive teaching program. I used a poster that has all the cursive letters written on it, capital and lower case. But there are very good cursive curricula on the market, and if you are not familiar with how to write cursive, I recommend that you use one. I will list them at the end of this chapter.

Before letter formation, your student will have to practice the strokes: lower case 'l' as in 'loop', then lower case 'e'. Continue with lower case 'n' and 'm'. You can figure out the basic strokes by looking at your poster, but again, a curriculum will make it easier for you if you are not familiar with it.

If you're comfortable creating your own cursive copy work, write a series of letters in cursive. Make sure you use a pen. Then have your student trace your letter formations. After that, they can copy it on a new line without tracing it.

After a few weeks of practicing strokes and basic letters, you can introduce one or two new letters, while still practicing the old one. In a semester or so, your student should be able to write most letters in cursive.

Keep at it, and copy off passages every day to improve speed, fluency, and accuracy.

What Kind of Print and Cursive Should I Use?

I had no idea, until my kids learned writing, that there are several print and cursive styles out there. Two of the common ones are D'Nealian and Zaner-Bloser. They look almost identical in their cursive form, but the printed version differs in the slant.

The printed D'Nealian letters are slanted so that the switch to cursive is more natural. You can google them and decide which appeals more to you. I happened to choose Zaner-Bloser for my youngest daughter simply because my older kids learned this in school.

Here is a list of writing curriculum choices.

Early writing practice
- *Get Ready for the Code* (available on Amazon)
- *Get Set for the Code* (available on Amazon)
- *Go for the Code* (available on Amazon)
- *Explode the Code* (several levels, available on Amazon)

Copy work
- *Draw Write Now* books by Marie Hablitzel and Kim Sitter (available on Amazon)
- *Draw and Write through History* books by Caryleee Gressman, Aaron D. Wolf, et al. for cursive copy work, also on Amazon)

Cursive instruction
- *Catch on to Cursive* www.masterbooks.com
- *Cursive Knowledge* www.iew.com
- *Handwriting: Cursive Practice* (Highlights Handwriting Practice Pads, available at Amazon)
- *Handwriting: Learn Cursive* by Peter Pauper Press (available on Amazon)

Spelling

Spelling is a daily but very short subject. IEW has a great spelling program that the student works on independently. Instead of purchasing a spelling program, however, you can choose words from the copy work selection that your student copies that day and practice these until mastered.

Spelling orally is an important skill, as well, so you can practice anywhere if you know a few words on the list. Have your student spell in the car or on walks. That can be very entertaining, especially if you have a student who likes challenges.

Spelling usually starts anywhere between first and third grade and continues however long you choose, but at least until seventh or eighth grade.

Curriculum Recommendations

- *The Phonetic Zoo* (starting in third grade, www.iew.com)
- *All about Spelling* www.allaboutlearningpress.com

Composition

Many kids find handwriting easy, but when it comes to composition, they feel at a loss. I was one of those children.

I remember thinking to myself, at the age of fifteen, "I really hate writing." With boredom and frustration I labored over yet another essay about something I didn't care about. In my mind, writing was pointless and tedious. It wasn't until years later that some of the content and reasons behind these writing assignments made sense to me.

I don't think I'm the only one with this experience. I have always wondered what could have been done differently to help create in me a better attitude toward my writing experience. What pieces were missing that might have pushed me in the right direction? I think I have found an answer, but unfortunately, I will never know for sure since I can't go back in time to try it out.

One of the ingredients I found to be helpful with my own kids is to connect any writing they are doing with something that is meaningful in the child's eyes, preferably a topic they enjoy. If the content of the writing assignment is relevant to the child, then the writing procedure will be more enjoyable.

I have seen this with my own kids and with many others as well. It's quite amazing how the content of the writing assignment impacts the outcome of the writing itself.

This doesn't mean that this subject will be every student's favorite one. What it does mean is that this subject will likely be more meaningful and enjoyable than the average writing class you will find in many schools.

How I Learned to Enjoy Composition

As a student, I never particularly enjoyed composition. Now that I am on the other end of it, I am a huge fan of teaching composition. What happened?

The summer before I started homeschooling my eighth-grade son, I found a company called IEW that publishes writing curriculum. Part of what they offer is talks by Andrew Pudewa, founder of IEW, about various topics regarding teaching writing.

That week, I needed to do some deep cleaning in my kitchen, so I searched for a long talk on something of interest to me. For whatever reason, I chose one of Andrew Pudewa's many talks, called "Nurturing Competent Communicators."

After my kitchen was clean, my mind and attitude toward several topics in the language arts department were completely changed. Until that moment, I did not look forward to teaching composition to my son, but now I saw this subject as one of the most exciting and important ones we would do together.

I assumed that my new-found interest in making this subject, composition, a priority for my son might soon evaporate. So, I hurried up and ordered some of the IEW curriculum, and after reading through it, I knew I had a winner. Composition has become, and still is, one of my and my children's favorite subjects.

Imitation Writing

Andrew Pudewa encourages the idea of imitation before you write compositions of your own ideas. He explains that writing what is in your head is a complex process and has the tendency to produce a dislike for the subject if your child is not properly equipped with tools to help him. Filling a page with sentences is one thing, but being able to compose those sentences for yourself—that requires different circuits in the brain, and if you haven't exercised those circuits, you'll be stumped and annoyed with yourself for being stumped.

I had never even thought about this, but looking back at my own experience, this makes complete sense.

Imitation writing is at the top of the list and is taught by providing short paragraphs about topics that are generally interesting to kids. The student then receives a specific assignment that does not require inventing new information but focuses on what is already there. She writes it in her own words, only using three key words from each sentence in the original paragraph.

Different methods of adding interesting language to each sentence are taught in a very gradual and systematic way. This fact makes teaching and learning composition easy and enjoyable.

All my children have learned composition using IEW's *Teaching Writing, Structure and Style* and all of them are good writers, even if they are not going to be English majors in college.

Composition is a skill that's frequently needed in life, and even my two sons, one a business and the other an engineering major, agree that in their work they use their writing skills—which go directly back to Andrew Pudewa—more than they ever thought they would.

What's the Point?

The skill of good composition is to be able to put thoughts together in a cohesive manner. It requires maturity and practice. This is not only a written, but also an oral skill.

Next time you look around and listen to conversations and people defending their opinions, pay attention to their thought cohesion. Some people are good at this, maybe because they have been trained, or maybe because they are just naturally good at this.

More often than not, people have poor thought cohesion and argue with reasons and words that do not really make sense. Many people believe what they believe because it feels right, without giving it a second thought.

Writing our thoughts down forces us to slow down in our thinking and give a step-by-step order of thought processes. This is not easy. Many times, kids (and adults, too), when they try to write, will jump around and become difficult to follow.

Having thought cohesion is a valuable skill regardless of what profession I am in. Fortunately, this is a learned skill, and it's never too late to practice it and improve our ability to express our thoughts orally or on paper.

The Benefits of Slowing Down

Most of us develop the skill to speak cohesively before learning to write. When we speak, we put words together at relatively high speed. Composition is a slow version of speaking, so why does it seem more difficult to write cohesively than to speak in that way?

Andrew Pudewa points out that writing is not merely a slower version of thinking, but one that requires several additional layers of brain function. When we talk to people, we use our hands and our surroundings to get our point across. Multiple attempts can be made to help us clarify and communicate.

But in writing, we get one chance. When writing anything, we must first decide what we're trying to communicate. That is usually the easy part. Now we must ask ourselves questions in order to figure out what we think about the chosen topic.

That's the difficult part. Coming up with thoughts and then expressing them clearly and cohesively is the step that makes this task unattractive. And in addition to figuring out our thoughts, we must know basic grammar rules, how to spell, punctuation, and other acquired skills. You get the point. It's not an easy job.

But something cool happens when we write our thoughts down. We read them as we write them down, and then we re-read. This process allows us to mull them over and evaluate whether they are cohesive and true. Writing down our thoughts aids in recognizing truth versus falsehood or possible fallacies in arguments.

Recognizing truth and communicating it with cohesive arguments is a skill I definitely wanted my children to learn. Composition aids with learning to think cohesively, which in turn makes you a better speaker. In other words, if I want to be a better speaker, it helps to become a better writer.

Connect Composition with Reading Aloud

I'll never forget the time when I was about twelve years old and reading a very well written historical fiction book about British prisoners being transported on a ship to Australia. I felt as if I was on board with them.

When my dad entered my room to ask me a question, I realized that my ears were ringing because the ship was in a storm and, in my mind, I actually heard the roaring sea.

I was enthralled by this book because it was a plot that I found relevant and fascinating. To this day I remember the plot and the historical setting. And since I was old enough to read independently, I was able to read it by myself.

Younger children might find certain books very interesting, but they cannot yet read it to themselves. So, by reading it to them, we can allow them access to these stories and broaden their knowledge base.

Being exposed to a wide variety of books allows children (and adults, too) to draw from those experiences they read about.

Even though I wasn't really on that specific ship, I had been on other ships on the rough North Sea, which enhanced my reading experience.

But it also goes the other way. I might read something in a book that I would probably never experience in real life, and I would feel as if I were really there.

When it comes to writing, the more experience we can personally draw from, the more creative our thoughts will be. More personal experiences will also help us ask more questions of ourselves, which will aid in our writing process.

How can we know what questions to ask of ourselves if we don't know what to ask? Having a broad basis of experience will provide the needed starting point for questions.

Conversations Lead to Good Writing Content

Besides broadening the ability to ask good questions, reading an interesting book or story aloud to the student will provide a good basis for conversation. This can give some great writing material, ideas, and opportunities to try out some reasoning skills on mom or dad regarding a topic that the student is thinking about.

Stories have a great effect on kids as their thinking skills are engaged, especially if there is an aspect of right and wrong in them. Kids enjoy discussing these topics, and this fact is in your favor when it comes to figuring out what to write about. Come up with your own question and try to answer it.

An example is, "Why did ———— do this? What was his motivation?" If you discuss it beforehand and come up with an answer together, writing the answer is not so intimidating. And since it is related to the read-aloud story, it will likely be relevant to your student.

Just Do It

Composition is the ultimate communication developer, but it takes time and practice. Did my child and I always agree on the most effective way to state something in her paper? No, we did not. How many times did I think that a sentence sounded wrong, while my student felt that it was just fine?

One strategy I employed was to have my students read aloud their own work, and I found that they hear their own mistakes or find a better way of saying it once I ask them to explain something they wrote.

However, in the end, we might still disagree. As Elsa in *Frozen* put it very nicely in her song: Let it go. I decided to give my student time to mature. It worked wonders.

My kids read some of their old papers from years ago and laugh at themselves. Pick your battles wisely. Correct their spelling errors, and gross grammatical mistakes, but thought cohesion is a matter of maturity and is best learned by writing. And writing. And writing some more. Just do it.

Recommendations

- *Teaching Writing: Structure and Style* by IEW (seminar for parents, then teach or do self-paced) www.iew.com
- *Structure and Style for Students* by IEW (self-paced, video based) www.iew.com
- *Writing and Rhetoric* by Classical Academic Press, www.classicalacademicpress.com.

  From the website: "The Writing & Rhetoric series method employs fluent reading, careful listening, models for imitation, and progressive steps. It assumes that students learn best by reading excellent, whole-story examples of literature and by growing their skills through imitation. Each exercise is intended to impart a skill (or tool) that can be employed in all kinds of writing and speaking."
- WriteShop Primary, www.writeshop.com.
  "Introduce beginning writing skills to your 5–8-year-old student through games, crafts, picture books, and one-on-one teaching time . . . an exciting, parent-guided writing curriculum with daily, easy-to-implement activities."
- WriteShop Junior, www.writeshop.com.
  "Using pre-writing activities, skill builders, and more, WriteShop Junior introduces students ages 8–13 to genre while teaching important writing, editing, and grammar skills."
- WriteShop I and II, www.writeshop.com.
  Provides 12–17-year-old students with a solid foundation in descriptive, informative, and narrative writing—and build self-editing skills—using the incremental WriteShop writing program."

Teaching Grammar

My favorite way to teach grammar is through learning a foreign language. The first foreign language I learned in school was Latin.

As a fifth grader, I remember how declining, conjugation, and translating sentences engrained in me correct grammatical use of the German language.

Just a few years later, I was able to transfer this knowledge to English, French, Dutch, and a few other languages that I was able to learn because of the basic knowledge I had gained.

German grammar as a subject was almost unnecessary for me because we covered most of the grammar content in Latin. Learning a foreign language that is based in the same root system of your native language (Romance or Germanic for most western languages) will teach you most of what you need to know in the field of grammar.

It would have been a similar experience had I learned French as my first foreign language. However, Latin is more complex and covers a wider range of rules than any other western language.

Just the act of forming a sentence in the foreign language forces you to exercise grammar rules. There is more on this in the chapter on foreign languages.

English Grammar Instruction

While learning a foreign language is the best way to learn English grammar as a whole, I do believe it to be helpful to teach students specifically English grammar.

Here's why: many Latin rules have no direct application in the English language. Gender, word endings, or the Ablative case do not exist in English in the same way as in Latin.

So, having instruction about some unique feature in the English language is necessary. A few more examples are comma rules (completely different from language to language), or run-on-sentences (equally inconsistent in different languages). However, these are concepts that can wait until middle or high school.

One way to include grammar into your day is to be on the look-out when your child completes a writing assignment. See if you find some grammatical error, then use this moment to quickly explain the problem.

Andrew Pudewa suggests turning it into a game. At the bottom of the paper, or if your child is younger, in the margin, mark how many mistakes, and what kind (spelling, comma, etc.). Have your student find her own mistake and try to correct it.

This takes some time, and you might not feel confident or comfortable enough to grade your student's papers this way, so IEW has a great curriculum that teaches grammar this way. As your student moves through the workbook, he reads an entire story, which keeps the lesson interesting.

Your student will hunt for errors in the text, and as he moves through the story, he corrects spelling errors, comma or contraction mistakes, and many other concepts that are slowly introduced. It is one sentence each day, and you are done.

Here are a few grammar curriculum choices.

ELEMENTARY AND HIGH SCHOOL

FIX-IT Grammar https://iew.com
- Grammar Galaxy by Melanie, PhD
  www.funtolearnbooks.com
- *Easy Grammar* by Dr. Wanda Phillips
  www.easygrammar.com
- Free Curriculum www.freedomhomeschooling.com
  www.grammar-monster.com

Highschool
- *Analytical Grammar* by Demme Learning
  www.christianbook.com
- *Fix-It Grammar* www.iew.com

Grammar through Latin
- *Latin for Children* by Classical Academic Press
  www.classicalacademicpress.com
- *Latin Alive* by Classical Academic Press
  www.classicalacademicpress.com
- Free Curriculum www.freedomhomeschooling.com

8

Public Speaking and Debate

Speaking in front of people is an acquired skill, for children and adults alike. It can evoke lots of anxiety, and the only way to really combat that is to provide opportunities to practice. In a home-school setting, this can be accomplished by assigning topics for your student to research and present orally.

If you can give your children practical experience in speaking aloud in front of other people, this can equip them well for later life. At first, the practice may be speaking to an audience of only one or two. A huge number of people say, in response to inter-views or questionnaires, that having to speak in front of other peo-ple is one of their most terrible fears: most people say they are far more afraid of having to make a presentation in front of an audi-ence than they are of dying. To take some of this fear away at an early age can be very helpful to kids.

Half the battle is to know what to talk about. Once there is a topic, say an animal or person of interest, the talking points will fall into place. It takes some practice to present the topic in a serious manner, and not giggle or start goofing off.

This is most fun if you have more than one student in your homeschool, or if you can arrange a time to meet with other homeschoolers or family so that the audience doesn't just consist of you. However, if there is only one student, you can take a video and let him watch his own speech. That will help with taking it more seriously.

Recitation from Memory

Public speaking does not mean that the speech must be composed by your student. Instead of an oral presentation about a topic, you can have your student memorize a passage and recite it in front of family at dinner or other occasions.

Reciting from memory is a skill that is largely being forgotten. It is still done in school plays and other productions, but the idea of memorizing poetry and famous speeches is not appealing to many and is often neglected in schools.

Who doesn't love watching a young child recite something? The younger you start, the better. To get your pre-schooler and kindergartener used to speaking in front of people, have them memorize poems or songs, then recite these at Thanksgiving or Christmas. It's so cute. For this I used the program called "Linguistic Development through Poetry Memorization," by IEW. It starts with very short poems, some of which are included in Primary Arts of Language curriculum for grades K–1.

Celery
by Ogden Nash

Celery, raw
Develops the jaw,
But celery, stewed,
Is more quietly chewed.

This isn't only for young children. As the student's brain matures, so does the ability to memorize more complex passages such as an entire passage from Shakespeare or a significant chunk of the Bible. It helps build vocabulary, improve the skill to use language in complex ways, and creates confidence in speaking in front of others.

Andrew Pudewa likes to tell the story of Frederick Douglass, who became a world-famous speaker by memorizing the best speeches of all time. His story is awe-inspiring and shows the power of memorization and self-motivation.

Plan Ahead

Practicing public speaking takes a bit of planning, but perhaps you have some opportunities already available. If you attend church, can your student participate by reading something in front of the congregation? What about Kiwanis or Rotary Clubs?

My children had opportunities to talk at Kiwanis meetings about certain special interests and community involvements that they participated in. We are also members of Civil Air Patrol which provides leadership and public speaking opportunities for the cadets.

What's your family already involved in that lends itself to speaking in front of an audience? Do you have any friends that might know of an occasion you could take advantage of? Or could you plan a family evening of storytelling (which is training everyone in public speaking) or student's presentations?

If you are super creative and have the energy, you could re-enact famous speeches by memorizing one, creating the backdrop, and finding the appropriate clothing, and have your student recite the speech.

If you are planning on studying Rhetoric, that will count as public speaking, so don't feel like you need to do both subjects. The important part of public speaking is the articulation and connection with the audience, all of which will be covered in Rhetoric.

IEW has a great program which is the only Public Speaking curriculum I've tried. But I found some others that look promising at www.cathyduffyreviews.com.

HERE ARE SOME EASILY AVAILABLE RESOURCES:

- *Linguistic Development through Poetry Memorization* by the Institute of Excellence in Writing, www.iew.com. Poetry and speeches are pre-selected and recorded for you to listen to and enjoy. Memorization is achieved by listening to the selected work every day. There are charts for you to keep track of the current memory work, as well as the previous ones to review. This program has five levels and will keep you busy for years to come.

- *Introduction to Public Speaking* by IEW, www.iew.com. Video instruction and easy to follow assignments guide the student through the steps of public speaking and teach several types of speech: self-introductory, narrative, expository, persuasive, and impromptu.

- *Free Curriculum Ideas*, www.freedomhomeschooling.com.

Debate

Learning to debate can be a bit trickier and more time-consuming than public speaking. The debater has to learn how to assemble relevant arguments for or against some opinion.

I have usually held the view that our discussions about books, historical events, and politics qualified, so I personally never signed my children up for an official debate class, unless I count the one-week debate camp that my son attended during the summer one year. If you're interested in joining a debate team, I know of one that I have come to respect. There are others, and you can soon identify them by asking around.

The National Christian Forensics and Communications Association (NCFCA), as the name implies, employs Christian principles to build arguments for debate.

Here's a short description from their website: "For more than twenty years, the National Christian Forensics and Communications Association has promoted excellence in communications through competitive opportunities where Christian students develop the skills necessary to think critically and communicate effectively in order to address life issues from a biblical worldview in a manner that glorifies God." www.ncfca.org.

Debate is an art that is currently in eclipse. It's a rare opportunity when you can witness a respectful discussion these days, especially in public, and especially in the political arena. So, this may be something you are drawn to and would like to foster in your middle- or high-school age children.

Some books that might help in this area are:

- *How to Argue with Anyone* by Thinknetic
- *The Art of Debating* by Luke Warren

9

Math

I felt like I had just wasted a whole week of math instruction. My seventeen-year-old son and I were working thorough the same set of Calculus problems again and again. He was lost, I was even more lost. All our momentum felt as if it was crumbling. We had started the year strong, so why were we hitting a roadblock? I simply couldn't figure out how to help him, and we had watched and re-watched all the instructional videos, and even scoured Khan Academy, to no avail.

Because I had several other students to take care of, I could not give him my undivided attention for more than an hour or two each day. And there were other subjects besides math. So, he had to figure it out completely by himself. After a day of leaving him to it, he found our 'roadblock'. I was very impressed, and he had a huge confidence boost because it was a truly tricky concept.

For my son, the real lesson, however, was not mastering the math concept, but one that he had learned before: sticking with it and getting more familiar with the concepts will eventually lead to success.

I, on the other hand, had completely underestimated my son's ability to figure out something that I could not; that sounds somewhat prideful of me, I know. I had somehow assumed that if it's too difficult for me, it's too difficult for my student, so I should assist. Nothing could be further from the truth.

So, once again, I was reminded of the strategy to leave my students alone with their assignments for as much as is reasonable so they can learn and grow independently from mom or dad. This is not always easy.

I have the tendency to notice where there might be a lack of understanding, and then try to jump in immediately, trying to fill the knowledge gap. I have to catch myself and back off in order to allow the student to become less dependent on me.

Math Teaches Problem Solving

Math teaches problem solving; I know—this is so obvious, it's almost too ridiculous to say. But if you look at it from a different perspective, it actually is profound. The problem my son had was not the math problem itself, but the fact that he was stuck. He could only figure it out by using non-math skills: patience and perseverance. These two characteristics play a major role in problem solving in the real world.

The subject of math, if used wisely, can aid in nurturing these virtues in our children. And since virtues cannot be taught by lecturing and talking, but only by providing conditions in which to apply them, using an intentionally hands-off method of teaching math can do just that. However, it needs to be done carefully so it doesn't backfire.

HANDS-OFF APPROACH

It's important to choose a math curriculum that has helpful guidance and advice on how to accomplish this. In my experience, short lessons that equip the students with the right tools to work independently are more effective than longer lessons.

After the lesson, we need to let our students wrestle with the problems as much as is reasonably possible. This hands-off method nurtures in the students the willpower and determination to become creative problem solvers.

In the case of my seventeen-year-old, up to this point, he had generally done most of his assignments independently, so he was used to figuring problems out for himself. But most of the time when he got stuck on a problem, he was able to sort it out very quickly. So, when we got to this zinger-concept, I knew it was different because it took much longer to sort it out, and then I started panicking because were getting way behind schedule.

And therein lay the problem.

FOCUS ON THE CHILD, NOT THE SCHEDULE

I was getting so hung up on thinking about following the schedule, that I forgot about the deeper lessons this subject teaches. Yes, numbers and operations are important, but if the math lesson itself does not impart a certain level of persistence and determination in my student to figuring something out, it only teaches an empty skill. Numbers and operations are relevant, but problem-solving skills on a higher functioning level are way more important.

So, as you look at your child, regardless of his age or math abilities, look beyond the superficial skill of juggling numbers. Keep an eye on the bigger picture and ask yourself how you're nurturing his approach to any kind of problem in the real world.

With younger children, this seems easier as the skills are directly transferrable to real life scenarios. For example, a six-, seven-, or eight-year-old does not feel silly walking through the store with mom or dad and adding or subtracting the number or cost of items while a fifteen-year-old would very likely not agree to this, at least not in my house.

But a fifteen-year-old might like to figure out how much sales tax I have to include and whether or not that means I can get the $6 bag of potato chips, and why on earth this bag costs $6. Would that count as wasting money, or is it worth spending $6 because we like the chips so much?

The level of problem solving has shifted by this age and involves drawing from other experiences. Math is the perfect subject to bring problem solving and reasoning skills under one roof. If we can somehow keep this in mind while teaching this subject, it would mean less pressure and more meaningful learning for parents and students.

Allowing my students to struggle with math problems taught them major problem-solving skills in the real world. Today they are excellent at figuring out creative solutions to any problem that comes their way.

This Is Great News

If you feel nervous about teaching math to your student, there is great news. The curriculum market is in your favor. There is something for everyone.

That has not always been so. Compared to the few math textbooks available in the 1980s, the amount of teaching materials you find today is overwhelming. Every level of math, from earliest math to Calculus, is available in every learning philosophy and in every medium (books, videos, self-paced, live-online, or combinations thereof).

This is great news, and extremely helpful for parents who have never themselves succeeded well in math or for whom it has been so long they feel like they forgot more than they learned. You can simply use your student's math curriculum as your own refresher course. And some materials are even designed in a way that the student can complete the lessons on their own with minimal guidance from the parent. The bottom line: there is a math curriculum for everyone's taste.

The Math Lesson

Math is a skill-based subject which means that it should be taught daily and separately for the different skill levels of each of your students. You can combine your students for some subjects, but each should have his math work at his own skill level.

One thing to be careful about is sibling relationships. Combining two competitively minded kids might end up being a distraction and leading to unnecessary frustration for both student and teacher. Teaching math one on one and having your students in separate locations is, in my experience, the easiest way to deal with this issue.

You can get one student started while another one is working on an easy, independent assignment (spelling, copy-work, memorizing, reading, and so forth). Give yourself fifteen to twenty minutes with your first math student, then let him work independently for the next fifteen minutes while you proceed to your other students. Move back and forth as needed.

If you have children that are very compliant and enjoy doing math together, there is nothing wrong with instructing them together. I have found it helpful to assess the dynamics of the math lessons throughout the school year. What works now might not work for you in three months. That is completely normal. Keep adjusting as you are able, and don't lose heart.

Messing up a few days or even weeks won't be the end of the world. Keep your eyes on the long-term progress, and, looking back, you'll be surprised how much you accomplished. Allowing your kids to conquer math problems by chipping away at them little by little will teach them skills that are far more valuable than merely teaching them to do number operations.

SHORT MATH LESSONS WITH FOCUSED ATTENTION

Over the years I have employed several math teaching philosophies and curricula, and depending on my student, the lessons looked different and had a different pace. Looking back, my favorite and most effective method comes from the Charlotte Mason approach: short math lessons with focused attention.

I sometimes have a hard time stopping a lesson when I feel like we're really accomplishing something. The problem is, depending on the age of the child, that, while my brain is still going, my student's brain is finished, attention in waning, and we are not using our time wisely.

Charlotte Mason has a maximum time limit for different age groups of children. When I stick to the time limit, the math lesson usually ends on a high point and the next time it's easier to get back into it, rather than when I push my student through "just one more math problem."

Here's a guideline for reasonable length of lesson (from Simply Charlotte Mason)

Grades 1–3	20 minutes maximum
Grades 4–6	30 minutes maximum
Grades 7–9	45 minutes maximum
Grades 10–12	45–60 minutes maximum

Also, the number of problems that are assigned to the student during each lesson is a suggestion, not a command. Allow your student to take the time he needs in order to be confident. This is not a race, but a slow and steady hike. If you as the parent are not anxious, your student will benefit.

There will probably be times of tears or frustration. Usually, and within reason, it's wise to move on to the next subject and make a mental note for the next math lesson to either review, switch topics, or slow way down.

WHEN FRUSTRATION HITS

There will be lessons that your student will breeze through, and then there will be days which bring frustration and struggle. At this point, my own attitude toward my student's level of achievement is important. How easily am I getting frustrated with my student's ability to grasp the current concept? How am I handling her attitude? How easily do I give up guiding her?

Should I slow down and achieve the desired result by cutting the lessons in half and turning it into two lessons? And when is it ok to close the book and revisit the topic at a later time so we don't actually waste time?

My rule of thumb is this: set a timer for a certain, maximum time. If the lesson is finished within this time, you are on target. Don't add more to it. If the student doesn't finish, it's okay, close the book and continue the next day. Before the next lesson, reassess what could have improved the learning process.

Questions to ask are:

1. Is the time of day during which we are doing our math lesson an issue? Perhaps we should move the math lesson to a different time slot?

2. Is there a skill that needs to be addressed (such as times tables, or basic operations) that my student needs to improve so he can succeed?

3. Is the pace of the curriculum too fast?

4. Is the curriculum a good fit?

If the curriculum is a problem, this can usually be fixed by supplementing with hands-on math manipulatives. You do not need to invest in brand new math books but simply follow the book you have, perhaps move at a slower pace, and add manipulatives. This will make it feel like you have a new curriculum.

For the next school year, reconsider the math curriculum you want to use and choose a different one based on your experience. Sometimes it's appropriate to switch a curriculum mid-year, but most of the time it's just as effective but a whole lot cheaper to add a few fun activities and break up the lessons.

PLAYING WITH MARBLES

One of my favorite activities that I frequently used in the early elementary years when hitting a roadblock was to get on the floor with marbles and 're-enact' the math problems. I would take several steps back and think of one or two essential skills that needed to be reinforced before moving on in our math curriculum.

Singapore Math, the math curriculum I had chosen for my youngest daughter during her early elementary years frequently included mental math. This requires grouping numbers by ones, tens, hundreds, in our head and then performing the operation.

This is a rather abstract concept, and frequently led to frustrating moments. Using marbles to illustrate each of the steps that had to be followed was extremely helpful for my daughter.

We started by using a group of ten marbles and making 'matches' that add up to ten. For example, she removed four marbles from the group of ten and saw that six were left. Therefore, six and four were a match.

Next, we practiced adding single-digit numbers to number ten. Two plus ten equals twelve, eight plus ten equals eighteen, etc.

After that, we moved on to simple addition problems. Let's say the problem was $8 + 4 = 12$. After making two groups, one with eight and one with four marbles, we separated the group of four marbles into two groups of two, then added one of these groups to the group of eight which gave us ten.

The rest was not so difficult since we had already spent time practicing adding numbers to ten. After doing this with a few other problems, my daughter figured out the idea behind this exercise.

For the next 'level' of our marble game, I put eight marbles in one of my hands, showed it to my daughter, and closed my hand. Then I put four marbles in my other hand, showed it to her, and closed this hand as well.

Next, I asked, "How many marbles do I have altogether?" Being able to see the actual number of marbles in my hands before I closed them made it a tangible problem to solve. And using marbles made it feel like a game.

I used a similar method with subtraction problems. If the problem was $12 - 8 = 4$, she watched me put twelve marbles in one hand. After secretly moving eight into my other hand, I showed her the four leftover marbles in my one hand and asked how many I had moved into my other hand.

For adding and subtracting numbers in the hundreds or thousands we needed to be creative in grouping and matching pairs that add or subtract easily. I wrote a number on a piece of paper and had my student use marbles to "build" that number by grouping the ones, tens, and hundreds.

We used three sizes of marbles, the smallest for the ones, the next size for the tens, and the largest for the hundreds place. When I ran out of sizes because the number went into the millions, we used different colors, with the largest marbles always being the greatest group. Being able to see this with objects rather than numbers on paper was a very effective tool.

MARBLES AND MANIPULATIVES IN THE UPPER ELEMENTARY GRADES

Multiplication and division add even more layers of complexity to the operations, so being confident and comfortable with the previous operations is a must. When my student was not confident with this and needed extra practice, I knew that we needed to practice grouping equal number of objects.

3 x 5 = 15 would look like three groups of five marbles, or five groups of three marbles. This immediately teaches the commutative property of multiplication, since you can reverse the numbers in the problem and still have fifteen as the product.

Division is simply the reverse of multiplication. If you start with fifteen marbles, how many groups of five can you make, or how many groups of three can you make? Your students will see that division and multiplication are related by simply arranging and rearranging the marbles.

The same strategy of getting on the floor and playing with objects goes for more difficult concepts, too. I love playing with cardboard pizzas that are cut up into fractions and can be added together. I also used card stock to cut out my own circles and fraction pieces and had my student label them.

Balancing equations is really fun when you draw a simple scale with two plates on each side and arrange equal amounts of marbles, or little paper circles and squares. Your students will learn that it is okay to remove matching items from both sides or add matching items to both sides.

Depending on the difficulty level of the concept that gave my student trouble, I decided how long our "math game lesson" needed to be. Sometimes we needed a week-long break from regular math lessons so we could review the needed skills. And sometimes only one or two days were needed.

My daughter loved these activities, and our math lessons were more attractive to her when I added "floor time." The best math lessons were usually when we started out with these games and switched after five or ten minutes to the lesson material. A timer helped keep us on track.

If you don't have marbles, you can use other small objects like buttons, dried beans, rocks, etc. Perhaps your student has a few favorite Lego bricks that can be used.

Measure Your Student against Herself

Your student plays the main character in the 'story' of her education, so allow her to be the main 'pace-setter' for her learning environment. Enjoy watching the natural learning curve that is taking place.

Some kids are naturally faster at grasping some of the concepts than others. Knowing this ahead of time gives us time to prepare ourselves for the temptation to compare our student with a faster or slower learner.

This is easier said than done, but we must force ourselves to look at only our student when comparing her. We need to compare her only to herself when we want to assess how much progress has been made.

Spiral Approach versus Mastery Learning

Math is a bit unique in that it has a few sub-methods within the philosophies we covered earlier. During your curriculum research you will encounter terms such as 'mastery-learning', and 'spiral-approach'. The difference lies in how soon a new concept is introduced and how often the old concepts are reviewed.

The mastery approach is more repetitive and ideal for students who need extra practice. It is also great for parents who prefer a slower pace. But it can be taken at a faster pace as well, so if your student gets bored and is ready to move on, don't have him do every problem.

The spiral approach introduces new concepts more frequently, but still revisits older concepts. This method is appropriate for students who feel very comfortable with math and like to move at a faster pace. It is also great for students and parents who enjoy frequent topic changes.

Both methods are effective, and you might even find yourself switching every now and then depending on your student's needs and interests.

A word of caution: spiral math curricula revisit topics from year to year, and you may not get the full benefit of the curriculum if you switch too often.

Math Facts

"Mom, why do I have to memorize these facts?! When will I ever use these?" Well, my kids now know the answer. You will use them all the time, whether you notice or not.

We skip count by twos every time we check to see whether we have enough eggs in the carton. And if you have a few quarters, you probably know how to count by twenty-fives. Memorizing facts is just a way of formalizing and accelerating the useful skill of skip-counting.

One argument I don't really like to use, is that eventually, your student will need to focus on more abstract concepts in math. It's true that having the basic facts memorized and being able to recall them quickly will make these more abstract concepts easier to master.

The reason I'm not a fan of this argument is that it reminds me of circular reasoning, even if it is not truly that. But I know that kids hear it exactly in that way. 'You have to memorize math to do more math'. Not a compelling reason at that age.

I preferred to stick with the real world and tried to notice whenever my kids were skip-counting. Next time they complained about memorizing math facts, I reminded them that they used this skill recently. And when I asked if it sped up their task of counting, they usually agreed. Math facts are, indeed, useful to memorize.

One way to practice facts is with flash cards. I had my students create their own flash cards by using blank index cards, writing the addition, subtraction, multiplication, or division problem on the front, and writing the answer on the back. My students then decorated them with stickers or drawings of their own.

In addition, I printed out two identical work sheets (available for free online, or it may be part of your curriculum), and get a cheap timer that your student can set for himself. He can then complete the first sheet and see if they can beat his own time doing the second sheet. This may not be the best idea for every student as he might get frustrated, but for several of my students this approach worked well.

Math facts are also fun to practice in the car. While driving to activities, all my kids enjoyed adding and subtracting when I put "thousand" behind it. For example, instead of five plus eight, it's five "thousand" plus eight "thousand." The same goes for subtraction.

However, it doesn't work quite as well with multiplication since you can't just put 'thousand' behind the factors and have the product in 'thousand'. For example, two times three is six, but two 'thousand' times three 'thousand' is not six 'thousand', but six 'million'. Then again, your student might just understand that concept, and surprise you. Nothing's impossible.

CURRICULUM CHOICES

The following list of math curriculum choices is what I have either personally used in my homeschool or would have used if I had the need. The purpose of this list is only to get you started. For a more comprehensive list of recommendations visit www.cathyduffyreviews.com.

Another great resource is the Rainbow Resource Center at www.rainbowresource.com, so if you need more help, check these out.

K–12

Traditional/Classical/Charlotte Mason:

- *Saxon Math* by Saxon: a traditional, spiral-approach curriculum. Many homeschool families and schools love this curriculum. I have personally only seen it used in a school set- ting when my older kids were in elementary school. Grades K–12. www.christianbook.com

  Online video lessons and auto grading for Saxon math courses is available with a membership at www.nicolethemathlady.com. Grades 3–12. Books sold separately.

- *Math Mammoth.* Use the printable worksheets as supplemental practice or use the full curriculum. Mastery based and very popular among homeschool families. You can purchase a downloadable version for each grade or purchase a printed version from vendors such as Rainbow Resource Center. Grades 1–7. www.mathmammoth.com.

- *Singapore Math.* This program has high reviews as it brings the Asian math method to the US. Japanese and Singa=porean children regularly out-perform the western countries in international math tests, so this curriculum is giving us a different style. It is heavy on word problems. For each semester there is a textbook, workbook, and extra practice book if needed. This is mastery based but has components of spiral approach. Grades K–8. www.singaporemath.com.

- *Math-U-See* by Steve Demme. A hands-on, visual math program that is mastery-based. It offers practice and extra practice problems but allows for a faster pace if needed. There is video instruction for the teacher, Lego-style manipulatives to visualize tens and hundreds, or fractions with over-lays. Each lesson has you 'build' the problem with the bricks. Grades K–12. www.mathusee.com.

Charlotte Mason

- *Math Lessons for a Living Education* by Masterbooks. In the

Charlotte Mason style, these math programs are based on real-life math problems as over-arching stories to engage the student. Christian worldview. Grades K–Alg 2 (as of now). www.masterbooks.com.

- *A Charlotte Mason Elementary Arithmetic* by Simply Charlotte Mason. A Charlotte Mason style math program that gently guides the student through real life and hands-on math problems. Grades K–8. www.simplycm.com

- *Kumon Method.* You may have seen the Kumon workbooks in multiple subjects, including math. Their approach is mastery based and follows the 'speed-accuracy' philosophy of quickly solving problems with high accuracy. Repetition is the key. Kumon tutoring centers are also beneficial to many families, perhaps even as a complete curriculum until the student has gained high speed and accuracy to move on to higher math levels. No grade levels.

GRADES 7–12:

Traditional/Classical

- Home Study Companions by David Chandler: The videos are thorough explanations of every lesson in the best math textbooks that have been successfully used in schools. Most of them are honors courses. All video courses are available as digital download. With the exception of the Geo-metry textbook, which is included in the digital download, textbooks have to be purchased separately. Grades 6/7–12. www.mathwithoutborders.com.

COMPLETELY ONLINE

Traditional/Classical

- *Thinkwell Math.* This is a comprehensive, online, video-based curriculum. Dr. Edward Burger teaches short lessons (5–10 minutes in the younger grades, longer in older grades). Each class is available as regular and honors level, which includes slightly more topics. The printable worksheets allow for practice and extra practice. Dr. Burger is a skilled teacher who uses his gift or humor to connect with the student. Automatically graded tests and quizzes are built into the course. Grades 6–12. www.thinkwellhomeschool.com.

- *CTC Math.* A solid and comprehensive math curriculum that offers tutorials and moves at the pace of your student. I have only tried a free sample but liked what I saw. It is highly rated by reviews. Grades K–12. www.ctcmath.com.

- *Khan Academy.* This free online video database offers countless subjects, including math. In addition to videos, you'll find assignments with solutions. This can be your main curriculum, or you can use it as a supplement. It's great for AP, SAT, and even MCAT practice courses. If you create a free account, it keeps track of your student's progress and gives feedback and help when he is stuck. There are no grades but energy points and levels. It is user-friendly and a great option if you are on a budget. Grades Pre-K–12. www.khanacademy.org

- *Redbird Math.* A fun, online, math-games based method. If your student enjoys math games and can resist the temptation to minimize the window and start doing something else on the computer, this might be worth checking out. I used this with one of my daughters, and she loved it. But it was not a good fit for us as a full math program because I could not easily keep track of how many concepts she mastered and how she was getting along. So, we used it as a fun way to practice math drills, and it was helpful for review. Mastery based with monthly or yearly subscription. Grades K–7. www.redbirdlearning.com

Great Math Supplements

- *Life of Fred* series by Stanley F. Schmidt, PhD. This can be used as a curriculum if it suits you.
- Doodle Math App www.doodlelearning.com/us/math-app
  IXL Math www.ixl.com/math
- Reflex Math (Math Fact Fluency Games)
  www.time4mathfacts.com

Free Worksheets

    www.math-drills.com
    www.dadsworksheets.com
    www.mathisfun.com
    www.khanacademy.org

10

Science

My youngest son has always been captivated by insects, reptiles, and similar creatures. He particularly enjoyed learning about animals with weird names. The stranger the name, the more interested he was.

One day, when he was about nine years old and playing outside with a group of friends, he found a fuzzy fly. He picked it up, and with much enthusiasm exclaimed that this was a red-footed cannibal fly.

Since he was known as the kid who knows about bugs, no one questioned him. When we looked it up, he was, indeed, correct. Now everyone in our family knows what a red footed cannibal fly looks like. How can you forget when your nine-year-old finds one and, with a completely serious expression on his face, looks at you and identifies it with the correct name?

The enthusiasm of a child is contagious. Wouldn't it be great if we could keep it going forever? Science is a school subject that has the potential of capturing children's fascination for years to come. There are so many scientific areas to choose from that it is possible to learn a different one every year for a decade or more without repeating anything that was previously learned.

The Younger Grades: Library Card and Outdoors

Science is a subject that, at least in the elementary school years, does not necessarily need a purchased curriculum. So, if you are on a tight budget, this is one of the subjects that you can easily save money on. Take your children to the library and check out books about insects, or birds, or rocks, planets, or oceans. Read the books aloud to your kids and talk about questions they or you may have.

Then go outside. The idea is to spend time being curious about nature. This is called interest-led or delight-directed learning. Science is the perfect time to let your children be curious and explore different natural habitats, find treasures such as rocks or seashells, and observe animals.

USE YOUR KIDS' CURIOSITY AS A GUIDE

Your kids probably already know exactly how to come up with lots of good questions, so you can use your science time to figure out the answers. It can be tricky to remember the questions from when they were first asked until you find time to research the answers.

In the past, I have used my phone to record questions as they come up during the day, and during the science lesson we listened to the recording and, if we were still interested in the question, we talked about it. Finding out the answer to a question is a lesson in itself.

Use books, your phone, Google, or YouTube to help you find the answers. Your kids will see how you go about it and eventually catch on. This is how they learn to eventually start doing their own research.

SPEND TIME OUTSIDE

Go outside as much as possible and play or take a walk. It does-n't really matter where you go as long as you're outside. This way of teaching science aligns with the Charlotte Mason method and is a very gentle approach to teaching this subject.

There are so many fun things that can be accomplished during these encounters with nature, from scavenger hunts to nature jour-naling.

I used to take my kids each Wednesday to a local state park. We packed the kayak, picnic blanket, sun umbrella and food into the car and headed out. It became their favorite day of the week.

They played by the lake, fished (many states don't require a fishing license until a certain age), kayaked, ate a picnic lunch, climbed trees, or hiked. We called it Nature Day, and when it rained, they played in the backyard building a tent with a tarp or jumping in the puddles.

To this day, these are some of their fondest memories.

These nature excursions are all part of exploring and studying science at this young age, but even during the high school years this special time outdoors should not be missing.

Some kids enjoy drawing things from nature, so you can bring paper and pencils if you like.

The point is to have the student build a relationship with the laws of nature before they can understand concepts of science that will be covered later in middle or high school.

Free Curriculum Ideas and DIY Science Lessons

The Internet is teeming with ideas about teaching science. There are free online guides available that will help with choosing topics, books, activities, and experiments. I will list a few of them below. You can then request the recommended books at your local library and decide which fits your needs.

You can also create your own science unit. Depending on the science area you are exploring, you can follow certain patterns that help study your topic. Here's an example.

BIRD STUDY

Here are some ideas to do bird study. Request a few field guides about birds in your area, put out some bird feeders with bird seed, wait for the birds to show up, and watch them. You could also go on a hike and see which birds you recognize using your field guides.

If you like, you can put some binoculars, a set of coloring sheets of various birds, their anatomy, names, and other information, and some coloring pencils next to a window. Your children can color it in and see if they can label the body parts of a bird or identify some birds with the field guide using the binoculars.

This is a great activity in the winter when it is easier to spot them since there are no leaves in the trees. It can be very entertaining if you have multiple birds playing together.

Voila, you are studying birds.

WHEN A CURRICULUM IS USEFUL

Coming up with the science topics by yourself can be exhausting over time. At some point, a curriculum guide might come in handy and will make life less stressful. Nobody wants to spend late nights on the internet in search of science worksheets or ideas for the next day's science lesson.

This is where you will appreciate a basic science textbook, and perhaps some field guides for rainy days when it is unpleasant to go outside but you still would like to study plants or animal life.

A single science textbook can actually last you for several years if you choose to split up the topics differently and use your own ideas in between.

For example, if your science book covers meteorology, geology, botany, and astronomy over the course of the school year, you can choose whichever topic you like, and once this topic is finished, plan a different topic yourself, if you enjoy planning your own lessons.

After finishing these, switch back to the textbook's next topic. There is no rule about the order in which students must learn science, so have fun with this process.

Only one point to remember: if you want your student to eventually take standardized tests, it does help to know ahead of time what kind of science concepts will be covered, so you can order a test-prep set that will familiarize you with some of the content.

SCIENCE IN UNIT STUDIES

Science lends itself very well as part of a unit study. Usually, a unit study begins with a book that is read aloud. Science, history, and math lessons follow based on the story. This is an effective learning method, as the concepts are usually tied to relevant, real-life, situations.

Unit studies can be designed by you or purchased online. I list some resources below.

LAPBOOKING AND NOTEBOOKING

A lapbook is a home-made book created by your student to display information in a creative and colorful method. Usually, a lapbook is created by glueing file folders together in such a way that they create a trifold or something similar.

Your student will then glue little booklets, pictures, pockets with information cards, and other materials, into this "book" and then decorate it. Usually, science topics lend themselves well to the creation of a lapbook.

Notebooking is simply a collection of thoughts on paper. This can be done in full sentences, keywords, pictures, and so forth.

The idea behind this is that the student captures her ideas and thoughts permanently which helps fix them in her mind.

This benefits the student in her learning and the teacher in the assessment of the learning progress. Nothebooking pages can be predesigned, printed out, and filled in, or your student can design and decorate them herself with her own illustrations.

Both lapbooking and notebooking are equally effective and can be incorporated in every type of teaching philosophy. Both of these are also appropriate for all grades and ages of students, depending on their enjoyment of creating these.

Ideas can be found for free or for purchase on the internet. I list links below.

GRADES 7–12

Science in the elementary years is an exciting subject to teach. But as the student gets older and the concepts become increasingly difficult, it's easy to slip into the checking-off-the-list mode and lose the joy of teaching and learning this subject.

With older students, it seems that the stakes are higher and each of my mistakes in teaching any subject has a more significant impact than with my younger students.

This is true to a certain extent, but I always have to remind myself that in a typical school setting, things would very likely be less exciting for my child. No one really cares whether the student enjoys learning botany or anatomy. In a school setting, the curriculum, scope, and sequence are set, and my student has no impact on these.

With homeschooling, this is entirely different. Our student has a great impact on the learning experience, including the curriculum, scope, and sequence. Who is to say that we must learn anatomy in eighth or ninth grade? Why not do it sooner? Or later?

So, even in the older grades, there is great freedom in choosing topic areas and making sure that the student stays engaged. It is important that we find books and other materials that explain scientific concepts well, keep the student interested, and cover enough topics so that the college-bound student will be well prepared.

The curriculum market is in your favor when it comes to choosing teaching materials. Each teaching philosophy has a large number of choices available in every grade, K–12.

Choosing your favorite method to keep science alive and engaging during the middle and high school years may seem a bit overwhelming at first, especially if this is your first year of home-schooling.

But remember that the first year is always a sort of experiment. You and your child will discover how to learn together. Your child will figure out how to learn independently, and you will find out different ways to make this work.

You'll probably switch your curriculum the following year to try something different. But then, you may have found one that works great from the beginning.

Keep an eye on your student's enthusiasm. If she's getting bored, you may need to make some changes. But if she's engaged, keep what you have.

A Typical Science Sequence for Grades 7–12

There is a general order in which science classes are usually taught. Traditional and classical teaching methods will usually follow this sequence, and the textbook publishers have them available in that order. It is as follows:

Grade 7: General Science

Grade 8: Physical Science/Earth Science

Grade 9: Biology

Grade 10: Chemistry

Grade 11: Physics

Grade 12: Advanced Science (choose from Biology, Chemistry, or Physics)

SCIENCE AND YOUR TEACHING PHILOSOPHY

This sequence is very typical in the traditional and classical philosophies, so if one of these is the method you chose, your textbooks will likely follow this path of science topics.

However, other teaching methods do not necessarily follow this sequence, even if the student is college bound with a science major.

For example, in the world of Charlotte Mason homeschooling, much of this subject can still be taught through nature study and nature journaling. There are topics, but they may or may not be related to the sequence I listed.

There will also be a wide selection of living books. These guide the interest of the student, and he can choose an area of interest for deeper, independent study, and then tell you, or write down, what he discovered.

This re-telling, either orally or in writing, is the key to learning. This teaching style of narrating what you have learned is one of the backbones of the Charlotte Mason method, but this can easily be incorporated into other teaching methods.

Getting Behind or Ahead

If you're using a textbook, it's important to understand the content rather than just zipping through the chapters, so if you're not exactly where you are "supposed" to be in the book, that's usually no reason for concern. Most students do not ever finish a textbook in a school year. Use the book to give you a guideline and try to finish as much as you can. You can continue with it next year if you like.

If your student is a quick learner, or loves science, or a combination of these, you can move ahead once the book is finished. You could also use this extra time to plan some extra activities, such as projects or field trips. There is no reason to keep pressing on. Follow your student's cues as to how much he would enjoy continuing on to the next book vs. doing a few different, yet science related activities.

Notebooking in the Older Grades

Notebooking is a way the student captures her thoughts on paper. Just like in the younger grades this teaches valuable skills, from ordering one's thoughts to putting them into words, and thinking about the topic for long periods of time in order to explain it.

Especially in high-school years, this skill leads to logical thought formation and good articulation.

Some parents use this method exclusively for all their learning, which is in line with the Charlotte Mason and unit study methods. Since I did not strictly adhere to any one specific method, I incorporated notebooking frequently but not every day into my lesson plan.

After a lesson, I printed out a set of pages from a notebooking website. These pages had pictures and designs that went along with the theme of my student's lesson which made the writing process more enjoyable. My student would then write a few paragraphs or a longer report about the recent topic he had studied.

Plus, when my student was writing a long report, I counted this for his writing lesson for the day. So that quickly changed his attitude about writing long reports in science since he was able to kill two birds with one stone.

PROJECT-BASED LEARNING

There's no better teacher than experience. When children are left to explore, experiment, and then explain what they have learned, they will never forget it. Each semester, whether your curriculum calls for it or not, should include some sort of project.

That means, the student is given a topic, and she comes up with questions, does research, designs the presentations, and finally presents her project in front of others.

Preparing some sort of food as part of this presentation is highly recommended. Using props is also a great idea. Have fun as a family, enjoy the food, the presentation, and the time spent together. These are the best times you'll ever have.

DIY HIGH-SCHOOL SCIENCE

You can still design your own lesson plans for high school, but it is important at this point to have an appropriate selection of topics. Especially during the high-school years, I recommend using a quality science textbook and following its table of contents as a guideline for topics. You can employ a series of science books for kids like the DK Eyewitness Books or the Wonders of Creation by Masterbooks for a variety of science topics. This is where the library will be a great resource.

Then check out a variety of additional books, preferably with lots of illustrations, and plan activities that teach the topic. Find YouTube videos, DVSs, or Nature shows on TV or your favorite network subscription (such as Netflix or Disney Plus).

If you're interested in the Nature Study approach of teaching science, check out the chapter about Nature Study and the curriculum choices listed at the end of that section.

Check out the websites I list below that offer free resources to help with this.

But I Don't Like Science

If you're not a science lover, rest assured that you will find something that will work for your family. One idea is to find a co-op that covers science. Another idea is to find friends (homeschoolers or not) that can help you out.

If none of these options are available, there are also online classes available. I have never personally used an online science class, but I will get you started with some options to consider.

Some of the curricula I am listing below require more, and some less, teacher involvement. Obviously, you will be required to participate in your student's science at some level, but there definitely are materials available that have done most of the work for you, and all you do is open the box and let your kids have fun.

It's difficult not to enjoy watching your kids explore and get excited about what they are discovering and learning. And who knows, you may yet unlock your hidden, inner scientist.

Choosing the Right Science Curriculum

If you love science, choosing the curriculum for this field may be the most difficult task of all your homeschool curriculum choices. Botany, Astronomy, Ponds and Streams, Weather, Geology, and all these with teaching materials that look so amazing. Yes, please! Sign me up for all of them!

I needed to be careful not to overload my young students with too much of this wonderful stuff. Choosing just one book from so many was difficult for me.

I found a great strategy: I made a list of the science topics I wanted to study over the next five years. Now I saw that we would eventually get to all the things I was tempted to squeeze into the current school year. My mind relaxed, and I was able to choose more easily.

But even if you're not so excited about this subject, I am sure you'll find something that will work for you. It may take a few curriculum trials, but you will get closer each time to what truly fits your need.

When you're shopping online for science curriculum, and you find yourself unclear what to get, or you like everything and want to get more that you know you should, a good method is to put everything in your shopping cart, go to bed, and sleep on it. See what you think the next day.

Perhaps your library carries some of the materials, and you can check them out and give them a try. Or perhaps you can read through the first chapter online which is many times available for free.

Whatever you decide, remember that most science curricula with high reviews will be just fine. You do not have to second guess your choice. Plus, you can change the next school year and try out a different one until you find what you like the most.

YOU WILL KNOW WHEN IT DOESN'T WORK

It will become very obvious when the curriculum does not work and causes drudgery. When that happens, there are several ways to remedy this situation, including switching educational philosophies, slowing down, or taking a break from the curriculum and filling the time with different activities that tach similar topics.

Usually, switching mid-year can be costly and cause turmoil. It's not the ideal choice, but sometimes it has to be done. I have only had that happen once or twice, and it was not without much debate about whether this will be the right choice.

BIOLOGY GONE WRONG

It was time for ninth-grade biology class. My son, the bug expert who identified the red footed cannibal fly, was all about life sciences. Bugs, mammals, fish, you name it. I just knew this would be a great year. Then we started. Chapter 1, twenty-seven definitions to memorize. Hmmmmmmm.

Then came Chapter 2, fourteen terms. This was better, but still caused this subject to become drudgery because memorizing terminology was not exactly the highlight of his day.

I was not creative enough at this point to turn memory work into something more fun, like a matching game. Assuming that it would eventually improve, we plodded on for another few chapters. Improvement never came.

RECOVERY

I finally took his cues, and a few months into the year, we switched to marine biology to make this subject more appealing. He immediately perked up because I ordered him the dissection kit with some cool marine animals.

This was a good move, I could tell, because his attitude changed instantly. Plus, it helped that I relaxed on the terminology part. Biology was now fun again, but I don't think he ever recovered from the trauma of the terminology.

I've changed my strategy since then, and for my daughters I turned the terminology memorization of each chapter into matching games. Eventually, the names stuck.

Switching curriculum mid-year was not a normal event. Usually, the curriculum choices I made were a good enough fit to use them all year. If needed, I switched to a different one the following school year. So, this was a bit of an unusual situation. But sometimes this is what needs to happen to stay on track.

Update: When my son read through this chapter, he informed me that he has indeed recovered from the definition memorization. Good to know.

RAISING A FUTURE SCIENTIST?

Usually at some point during the high school years, it will become somewhat clear whether or not your student is interested in any particular science, or whether science is not on the agenda.

You have to assess your student's enthusiasm and grasp of this subject. You should also watch for certain special interests he displays in the different areas of science topics. Is he more interested in earth or in the life sciences? What about the physical sciences?

If you see special interests, you can foster these by allowing extra time to study them and requesting books from the library to help with this.

Let your student be your guide in choosing the sequence of topics in your science curriculum. Sometimes, topics need to be covered in a certain sequence to build a foundation of knowledge, but some topics are stand-alone topics and can be taught in any sequence.

Certain science curricula are more rigorous than others, so you can look at the table of contents before choosing your textbook and see how much ground is covered. Remember, you can always go slower or faster, or skip around in the book if needed.

IS YOUR STUDENT NOT SURE ABOUT SCIENCE?

Science is not everyone's cup of tea. If your student shows strong interest in a different subject, allow extra time for that subject. You have to make the decision how much you focus on various subjects. Science does not need to be a focus subject.

Each teaching philosophy views the amount of time spent on a subject each day, and the method of teaching and learning, slightly differently. So, follow your method and see where it leads.

At the same time, just because your student doesn't like biology one year, that doesn't mean he won't like physics a few years later. Be in tune with your student and see how much can be expected of him.

If it's unclear whether your student is inclined toward choosing a scientific career in the future or not, it is a good idea to keep exposing her to a wide variety of science topics. You may choose to go slower, add extra review time, and focus on areas your student enjoys more than others.

And unless you are absolutely sure that she won't be going into a science field, keep the science instruction going as much as possible so that your student will be exposed to a large variety of concepts in case she chooses a science major.

That doesn't mean you need to teach science every day for an hour, but you should follow your chosen teaching philosophy's recommendation.

Our Kids Will Learn When They Set Their Mind to It

Let's say you wake up one morning and realize that your student never got to a certain topic within biology and now wants to go to college and study biology. You might scold yourself and think, Oh, no, how could I let this happen! What a nightmare!

Here's the amazing thing: she has now made up her mind to study this field. She will learn quicker now than perhaps years ago when you tried to convince her, and she was not very interested.

I have personally experienced this. My daughter had to take several biology and chemistry classes in college. I thought that we didn't do a very good job covering all the chapters in her high school biology book, but she excelled by studying hard.

Obviously, our students won't learn everything there is to learn while they're still at home. But we can teach them how to learn so that when they encounter something unfamiliar, they are ready and motivated to pick it up.

Final Words Before Choosing

When choosing a science curriculum, trust your gut. If it looks good to you, and you've read the table of contents, a few pages of the teacher guide, or whatever there is to preview, try it out.

Keep a record of what you are using this year so that next year you can assess what you liked, didn't like, or whether you want to switch.

Then enjoy this beautiful subject and your children.

Free Online Ideas

- www.amblesideonline.com
- www.freedomhomeschooling.com
- www.thehomeschoolmom.com
- www.wholechildhomeschool.com

Notebooking and Lapbooking

- www.notebookingpages.com
- www.dailyskillbuilding.com
- www.juiceboxhomeschool.com

CURRICULUM CHOICES

GRADES K–6

Apologia Science: Exploring Creation: Young Explorer Series

These are quality textbooks with conversation-style lessons, quality color photo illustrations, and written to be read aloud to your child or read independently. Books are available as audio books. You can choose between doing a notebook or a lap-book. The notebook is from the same publisher, lap book materials are from a different publisher. There are many experiments, and the Instructor's Guide is clear and easy to use. This curriculum has a Christian worldview. Grades K-6. www.apologia.com, lapbook materials are found at www.apologia.com.

Sonlight Science Curriculum

This is a literature-based, Charlotte Mason–style science curriculum which uses quality children's books like Magic School Bus and Usborne. The experiment kits are very well supplied with everything you need. Video instruction for the experiments is available, and well made. The Instructor's Guide is clear and explains each step. There are fun worksheets, and the student will work on a scientific notebook for the experiments. Christian and secular worldview. Grades K-6. www.sonlight.com

Book Shark

Book Shark is similar to Sonlight Science curriculum. It uses a Charlotte Mason approach with living books. Grades PreK-10. Secular worldview. www.bookshark.com

Berean Builders: Discovering Design

Dr. Jay Wile, you might recognize his name from some Apologia Science books, covers science in a historical fashion, starting with the creation account and connecting this with the study of light, water, energy, botany, and so forth. Textbooks are written in conversational style, and there many experiments are included.

These books are designed to combine students of different ages. Starting in middle school there are live online or self-paced classes available for purchase. Christian worldview. Grades K–12. www.bereanbuilders.com

Noeo Science

Similar to the Sonlight curriculum, this curriculum is based on a selection of quality, non-fiction, living books that are enjoyable to read. There are many experiments, some of which have a video to go with them which you will find on the Noeo website.

The open-and-go instruction guide offers both a two-day and a four-day schedule. Written by Christian authors, but not distinctly Christian worldview. Grades K–6. www.noeoscience.com

Elemental Science

Based on a wide selection of factual children's books, this curriculum uses aspects of Charlotte Mason and the classical method. Assignments include narration and note booking. The name of each course reveals the classical nature of the content. Secular worldview. K–8. www.elementalscience.com

Timberdoodle

Timberdoodle is an online store and a great resource for various curricula and unique toys and activities. They sell a selection of Apologia, Building Blocks of Science, and Evan-Moor workbooks.

Especially for the younger grades, Timberdoodle sells many unique toys, educational electronic toys, games, and puzzles, that you might not otherwise ever stumble upon. It's definitely a helpful resource if you are looking for unique, hands-on, and fun educational materials. They offer Christian and secular kits. Grades Pre-K–12. www.timberdoodle.com

Master Books

Master Books has been long known for printing high-quality books. For several years now, they have also been producing high-quality curriculum based on these books and keep publishing new materials faster than I can type, it seems like.

All their science curriculum is written with short, clear, lessons in mind, and in conversation-style using the Charlotte Mason method. The instruction manual is open and go, and very easy to adapt to your needs. Master Books offers many online classes and video lessons. This publisher has an explicitly Christian worldview. Grades 1–12. www.masterbooks.com

Nature's Workshop Plus

www.workshopplus.com

This website is great for lab materials and science equipment. It's also great for getting gifts for the nature and science lovers in your life.

MIDDLE SCHOOL AND HIGH SCHOOL

Several of these I described in the last section, so I will share my personal experience here.

Apologia Science

"Exploring Creation" Series. We've used every level of science they offer and liked all of them. These books are rigorous and well written. Experiments are included but supplies need to be purchased separately. Your student will be prepared for college. Christian worldview. Grades 1–12. www.apologia.com

Berean Builders

I love Dr. Wile's conversational style of bringing science to life in these books. He also wrote some of Apologia's books, so they are similar in content and style. Experiments are included in the books, but supplies need to be purchased extra. Great college preparation. Christian worldview. Grades 1–12. www.bereanbuilders.com

Discovery Education.

A subscription-based online science streaming service with

thousands of videos covering a large number of science topics. The website has a tool that can be used to create lesson plans and assignments. This can be a full curriculum for elementary through high school. I have used this as a supplement, and we enjoyed the large selection of videos. K–12. Secular worldview.
www.discoveryeducation.com

Logos Press

I used the biology curriculum called "The Riot and the Dance" by Dr. Gordon Wilson with one of my daughters. This is one of my favorite biology curricula. There are two delightful video documentaries that accompany the book. Christian worldview. Grade 8–10. www.logospressonline.com

Master Books

We've used the Chemistry curriculum and the Advanced Pre-Med Studies. The student books are filled with easy-to-understand lessons and every topic the student should be familiar with. The open and go format makes it easy and fun to use. Every lesson is taught from a Christian worldview. Grades K–12.
www.masterbooks.com

Supercharged Science by Aurora Lipper

This is a completely project-based science curriculum and very different from what you would normally find in a science textbook. She gives you exactly enough (not more, not less) information as you need to complete the projects. Secular worldview. Grades K–12.
www.superchargedscience.com

Thinkwell Science Courses Online Physics 1, Chemistry and Biology courses. Texts are included in the monthly or yearly subscription. Videos and assignments help the student complete this subject independently. Secular worldview. Grades 10–12.
www.thinkwellhomeschool.com

Noeo Science

Noeo Science publishes curriculum up to eighth grade. So, if you have used it and enjoy it, continue until eighth grade. Then switch to a high school science curriculum. Noeo has Christian authors, but not distinctly Christian worldview. K–8.
www.noeoscience.com

ONLINE LIVE AND SELF-PACED SCIENCE CLASSES

Apologia

www.apologia.com
Teaching style: traditional, classical, Charlotte Mason. Self-paced courses include videos, e-books and auto-graded tests and quizzes. Live classes meet once a week online and interact in real time. Christian worldview. Grades 7–12.

Berean Builders

www.bereanbuilders.com
Teaching style: traditional, classical, Charlotte Mason. Live classes are graded and include lab instruction. Lab materials need to be purchased separately. Self-paced classes consist of pre-recorded videos but are not graded. Christian worldview. Grades 7–12.

Masterbooks Academy

www.masterbooksacademy.com
Teaching style: Charlotte Mason. You will have access to these pre-recorded classes for eighteen months. Students will not be graded. Christian worldview. Grades 4–6.

Time 4 Learning

www.time4learning.com
Teaching style: traditional, classical, Charlotte Mason. You will have access to various classes, all included in the subscription. Lab instruction is included, but you need to purchase equipment. Secular Worldview. Grades K–12.

Thinkwell Science Couses

www.thinkwellhomeschool.com
Monthly or yearly subscriptions to individual classes. Teaching style: traditional, classical, or Charlotte Mason. Interactive videos, assignments, and reading material/lesson notes included. No separate book needed. Auto-graded tests and quizzes. No labs included. Secular Worldview. Grades 9–12.

Nature's Workshop Plus

www.workshopplus.com
Lab materials and science equipment.

11

History

During all of my school years, history was never on my list of favorite subjects. I remember the days of drudgery and boredom, having to memorize the dates, people, and wars of medieval Germany and Europe, and I had no interest in them whatsoever. Much of it didn't even make much sense to me because there were just too many details.

As a first-time homeschool mom, I looked back on my days of being a student and thought to myself, "I will not teach history to my kids in that way." But which way is a good way? And why exactly should I include it in our curriculum? As a teen, I didn't think studying history was all that important. So, now what do I do? I stumbled upon the answers to my questions quite by accident.

How I Found an Effective Teaching Method

My oldest son was in fourth grade at a private school and had to present a biographical report of a famous West Virginian. He had chosen Stonewall Jackson, a name that both he and I were not too familiar with at the time.

The day he came home with the assignment, we took a trip to the library to check out a few books. Back home we sifted through the tall stack of library books. That's when one of them stood out to me.

It was a well-written biography that was just detailed enough to learn about Stonewall, but not so detailed that you get lost. I remember reading most of the book aloud to him that afternoon. Neither of us could stop. We were there with Jackson during his childhood, his West Point years, and the various wars he fought. We felt like we knew him personally.

From that afternoon on, my son was hooked on US history, specifically the Civil War era. The best part of it was that I learned an effective way to connect my son with any period in history: get to know a person from that time and walk with them.

Get to Know Historical Characters

When we read Stonewall Jackson's biography, we not only met him and his friends and family, but also his circumstances, his challenges, and the events that he had to face. Suddenly, the same historic events that bored me so much during my own school years came to life, made sense, and became even—dare I say it—exciting! A word I would *never* have used in the same context as history.

Reading this simple children's biography started an avalanche of further research into other interesting people and events, using the same method. I regularly added biographies as read-aloud books to my sons, since my daughters were not yet old enough to care.

Without even noticing or intending to do so, I helped both my sons build a frame of historical knowledge that has served them well over the years. Both of them were avid readers of historical fiction, some as a family read aloud and many more by themselves. And we hadn't even officially started homeschooling yet.

When I started homeschooling several years later, this method became my primary mode of teaching history. My daughters were not as excited about reading biographies to themselves but were always very interested when I read one aloud. So, I made sure I had several biographies lined up for our Morning Time read-alouds.

Advantage of Homeschooling

It's difficult to duplicate this type of teaching history in a school setting because the comfort level is simply not there. I can't remember how many times I have been too embarrassed to ask a question in a classroom full of peers because I felt all eyes resting on me. Being in a non-threatening environment makes it easier to ask questions and make comments without risking humiliation.

Who Is Right?

Because homeschooling is more personal than the classroom setting, it is also easier to gauge whether the student is able to make connections. As students enter their teenage years, their brains start processing information through an increasingly critical filter.

This means that mom or dad are many times simply wrong from their perspective. After many failed attempts to convince my student of my opinion, I have adopted the attitude that if I disagree with one of my kids, and they have listened to my side and still disagree with me, I let it go. It proves that she's thinking on her own and wants to make connections without being told what to think.

Open-ended questions are a great way to guide them in this process, and when I set an example by setting my own opinion aside and listening to my student, it not only teaches him to articulate his thoughts but also to listen to my opinion.

If our kids don't nail it, it's okay. If we stick with this conversational style, our kids will naturally come to the right conclusions.

Aha! I Do Not Have to Teach All of History

As a new homeschool mom, I felt the weight of having to teach all of history to my kids, or else depriving them of important information. After a year or so of homeschooling, I noticed that even with my own limited knowledge of history, I had a good basic "skeleton" of events that helped me categorize and connect new events I was learning to what I already knew.

When I realized this, I felt the pressure that I had on myself lift. I do *not* have to teach all of history to my kids. Not even close. Since I want to create lifelong learners, my task is to help create a basic framework, instill curiosity, and teach how to ask good questions. And this leads right back to teaching critical thinking.

COMBINE HISTORY AND LITERATURE

Regardless of your child's age, reading a well written biography or a suspenseful work of historical fiction is a fun and effective way to introduce any historical event. History lends itself to being paired with literature since every book ever written has a unique backdrop of historical events, including fiction.

Surprisingly, most schools do not use this approach of teaching literature and history as part of the same class. But many homeschool curricula do just that. These two subjects make a lot of sense together, plus you're knocking out two for one. It's a win-win.

Does that mean that every book we read leads to a history lesson? Not at all. Usually, we have several books going at the same time. One of these will be our book that will be paired with history. The others, we simply enjoy. But I did notice that once my student had caught on to looking at the historical backdrop (characters and setting), they naturally observed many historical connections, if there were any, to what they had learned in the past.

WHERE TO START AND HOW TO FIND GOOD BOOKS

Among homeschool curricula, there is a commonly used division of history which breaks up the time periods into ancient, medieval, and modern. If you cover a time period over the course of one school year, you will be able to repeat this cycle four times between first grade and twelfth grade.

It makes sense to start at the beginning. But depending on the age and interest of your student, you can pick it up anywhere. So, begin by choosing a time period to study. Personally, at this point, I like to have a history textbook to help me dig deeper. Many of these have book lists that go along with the specific period in time. If there is no book list, I usually go online and search for recommended books on my favorite homeschool websites.

Before purchasing any book, I request it at the library. Once I look at it and decide if it's a keeper or not, I will then either use the library copy or order it online. The problem with using any library book is that you never know how many times you can renew it before someone else puts a hold on it. But when I knew that we could finish the book within the renewal period, that's what we did.

I kept track of the books we especially enjoyed, and when I saw a copy at a used book sale, I bought it. After over a decade of doing this, we have a considerable collection of books that we have enjoyed over the years. And I did not feel like I was constantly spending money on books because I took advantage of the used book sales that our library had every year.

The Great Books List

For those moms and dads who are themselves avid readers and enjoy a challenge, "The Great Books" collection will give you great starting points for historical literature throughout human history.

You may think this is too advanced for your younger student, but titles like *The Odyssey*, for example, is a wonderful read-aloud for any age. Again, use this list as a starting point, then request them at the library and see what you think.

I also really like using adaptations of certain books for younger children. Shakespeare's plays or *The Aeneid* are two examples.

While the language and sentence structure are different from the original, the ideas and problems they deal with are still maintained, although perhaps on an easier level.

If you choose a more literal translation over an adaptation, you can start slowly. Reading from these as much or as little as you can every day will get you some amazing results. There's no need to rush through it, but don't be surprised if your students ask for more.

Project-Based Learning

I found it very effective to have my students choose a topic from within our history time period and work on a project. This could be a few facts about a battle, historic person, or historic place, for young kids, or an in-depth presentation about these things for older kids. When my students were required to do research by themselves, the information stuck with them. I usually had them prepare food as well.

Depending on the age of the students and the length of the written part of the project, I would allow time from their composition class to be spent on this research and writing project. I had them take a one or two week break from their regular composition assignments, and put the subjects of history, literature, and composition back-to-back. That gave them a good chunk of time to work on their research.

These projects are still among the favorite memories my kids have. They also still remember much of the information they learned. Plus, I didn't have to cook dinner that night. It was a win for everyone.

My Personal History Reading List

Below is a list of some of my favorite books I have encountered over the years. This is not even a fraction of the wonderful books that are available in this genre. They are somewhat organized chronologically and include a few works from each epoch of history.

Ancient

- Books by G.A. Henty
- Books by R.M. Ballantyne
- *Tales of Ancient Egypt* by Roger Lancelyn Green (Puffin Classics)
- *The Golden Goblet* by Eloise Jarvis McGraw

- *Black Ships before Troy* by Rosemary Sutcliff
- *The Wanderings of Odysseus* by Rosemary Sutcliff
- *The Saga of the Volsungs*, translated by Jesse L. Byock (Penguin Books)
- *Myths of the Norsemen* by Roger Lancelyn Green (Puffin Classics)
- *Tales of the Greek Heroes* by Roger Lancelyn Green (Puffin Classics)
- *The Eagle of the Ninth* by Rosemary Sutcliff
- *The Silver Branch* by Rosemary Sutcliff
- *The Lantern Bearers* by Rosemary Sutcliff
- *The Bronze Bow* by Elizabeth George Speare
- *Detectives in Togas* by Henry Winterfeld
- *Mystery of the Roman Ransom* by Henry Winterfeld
- *The Roman Mysteries* series by Caroline Lawrence
- *Augustus Caesar's World* by Genevieve Foster (this is actually a history book, but told as stories)

Medieval Times

- *Rolf and the Viking Bow* by Allen French
- *King Arthur and His Knights of the Round Table* by Roger Lancelyn Green (Puffin Classics)
- *Robin Hood* by Roger Lancelyn Green (Puffin Classics)
- Books by Louise Vernon (Stories of famous people at the time of the Protestant Reformation)
- Books by Douglas Bond (Stories about the Scottish and English Reformation)
- *Heroes of History*, books by Janet and Geoff Benge

US History

- *Voyage to Freedom*. A Story of the Atlantic Crossing 1620 by David Gay
- *Johnny Tremain* by Esther Forbes
- *Annie Henry* series by Susan Olasky
- *Childhood of Famous Americans*, books by various authors.
- *Chalico Captive* by Elizabeth George Speare

- *Indian Captive* by Lois Lensky
- *Alone Yet Not Alone* by Tracy Leininger Craven
- *The Witch of Blackbird Pond* by Elizabeth George Spear
- *Caddie Woodlawn* by Carol Ryrie Brink
- *Kathleen McKenzie* books by Tracy Leininger Craven
- *Iron Thunder.* The Battle between the Monitor and the Merrimac by Avi
- Books by Jean Fritz
- *Bud and Me*, Alta Abernathy (a true story about two little boys riding alone to cross the country)
- *Heroes of America* by various authors

Holocaust

- *When Hitler Stole Pink Rabbit* by Judith Kerr
- *Journey to America* by Sonia Levitin
- *Number the Stars* by Lois Lowry
- *Hideout in the Swamp* by Piet Prins
- *The Watchmaker's Daughter* by Jean Watson

The Value of Learning History

It takes years to form and mature ideas and opinions. The only way kids can effectively learn to form an opinion is to be exposed to a variety of ideas. But the ideas in themselves are not enough. They need to be learned in the right context so that our kids see what kind of impact they had. Without seeing the ideas play out in real life, how should we know what opinion to have? This is where history becomes of great value.

Winston Churchill once said, "Those who fail to learn from history, are doomed to repeat it." A quote attributed to Mark Twain states that "History doesn't repeat itself, but it does rhyme." Looking at historical events, we see patterns which recur every so often. Being aware of these patterns gives us reference points and helps us and our students be better prepared for our future.

UNDERSTANDING OUR PLACE IN HISTORY

Ancient and medieval history is important to learn, but if you have a high schooler and only a few years left to homeschool him,

I highly recommend focusing on the last hundred to hundred-fifty years, so she can better understand some of the events that are taking place today.

Indeed, since every event had a reason that goes back further, you can keep going back in time, but in my opinion, the last hundred years or so of historical events give a good idea and solid base. So many events took place during that time frame that it includes most aspects of human failure and success. Understanding these gives us a broader perspective of the news we read in the paper or on the internet today.

We Are History

I wonder how many times the average person thinks about themselves as a person making history. Every action of every person around us affects us in several ways. It affects our thinking, our actions, and our future plans. It is part of who we are. Knowing our own personal history helps us preserve our identity. If I don't know where I came from, I don't know who I am or what my purpose is.

People generally live in community, and the traditions, culture, habits, and personal characteristics past and present, impact their principles, struggles, and direction. Studying history teaches us about how intertwined and connected we are, and how every event and famous historical person affects us personally, whether we see it or not. All this may sound somewhat broad and fuzzy, so I will illustrate with an example from my own life.

> Mr. Gorbachev, tear down this wall!
> —President Ronald Reagan's Brandenburg Gate Speech

November 9th 1989. My family ate breakfast together, and I headed to school. The sun was not up yet, so I walked to the subway station in the dark. But that was normal. Winter days are short in Germany.

I was looking forward to the following week, because I would celebrate my fifteenth birthday. School was uneventful, and after getting home and starting on my homework that afternoon, my parents told me of some strange news that was being reported on TV and the radio.

There were people on the East Berlin border trying to get into West Berlin. And the East German police did not know what to do. The people persisted and eventually were allowed to pass. An avalanche of change had started. And I had no clue.

I had no real appreciation for history or even the unique status of my hometown. From an early age on, I was inundated with horrible pictures of the holocaust and the terrible guilt my native country had to bear. This was one of the reasons that history was not enjoyable to me.

COLD WAR

You may be familiar with the candy bomber. I was not alive yet, but my dad was a five-year-old boy at the time. In 1948–49 the Russians besieged and blocked Berlin to prevent food and other items to enter the city. The western allies responded with the Berlin Airlift, or the 'Air Bridge', as West Berliners call it.

For over a year, every thirty seconds a plane either took off or landed at Airport Tempelhof, just a few miles from the apartment in which I would one day grow up. The planes were carrying food supplies, and even candy for the kids.

The apartment I grew up in was located in the final approach line of the runway of Airport Tempelhof which the American military used. I could almost touch the American military planes as I stood by the window in my family's third-floor apartment and watched them approach. Some of these planes were so loud, they made the whole building quiver.

GROUND ZERO

I didn't really understand the seriousness and implications of the Cold War, mainly because I grew up at Ground Zero. Knowing that I lived in the American Sector in West Berlin, I never questioned the presence of American troops. Growing up in the danger zone of the Cold War was so normal for me, I did not grasp the implications.

Within the city of West Berlin, life was free and normal, just like any American city today. I walked to school in grades K–6, and when I entered high school, I took the subway. We walked or drove to stores which were well stocked with every kind of produce and goods imaginable, visited friends, all normal things to most Americans.

However, despite living in the free part of Berlin, my family could not simply get into a car and drive to West Germany or any other western European country. West Berlin was an enclave inside

East Germany and traveling outside its boundaries meant traveling through East Germany, which was a big hassle.

"DIE WENDE" (THE TURN-AROUND)

In 1987, Ronald Reagan visited Berlin, and gave his famous speech at the Brandenburg Gate, asking Soviet General Secretary Gorbachev to tear down the wall. This created quite the buzz in West Berlin, and for a long time, people talked about this.

In the summer of 1989, things heated up. Miracle after miracle occurred. Peaceful demonstrations in Dresden, Leipzig, and other East German cities were not violently ended by the Soviets, so they continued.

Every day, the news media was full of images of trains leaving Czechoslovakia with people clinging to the outside of them. They were going to the West. For several months, my favorite radio station, 100.6 FM, was jammed every time the news came on. I could feel in the air that something was going to happen.

On November 9th 1989, just a few months after East Germany had celebrated its fortieth anniversary, a chain of little events started a domino effect, from a newscast announcement that the border is seemingly open, to East German border officers being unsure of what was going on and letting people from East Berlin cross into West Berlin. You can watch some of these events on YouTube.

Of course, my dad, who saw the wall go up in 1961, understood very well what was going on, so, the very next day, November 10th, he took me to the Brandenburg Gate where all this commotion was going on. Ronald Reagan had stood here just two years earlier. Now there were Soviet tanks and soldiers, all armed and ready to attack the crowds. People threw Molotov cocktails at them.

We climbed onto the part of the Berlin Wall that was wide enough at the top that you could stand on it. From there we could see into East Berlin which you normally couldn't because of the wall.

The East German Border Police was as confused as ever, and the Russians waited for a command from Moscow, but it never came.

A HISTORIC LITTLE WALK

My dad decided that we should walk through the Brandenburg Gate to "Unter den Linden" (historic downtown Berlin, located on the east side), so we did. I remember being in awe as we walked under the Brandenburg Gate because I knew this had not been done by anyone in decades as this was no man's land, and stepping ono it would be an act of aggression on either side. Looking up at the artwork inside the arches of the gate, I felt a sense of historic wonder and amazement. We went to a little café in East Berlin and ordered coffee and some chocolate cake.

TRYING TO MAKE CONNECTIONS

All this happened right before my fifteenth birthday. And while I intellectually understood that this was a historic event, it wasn't until years later when I was teaching my own children about these events that the significance occurred to me.

You see, having witnessed the harassment of the German Border Police, and observing the presence of American military my whole life growing up, I was conditioned to think these events that were taking place were normal.

The images of Soviet tanks and soldiers were not unusual for me because that was something I was familiar with from simply crossing the border into the East. I had been shaped by what I saw, and what would seem scary under normal circumstances, was not scary because I was used to it.

Looking back to that time in my life, I realized just how much more sense I am making of the way people behave, countries interact with each other, and that there are really no new events taking place nowadays that have not happened before. I was using my past experiences to make connections in the present.

SHAPED BY HISTORY

I'm telling you all of this to illustrate how current and past events shaped me while I didn't even notice it. Even my husband has trouble relating to all these events that I witnessed as a child. I saw firsthand the terrible results of communism.

Through my grandmother's accounts and a school curriculum that instilled national shame in the students, I learned second hand the terrible result that Hitler's rule left on Germany. My entire childhood was characterized by the shadow of historical events, two terrible wars which left visible and invisible marks that are still seen today.

I was immersed in this aftermath. It defined my surroundings which, in turn, shaped me.

Your Historical Backdrop

What about you and your background? How were you shaped by the history of your surroundings? Making history come to life by reading direct accounts, biographies, or historical fiction is a very effective way of creating a sense of connectedness.

We are all woven together with historical events and the repercussions of them. Some people understand that more than others. The realization of that fact helps to make sense of our surroundings and current events that are taking place.

I was not very history-literate when I started homeschooling. I felt very inadequate to teach this subject to my eighth grader, so I had to come up with a strategy. Fortunately, I had stumbled upon the effective method of using children's biographies and conversations to make it come to life.

THE MYTH OF CLAIMING TO BE OBJECTIVE

As I started to teach my own children US history and we read the accounts of those who made great sacrifices in the Revolutionary War, or in the Civil War (regardless of North or South), we were fascinated to learn about the issues, problems, misunderstandings, loyalty, steadfastness, love, honesty, and betrayal that were going on.

We are products of our time and circumstances. Just as I was shaped by my surroundings as I grew up in Berlin, we all have our place in the world. We are by default on one 'side' of history. To say that we are above it is not an honest statement.

There are basic assumptions and experiences that each person has, and that puts everyone on one side or another. Many times, especially during long periods of peace, the reasons behind certain events become fuzzy. The more time passes, the fuzzier things get, and the more difficult it becomes to sort them out.

Finally, it becomes all too easy to jump to the conclusion that certain historical figures made too many mistakes and don't deserve to be remembered. When I am studying history, I try to allow myself and my student to build a relationship with the people of the time period we are studying.

The best books for this are original works or books that are based on certain original work. After getting to know a person better, I find it more difficult to pass judgement and pretend I could do a better job.

Curriculum Choices

GRADES 1–4

Christian content

- *Our Star-Spangled Story* by Charlene Notgrass, Bethany Poore, and Mary Evelyn McCurdy

  From the Notgrass Website: "This one-year course combines narrative lessons about children and families in American history with songs, dances, and hands-on activities"

- *Our 50 States* by Mary Evelyn Notgrass McCurdy.

  From the Notgrass website: "This one-year course takes elementary students on a journey across our country, introducing them to the natural wonders, the fascinating places, the factories, the farms, and the people that make America."

- *The Mystery of History* by Linda Lacour Hobar. Easy to understand history lessons in conversation-style narrative. Great to read aloud or let the student read independently. Includes suggestions for activities and further study.

- *History Courses* by Veritas Press (various time periods from Creation to modern, parent led or self-paced)

- *Biographies of the Revolution* by Masterbooks

Secular Content

- *A History of US* by Joy Hakim
  From the back of the book: This "is a ten-volume, award winning series about the birth and development of the United States. Master storyteller and lifelong student of American history Joy Hakim takes readers from 9 to 99 on a breathtaking journey through time, from the Ice Age to the 21st century."

GRADES 5–8

Christian Content

- *America, the Beautiful* by Charlene Notgrass
- *Uncle Sam and You* by Ray and Charlene Notgrass with Mary Evelyn McCurdy
- *From Adam to Us* by Ray and Charlene Notgrass
- *History Revealed* by Diana Waring

- *History* by Veritas Press (various time periods from Creation to modern, parent-led or self-paced
- *The World's Story* by Masterbooks
- *The Mystery of History* by Linda Lacour Hobar

Secular Content

- *Classical Historian* by John De Gree
- Books by Genevieve Foster

HIGH SCHOOL

Christian Content

- *Exploring America* by Ray Notgrass
- *Exploring Word History* by Ray Notgrass with Charlene Notgrass and Mary Evelyn McCurdy
- *History Revealed* by Diana Waring
- *The Mystery of History* by Linda Lacour Hobar
- *Stobaugh's American and World History* by Masterbooks
- *The History of Religious Liberty* by Michael Farris
- *Dave Raymond's History Series*, found at www.compassclassroom.com

Secular Content

- *Land of Hope: An Invitation to the Great American Story* by Wilfred M. McClay
- *The Nomadic Professor History Courses* by Dr. William Jackson and Kate Noorlander
- *Books by Genevieve Foster*

Government

Anyone living in this country, especially homeschool families, should study the US government and constitution. This does not mean becoming an expert, but simply gaining enough knowledge to understand how the government works, the differences between federal and state regulations, my rights and responsibilities, and to understand how the US constitution is unique in the world.

I am really encouraging homeschooling families to study government and the Constitution because there may be a day when you really need to know your rights. If you recall the chapter about homeschool laws and regulations, there are plenty of scenarios that illustrate this.

Constitutional Literacy

I had no idea where to begin with this subject, so I learned right along with my kids. We used a curriculum for Constitutional Literacy that was written by Michael Farris, founder of HSLDA and Patrick Henry College.

There are twenty-five videos, each of them featuring a lecture by Michael Farris about important points to know about the constitution. He explains different clauses and shows how some of them are being interpreted by the Supreme Court through court cases that established certain precedents. It is a bit dated, but still a great resource.

There is a student workbook and a teacher handbook with all the answers (which I needed badly!). This is a high school class, but younger kids can watch and participate. I had all my kids, regardless of age, memorize the five rights guaranteed in the first amendment. This is one of those things you can have your students learn so they can make you look good as a parent. Of course, the real reason is for their benefit, but it sure feels good when your kids can show off a little bit.

Curriculum Options

- *Constitutional Literacy* by Michael Farris, Esq and HSLDA
- *Constitutional Law for Enlightened Citizens* by Michael Farris, Esq
- *Understanding the US Constitution* by Mark Strange
- *Civics and the Constitution: An American View of Law, Liberty, and Government* by Jake Macaulay and Ricki Pepin
- *Our Constitution Rocks* by Juliette Turner
- *Exploring Government* by Ray Notgrass

Economics

Sometime during high school, even if it is only one semester, every student should learn some basic economics. When our students graduate, we want them to be able to balance a checkbook or the digital version thereof. This is an important skill, and many kids are never taught how to be good stewards of money and how to keep track of it. There are different types of classes available, some about home economics, and some more related to the economic systems of the world. But each of them has the goal of teaching the student to understand the power and use of money.

- *Intro to Economics: Money, History, and Fiscal Faith* by Masterbooks
- *Exploring Economics* by Ray Notgrass
- Find more ideas at www.cathyduffyreviews.com.

Theology

No matter where you stand regarding the Christian faith, it is part of the western worldview and should not be ignored. I already touched on this topic in the section on worldview. The Christian worldview is the backbone of the US constitution and morality, and it is under attack.

Many influential thinkers and writers over the centuries chose to reject the Christian God but a great number of them still lived their lives as though God existed because they recognized that the basic foundation of western morality is linked to Christian values.

Studying the basic principles of theology will give your student a good understanding of many historical events and the origin of the western worldview.

You may wonder how studying theology will help understand history. The reason is simple. Wars are generally religious in nature. Every war fought in Europe within the past five hundred years has been tied to religion in one way or another. This is a huge topic, but the short version is that most, if not all, significant shifts in societies are related to religious beliefs.

GEOGRAPHY AND RELIGIOUS FREEDOM

From a geographic point of view, you might notice that countries without religious restrictions prosper with freedom. Look it up on a map if you are not sure about that. I was curious about this and googled it. What I found was interesting.

Pew Research published a list of countries whose governments are highly restrictive on religion. In every one of the listed countries, people are persecuted for their beliefs. By that I don't mean not getting a wedding cake, but actually lose their life.

Many Middle Eastern and Asian countries, including Russia, are listed as heavily restrictive. People living in these countries do not have much freedom despite what the governments like to report in the news. If you read the stories from common people in these countries, there is much oppression. Many South American and African countries have the same symptoms.

What I found interesting is that not a single country which has ascribed to Christian values within the past few hundred years or less was on that list. That would include most of Europe, North America, some of Latin and South America, a few African countries, and Australia.

You could call this a correlation or coincidence, however, in my opinion it is so regular that it is difficult to ignore. At least it is an interesting observation that is worth looking into. From my perspective, the best way to form an opinion is to study this yourself if you are interested. Studying theology as part of history will shed some light on this topic, no matter where you find yourself regarding this issue.

Curriculum Choices

My family adheres to the Protestant faith, so the materials we use are Protestant.

- *Foundations in Faith* by Masterbooks
- *Table Talk Magazine* by Ligonier Ministries
- *The Christian Almanac* by George Grant and Gregory Wilbur
- *Renewing Your Mind* daily podcast by Ligonier Ministries
- *Voices of the Martyrs* magazine
- *Essential Truths of the Christian Faith* by R.C. Sproul
- For more ideas, visit www.cathyduffyreviews.com.

BIBLE CURRICULA

- *God's Great Covenant* by Classical Academic Press
- *Bible Curriculum* by Veritas Press

12

Foreign Languages

Boys speak English, and girls speak German. That was my four-year-old son's logical explanation for why he should not speak German anymore. Even when I spoke German to him, he answered back in English. He explained that since Daddy does not speak German, neither should he.

I reminded him that it is okay to speak English with people who don't understand German. But with Mommy, he should speak in German.

A few weeks later, the day came to be evaluated for kindergarten readiness at a private school. I could tell that the teacher was slightly confused after the assessment, but she didn't go into details because my son did well. So, he was all set to begin school in the fall.

Several years later, this same teacher and I were setting up books for a book fair. We were just chatting, and then she told me the full story of what had happened during my son's assessment several years ago.

She had given him instructions to do certain things, which he had quickly and correctly completed. But when it was time to answer some of her questions, he answered only in German. She tried to convince him to speak English, but he continued to speak German.

This went on for a time, and then she moved on because she knew he understood everything, and she had witnessed earlier that he was, indeed, capable of speaking English.

This was too funny, and I was glad she told me that story. Remembering the confused look on her face a few years back, I explained to her that he had in his head that boys should only speak English, but that I had corrected him. And now it seemed that he took it to the other extreme. If you ask him today, it all made perfect sense to him. Since this was a teacher, he assumed she could speak German. Plus, she was a girl, so that settled it for him.

How Do Kids Learn Language?

Watching my children grow up bilingually was an amazing lesson for me. I had never thought about this question: how do kids learn language? If we can figure that out, it will help us teach languages more efficiently to kids and adults.

Looking back, I realize that when kids learn multiple languages at a young enough age, to them it counts as all one language. They just have more words for the same thing. Car is also Auto, tree is also Baum, and moon is also Mond.

At the same time, they're capable of distinguishing the languages because, in general, none of my kids mixed German and English in the same sentence. After thinking about this for a long time, I came to the conclusion that this distinction is not learnt by studying the language, but by simply listening to others speak German.

They quickly learn which category the words 'car' and 'Auto' belong to and which other words to pair it with. So, by hearing a lot of the language, they know how to combine the correct words from the correct language.

You can relate to this when you hear someone say, "He run home." You know it should either be "runs," or "ran." Do you first think, "This is third person singular and needs an 's' at the end?" Or "It's past tense, which mean it should be 'ran,' and it needs no 's' at the end?"

My guess is that your thoughts do not immediately go there. You first know something is wrong because it doesn't sound right. And then, perhaps, you start thinking about what the problem might be.

Immersion

Kids learn correct language patterns because they listen to a lot of the language in their home and everywhere they go. This is called 'immersion', and is the most natural learning method because it gives the brain no choice but to pick it up. The brain is so amazing. After listening to enough spoken language, it subconsciously knows if something sounds right or wrong.

Learning by 'immersion' means that you focus on speaking phrases in your everyday life as they make sense. No grammar lesson is needed unless it comes up naturally. The younger the child, the less grammatical explanations are required.

Older kids might be curious as to how certain phrases can be applied in different scenarios, and they will start using them in various contexts trying to be silly. At that point, specific grammar instruction might be useful, and they will gladly receive it.

What's the point of studying a foreign language?

That's a common question for many English-speaking students. After all, the whole world speaks English, and most if not all the scientific community has adopted English as the normative language. So, if English is your native language, why bother?

Practicality

Many American tourists don't speak a foreign language, so when traveling, English is the main language. If you're an American traveling to Europe, you want to shock those Europeans by being able to communicate in their language, even if not amazingly well.

Grammar

The second reason is that learning a foreign language teaches you your native tongue better. Even if you don't become fluent in the foreign language, simply observing the sentence patterns and grammar will teach you English sentence patterns and grammar. Learning grammar in this way is far more effective than rote memorization of grammar rules. Think of it as a hands-on teaching tool.

THREE RULES

There are three rules regarding any language:
1. The younger the student, the easier the language learning process.
2. The teaching method matters.
3. Be consistent (use it or lose it).

The younger the student, the easier the language

Young children (before the age of around eight) have the ability to learn foreign languages with much more ease and better pronunciation skills than older children or adults. You probably already heard that somewhere. It is called 'the window of opportunity'.

And the older you get, the more difficult it is for the brain to learn new words and language patterns. This fact has clearly not made it into most schools where foreign languages are typically introduced in later grades. By then it takes hard work and determination to make it through.

It's Never Too Late

On the flip side, even if that's the case, it doesn't mean we shouldn't try. It is never too late to learn a new language, it just requires a bit more effort, that's all. So, if you have an older student, don't think that it's impossible or a waste of time to start learning a different language. There are great resources to help you with this.

How I found an effective method

I learned foreign languages in various ways. My mom is Dutch, so we visited her relatives frequently, and I quickly learned to say hello, goodbye, ouch, and windmill in Dutch. These words were not so difficult for me since the German language shares common root words, and I could piece some of the spoken words together.

Later, in school, I learned English and French in the classroom setting. This can be effective, but I did not become fluent in these languages until I spent time in England and France and was forced to use the language. It just clicked one day, and I was fluent.

That's difficult to duplicate in the US, simply because of the distances to other countries.

With my own kids, I spoke exclusively German to each of them. So, every one of them was fluent as a four- and five-year-old. But as they started attending school, speaking German with them became more and more difficult.

They had homework, which needed to be completed in English. They had friends, who spoke English. And my husband does not speak enough German to have a conversation, so the language spoken in the evenings was also English.

MY FAVORITE FOREIGN LANGUAGE TEACHING METHOD

I came up with a plan which worked well for us and where you can pick it up, as well, even with no prior experience. I came up with four steps to be implemented throughout the week to create an immersive atmosphere. Many times we simply stuck with step one.

1. TV Shows and Movies
2. Gouin Series or TalkBox
3. Stories and music from the country of origin.
4. Memorize and have fun.

TV shows and movies

First, we started watching German children's shows. This is probably the most effective tool out there, and the biggest reason that European kids learn English so quickly. Virtually every TV show is in English, and they watch it.

In Germany, TV shows are usually synchronized, but they are still available in English. In other European countries, they are usually broadcast in English with subtitles in the native language.

Here is a list of shows you can find on YouTube in case you are interested in exposing your children to German through watching shows. Visit YouTube and type the following words into the search bar:

Rock'N'Learn—Learn German for Kids

German for Kids with Frau Collett (great for preschool—second grade or so)

Der Mondbär (animated show about a little bear and his friends, this is different from "Little Bear")

Benjamin Blümchen (animated show about a talking elephant)

KinderKlubTV (several animated shows)

Das Kätzchen und die Zaubergarage (a kitten and the magic garage)

Franklin—Eine Schildkröte erobert die Welt (German version of "Franklin, the Turtle")

Mascha und der Bär (stories about a little girl and her friend, the bear)

Wilde Tierwelt—Anna und die Tiere (a show about wild animals)

You can search for other languages, as well. I found educational shows in French and Spanish, so just search for "Learning French for Kids" or similar words.

Most movies, whether on DVD or streaming, are available in Spanish and French. Since your kids may already know the content, it becomes easier to understand.

Gouin Series or TalkBox

Secondly, I still wanted a pre-made language program, but one that uses a slightly different approach than what I had found so far.

After further digging, I found some interesting ideas, again inspired by Charlotte Mason. She exposed her students to French, Italian, Latin, and German and used a unique method that reflects the way babies learn to talk.

When you teach a baby how to talk, you repeat the word over and over again, then get very excited when baby says the word. Next come sentences. We repeat them to Baby, and if she says it correctly, we praise her.

If she uses the wrong grammatical part of speech, we correct her. Baby says, "Me like apples." I reply, "I like apples." It's no big deal, we eat an apple and move on. Eventually, Baby will say, "I like apples."

I praise her and give her an apple. If we look at our student, regardless of age, in the same way and adopt this way of teaching, foreign languages wouldn't be quite do intimidating.

Charlotte Mason used what is called the Gouin series. Sonya Schafer explains how it works.

"For example, the students might learn a series like this:

I take the box.
I open the box.
I close the box.

"Here's how it works. Students say the series of statements aloud a few times as they do the actions: take a box, open it, close it. Once they know the series, it is simplified to just the verbs: take, open, close.

"They learn each of those verbs in the new language and practice saying it aloud as they continue to do the corresponding actions. They learn the one phrase needed to finish the sentences (the box) and practice the entire series in the new language with actions.

"The beauty of this method is that by coupling everyday activities and actions, they begin to think in the new language. What other things do I open and close? A book, maybe. By learning one more new word (book), they can then narrate a new activity and are beginning to feel at home with using the language for themselves."

TalkBox

A similar program to the Gouin series is TalkBox.mom. Adelaide Olguin, founder of TalkBox.Mom, uses a similar method to the Gouin series, but the format is a bit more accessible and adaptable.

Each box includes cards relating to specific everyday scenarios. Kitchen, bathrooms, etc. I placed the cards throughout my house, labeling various items. My kitchen counter has cards by the fruit bowl labeled with "der Apfel, die Äpfel," and "the apple, the apples," along with various phrases to use with "apple."

It reinforces vocabulary and is a fun way to quiz each other when a card is encountered. Each box has a theme, from kitchen, to bathroom, games, and entertainment.

Along with the boxes, you get access to an app that tells you the exact pronunciation wherever and whenever you need it. The idea is to practice alongside your kids. It's very easy to keep track of what you've learned and what you want to learn next. These are some of the most effective language lesson tools I have seen.

READ STORIES, LISTEN TO MUSIC

Thirdly, we spend some time each week reading German stories. Since I speak German, I can easily do this, but even if you do not speak any language besides English, there are a few wonderful bilingual children's books, or German, French, or Spanish versions of already familiar books available at Amazon. You can also try audiobooks online.

For our music, I found folksongs on youtube. Once a week, we listened to them and tried to see how many words my kids recognized.

Even if you don't understand anything at first, just repeat listening to it and observe how over the next few weeks, your familiarity with these stories or songs will make it more enjoyable, and you'll very likely be able to pick out a few words that you've learned, especially if you find videos with subtitles. Make it fun and enjoy the learning process.

NATHAN THE WISE

When my two sons were in high school, I gave them each an English version of Lessing's "Nathan the Wise" to read as part of their German reading assignments. It's a German classic.

My sons read the parts aloud, used sound effects for each character, and enjoyed the process very much. Every now and then I listened in and had to laugh because among some of the sound effects were Darth Vader's breathing, and low rumbling sounds from dramatic scenes of various movies.

On the last day of their "enactment", I heard loud shouting and laughter, so I went to find out what had happened.

As it turned out, the names are not exactly revealing of the gender of some of the characters, and they had missed that Sittah (the Sultan's sister) was actually a woman, not a man.

From her first appearance in the story, they had been giving her a low man's voice with a dramatic rumbling background noise. Then, on the last day, it became clear to them that this was no man.

To say they were in shock is an understatement, but it made the book extremely memorable. We frequently laugh about that misunderstanding, and many inside jokes exist because of it.

Here are some ideas for children's books in different languages you can find on Amazon. If you don't know how to pronounce the words, you will find several of these books as a read-aloud on YouTube.

German

- *Wer wohnt im Wald?* (Who Lives in the Wood?) by Chatty Parrot
- *Der Regenbogenfisch.* (Rainbowfish) (any in the series) by Marcus Pfister
- *Die Kleine Raupe Nimmersatt* (The Very Hungry Catterpillar) by Eric Carle
- *Gute Nacht, Lieber Mond* (Good Night, Moon) by Margaret Wise Brown
- *Gute Nacht, flüstert der Mond* by Susanne Lutje

French

- *The Cat in the Hat* (English and French) by Dr. Seuss
- *Madeline* (French edition) by Ludwig Bemelmans
- *Bonsoir Lune* (Goodnight, Moon) by Margaret Wise Brown

Spanish

Amazon is overflowing with children's book in Spanish, so if this is your language, then you'll have a large selection to choose from. Yay for you! Here I am only listing a few. Also, I bet your library has a good selection of Spanish children's books.

- *The Cat in the Hat* (Spanish edition) by Dr. Seuss
- *One Fish, Two Fish, Red Fish, Blue Fish* (Spanish edition) by Dr. Seuss

- *The Very Hungry Caterpillar* (Spanish version) by Eric Carle
- *Brown Bear, Brown Bear, What Do You See?* (Spanish version) by Eric Carle
- *From Head to Toe* (Spanish version) by Eric Carle

Talking around the Hot Mash

Language and culture are intertwined, and certain expressions are specific to each culture. Usually, someone used a phrase in a time of frustration or success, and it stuck. Some examples in the English language are 'riding shotgun', going back to the time of the Wild West, when the seat next to the stagecoach driver was reserved for the armed guard who had the shotgun.

The American and British expression 'burning the midnight oil' refers to working late. People used to burn oil lamps when it was dark, hence the idiom.

German idioms originated in the same way, but rarely can you directly translate it into English and mean the same thing, which can be a hilarious activity. For example, 'someone is behaving like an axe in the woods' refers to someone being rude and inconsiderate.

When a German says 'He stands on the hose', it means he's stumped. Beating around the bush in German is 'talking around the hot mash'.

The Poor Sausage

Here's my favorite idiom, as it clearly demonstrates the German spirit of optimism: Everything has an end, only the sausage has two. In other words, sadly, everything must eventually come to an end, but it could be worse. The poor sausage must deal with two ends.

COLLEGE REQUIREMENT

It is usually required by colleges to have two consecutive years of the same foreign language sometime during high school. So, if there is even a remote chance your child will attend college, add this to your list of subjects. Being fluent in a foreign language might even allow your student to receive credit without taking a class in college.

GRAMMAR AND LATIN

A big problem with the English language is that many grammar rules are invisible and hidden to the novice, so how are you going to explain these to a young learner who has perhaps just now mastered English phonics rules with its numerous exceptions?

Latin is the textbook language with all grammar rules visible to the naked eye. Here are just a few examples of hidden rules.

Hidden Grammar Rules in English: Gender

For example, one of these hidden rules is gender. Most western languages (Latin, French, German) have at least two of the three genders (male, female, neuter). While the idea of gender exists in English, the actual sign of it is invisible. Each noun's article is 'the'."Here's the million dollar question: Is this article, 'the', a masculine, feminine, or neuter 'the'?

Let's look at the German word for 'the tree': 'der Baum'. 'Der' is the masculine article and goes, just like the English article, in front of masculine nouns. So far so good. But what on earth is the logic behind the genders of each noun in German? Why is tree masculine? Is there a rule? Nope. Tree is masculine, couch is feminine, bed is neuter, rug is masculine, drawer is feminine, leg is neuter.

This concept is invisible in the English language. And while it doesn't keep children from learning good English skills, it will keep them from learning foreign language skills.

Latin does not have articles in the traditional sense. Latin has endings, determining the gender. The gender of the word is built in, so to speak, so that, as you memorize each word, you automatically memorize the gender.

More Hidden Grammar Rules: Cases

Do you remember learning about subjects, and direct, and indirect objects in grammar? These represent the equivalence of cases in the Latin language. The case of a noun determines its purpose in the sentence.

Latin has five cases, and they are not difficult to spot. Each noun (and its adjective if there is one) has a specific ending that determines the case. English has four cases, but they are not very obvious unless you understand what you are looking for.

While the ending reveals the purpose of the noun in Latin, the English language relies on the position of words. For example: 'The mother praises the child', or 'The child praises the mother'. Both sentences have the same words, but in a different order.

In the English language, the order matters with regard to the meaning of the sentence. In Latin the order does not matter.

The word ending determines the subject, that is, the person doing the praising, and the direct object, that is, the person receiving the praise.

So, the English language has cases, but they are hidden. It's difficult to explain concepts that are not obvious to kids. Latin helps teach these concepts that are hidden in English, but obvious in Latin.

Not Ready for Foreign Language?

Before I move on to curriculum options, I do understand that learning a foreign language is not a top priority for everyone, at least perhaps not at this point. If that is the case for you, do make sure that your student learns some basic English grammar skills. Check out the curriculum options in Chapter 7, page 93, on Composition.

Curriculum Options

GRADES 1–3

Classical Approach

- *Songschool Latin* by Classical Academic Press.
  Catchy memory songs and chants make it fun for little ones to memorize the Latin alphabet, Latin vocabulary, counting, and more. The workbook and games are easy to understand and enjoyable for any age. There is an online practice program that includes games, videos, and putting together lap books.

- *Songschool Greek* by Classical Academic Press: The same as above, just in Greek.

- *Songschool Spanish* by Classical Academic Press. The same as above in Spanish. www.classicalacademicpress.com

Charlotte Mason

- *Speaking German with Miss Mason and François* by Cherrydale Press www.simplycm.com

- *Speaking Spanish with Miss Mason and François* by Cherrydale Press www.simplycm.com

- *Speaking French with Miss Mason and François* by Cherrydale Press www.simplycm.com.
  These books explain how to use the Gouin series with your students. www.TalkBox.Mom, explained above, boxes with themed phrase cards.

GRADES 4–6

Classical

- *Latin for Children* (Three Levels: A, B, and C) by Classical Academic Press: www.classicalacademicpress.com
  This is the continuation of Songschool Latin without the songs. The thirty-two videos are well done and easy to understand for the Latin novice. Each lesson takes approximately one week to complete, and review is included. The chanting of vocabulary, conjugations, and declensions reinforces each lesson. The thirty-two lessons in the supplementary Latin History reader follow the history card by Veritas Press (see in the history recommendations).

- *Greek for Children* by Classical Academic Press: www.classicalacademicpress.com
  The lessons on DVD will guide your child (and you) through each lesson. This is a curriculum I used for many years in my homeschool, and every time I used it, I liked the flow of the lesson and the pace they used. This is a well-made and easy-to-use curriculum and easily adjustable to every schedule. There are online games to reinforce vocabulary, word endings, and grammar rules.

- *Hey, Andrew, Teach Me Some Greek:* www.greeknstuff.com
  This program moves at an extremely slow pace and can be used starting in second or third grade if you only focus on learning the Greek alphabet for a while. Slowly, words are introduced. This works best for very short (10 minutes or less), but everyday lessons. This is a great program if you have absolutely zero background in Greek or Latin. There are no videos, just workbooks, but the pace is slow and very easy to follow.

Unschooling/Classical/Charlotte Mason

- *Visual Latin* by Compass Classroom. www.compassclassroom.com
  Compass Classroom has some fantastic curriculum, and Latin is no exception. Dwane Thomas is funny and easily connects with the students. His method is effective, and your student can watch the videos alone or with you. You can either buy a monthly subscription for the entire Compass Classroom curriculum selection or purchase the

Visual Latin program. This is a streaming service, no DVDs.

- *Rosetta Stone* (any foreign language)
  www.rosettastone.com
  you purchase a subscription to an online program that teaches by immersion into the language through many pictures, repetition, and slow progress in conversational language skills. It features audio samples, and assessments of the learners pronunciation.

- *Duolingo* (in the app-store) a free app or online program that teaches translation in many different languages. This is a good way to practice sentence building if you can already read and write.

- *Mango*, www.mangolanguages.com
  an online program that teaches speaking, vocabulary, writing, and conversational skills. It's similar to Rosetta Stone, and even offers Pirate as a language. Shiver me timbers!!

- www.TalkBox.mom, explained above, boxes with themed phrase cards.

- *Speaking German with Miss Mason and François* by Cherrydale Press www.simplycm.com

- *Speaking Spanish with Miss Mason and François* by Cherrydale Press www.simplycm.com

- *Speaking French with Miss Mason and François* by Cherrydale Press www.simplycm.com

GRADES 7–12

Classical

- *Latin Alive* by Classical Academic Press: A continuation of Latin for Children www.classicalacademicpress.com

- *Henle Latin* by Loyola Press—Memoria Press www.memoriapress.com

- *Basics of Biblical Greek* by Zondervan:
  www.christianbook.com
  A rigorous, college-level Greek program that your junior or senior in high school might enjoy. This is a very structured, fast moving, but clear program. You should be somewhat familiar with the Latin form of grammar to better understand this language. Not only is it somewhat different grammar

than Latin, but an entirely new alphabet. Being familiar with Greek letters and basic declensions and conjugations from an earlier Greek program will definitely help.

Charlotte Mason

- *Speaking German with Miss Mason and François* by Cherrydale Press: www.simplycm.com
- *Speaking Spanish with Miss Mason and François* by Cherrydale Press: www.simplycm.com
- *Speaking French with Miss Mason and François* by Cherrydale Press: www.simplycm.com
- www.TalkBox.com explained above, boxes with themed phrase cards.

Sample Schedules for Teaching Foreign Language Every Day

MONDAY: 20 minutes Gouin series, watch a 5-minute YouTube song

TUESDAY: 10–15 minutes Gouin series, review if needed, watch same YouTube song as Monday

WEDNESDAY: Story Day: read from a story book (in English or your foreign language) for as long or as short as you like (10–30 min)

THURSDAY: 10–15 minutes Goiun series, same YouTube song

FRIDAY: 5–10 minutes Gouin series, 5–10 minutes play vocabulary game (point to objects or perform an action and see if your kids can say it without using the Gouin series), then movie time. Check your DVDs or Blue rays for language choices, make some popcorn and watch a movie in your foreign language. Or watch a show on YouTube. These are shorter, but that may be a better choice sometimes.

LEARNING BY TALKING

Using TalkBox: there is no schedule for TalkBox because it is used throughout the day. If you put the cards in the right places, they will be reminders. Use TalkBox in conjunction with youtube, and you have an immersive language experience.

MONDAY: 15–20 minutes YouTube show, practice a TalkBox phrase.

TUESDAY: **20** minutes Mango if you have it, otherwise review TalkBox phrase cards.

WEDNESDAY: Story Day: read from a book (same as in above sample schedule)

THURSDAY: **20** minutes Mango, or spend extra time in the locations for TalkBox phrases (kitchen, bathroom, etc.)

FRIDAY: Movie (same as above sample schedule)

Important to Remember

- Some knowledge in foreign language is better than none, and
- Consistency is the key.

13

Logic (A.K.A. Critical Thinking) and Rhetoric

Fake news. Fact checking. Misinformation. What do all these have in common? Every one of these requires a healthy dose of critical thinking skills, to interpret what is true or false. Where do I learn how to do that?

Many parents assume their kids learn all these skills at school. But studies show that schools are not getting the job done. This continues to lead to the problem that a substantial number of Americans does not possess proficiency in this area.

Sadly, the most common way for people to get their political news is through social media, so in the face of information overload, fake news, and misinformation, critical thinking skills are nowadays most desperately needed.

Where exactly do children learn how to use reasoning and thinking skills? The simple answer is: In the home. Watching mom and dad, siblings, or other relatives converse, disagree, question, or explain issues is the first and most impressionable interaction a child experiences.

Kids learn very quickly how to best convince mom or dad to get what they want. And even if it didn't work the first time, they don't give up but try again, with adjusted strategy. So, the first lessons of reasoning are learned by imitation, trial, and error. This is about as 'hand-on' as it gets.

Window of Opportunity

As kids get older, their reasoning skills shift to a higher level. From about twelve years old (sometimes sooner, sometimes later), their logical reasoning skills begin to develop to a more sophisticated pattern.

If we jump on board, when this development occurs, and begin to guide our students as they expand their 'reasoning base', we can equip them with important tools to successfully navigate this maze of information overload that is surrounding them.

CRITICAL THINKING THROUGH READING BOOKS

Reading a variety of books, or even watching movies and talking about them creates critical thinking skills. You have seen this in action. Think back to when you had just finished an exciting story or watched a great movie. It's hard not to think about it constantly, and every conversation you have reminds you of some scenario from the book or movie. This is critical thinking in action.

Applying what we've read or watched to new situations means we're dealing with the heart of the issue. The more we think about it and apply it, the more we realize the depth of it. This is just one good book or movie. Imagine doing this a lot. Before we know it, we have our head full of ideas which help us form opinions.

What is critical for kids at this point is feedback from someone who understands the topic and the child. Kids need someone to talk to. We don't have to have the right answer, but we can give them new ideas to consider, and questions to ask.

Books versus TikTok

In the past, building a knowledge base has been done by exposing children to carefully selected literature. However, if you recall the studies by Pew Research and Dr. Hutton, the average interest in reading books has been decreasing. What is it that kids are spending a lot of time absorbing these days?

Statistics show that TikTok has skyrocketed in the last few years, and a large portion of viewers are kids. This is an indicator for how kids like to learn: not by reading, but preferably by watching, listening, and interacting. Reading is hard work, so if I have a choice between hard and easy, I'll take the easy path.

As parents, let's deal with reality, and attack the problem not by belaboring our kids with criticism and threats to take away their phones, but come up with real solutions.

If my kids have already been exposed to TikTok or any other place that offers this kind of content, I would like for them to tell me what the latest trending video is.

What kind of videos are they watching? What are they about? Chances are that it's not only cat videos.

Usually, the videos are relatively short, so it shouldn't take too long to explain. You can also watch a video together. Is there any underlying message? Can your child articulate it? Have a conversation about it.

Be an example of how to ask questions. Then, find a story to read aloud which you can relate to the video you watched. Can your child make the connection between the two, story and video? This is critical thinking in action.

Critical Thinking through Composition

In addition to reading, one of the subjects that helps develop critical thinking skills is Composition. One of the difficulties that students of all ages face when writing anything is figuring out what to write.

The entire process of writing anything, from a short sentence to an essay, requires thinking through multiple levels of ideas, language rules, order of thought, communication rules, etc. It's not an easy task, but an essential one.

If you listen to any talk given by Andrew Pudewa from IEW, you will quickly learn that composition forces you to ask yourself questions to get information "from your brain." Critical thinkers are skilled at asking the right questions to get to the bottom of things. Composition aids in exercising this muscle of asking questions.

Critical Thinking through Literary Analysis

Does this term 'literary analysis' make you nervous or excited? I was on the nervous end of the spectrum, that is, until I found Adam Andrew's curriculum *Teaching the Classics.* The instructional video was so inspiring and enjoyable that this quickly became one of our favorite parts of the day.

If you have ever analyzed a literary work, you remember how difficult it can be to come up with any of the elements of the story. This requires insights that are too abstract for very young children, yet they can be trained to recognize a few aspects of it.

Characters and setting are easy enough for most kindergarteners. How about the climax? You can ask, "What's the most exciting part of the story?" In all likelihood, your kindergartener will know the answer to this one as well.

But conflict and theme are a bit trickier. A more mature brain can figure these out. But what's interesting is that the more this exercise is done, the quicker the brain recognizes patterns, signs of conflicts, and manifestations of the themes. These were once difficult to identify, but after just a few practice-runs, this task becomes easier each time we do it. We begin to transfer and apply familiar concepts to new situations. Again, critical thinking in action.

Critical Thinking through Logic

Logic is 'the art of reasoning well'. Reasoning, or 'arguing', in order to convince others of our opinion is a natural desire we all possess. This is a subject that puts our thinking skills to the test.

In Informal Logic, we learn about logical fallacies, and the make-up of good and bad, consistent and inconsistent arguments. Formal Logic feels many times like math, except with words instead of numbers. This is where we learn to dissect and analyze each component of a whole argument set.

For some, this might sound a little too theoretical, which is true if you start too soon with formal logic. This is the reason I started with informal logic in seventh grade and had fun discussions about ridiculous arguments.

Several years later, the student's brain is ready and mature to tackle more abstract concepts. Formal logic is not for everyone, but I added it to my curriculum because I find it useful for building thinking skills.

Abstraction and Discernment

We've covered the importance of reading, comprehending, and articulating. What about abstraction and discernment? Let's start with abstraction.

This is a skill that depends on maturity and experience. Both of these are key factors. Maturity is achieved twofold: natural brain development and practicing the abstraction process. The first occurs naturally, the second is taught. How? Through math and logic.

We start teaching math in kindergarten, using numbers and operators to train our children how to think in abstract terms. Formal logic is taught at a much older age. It feels like math, except it is not based on numbers, but on language relations.

This leads to the actual benefit of abstraction: discernment. Practicing the skill to look beyond words and realize the meaning behind statements equips our students with discernment.

They cannot memorize every scenario they will encounter in life to discern between right and wrong. Or perhaps it's in the gray zone.

Abstraction allows them to take the concept of one scenario and transfer it to a different one. This is what makes abstraction an important skill. It's necessary for everyday life.

How We Think

Thinking occurs when our brains have encountered a problem that it deems relevant enough to solve. How do we actively think? In one of his talks, Andrew Pudewa explains that asking yourself questions is a way to engage yourself in thinking thoughts.

But what questions should we ask of our brain? Teaching our children to ask good questions is equipping them with critical thinking skills. Some people are more natural 'question inventors' than others, but all of us can do it well if given the opportunity and proper training. It is a learned skill.

QUICK THINKING

Life sometimes puts us into situations in which we must think quickly to figure out whether to agree or disagree with a stated proposition.

If you have a four-year-old, you already know that each time you tell him 'No', the automatic reply is, 'Why?' Even if I don't need to justify my answer, I need to have one. What is my basis? What are my non-negotiables?

What if a forty-year-old asks me, 'Why?' What do I say now? In order to make quick decisions, I must be ready to give an answer to questions that challenge my fundamental beliefs and thinking, even if it's just to myself.

Not every question or decision has that urgency of choosing between right and wrong or good and evil. But some do. We want to be ready when they come our way.

THREE STEPS TO CRITICAL THINKING

Step one: Reading aloud and conversations.
Step two: Continue step one, plus literary analysis and informal logic, perhaps formal logic.
Step three: Step two, plus Rhetoric. This step requires being comfortable with steps one and two. Your student combines correct language, well-ordered content, and articulates complex topics.

IF YOU'RE A CHRISTIAN

Having answers to certain questions that people ask forces me to think about my worldview and my basis for morality and decision making. This process is called Apologetics and refers to the training in debate and understanding the Christian worldview. In the Bible, Christians are told to "always be prepared to make a defense to anyone who asks you for the hope that is in you; yet do it with gentleness and respect" (1 Peter 3:15). Studying logic, and later, rhetoric offers a structured way of doing that.

Literary Analysis
- *Teaching the Classics* by the Center for Lit
  www.centerforlit.com (Grades 2–12)

Logic
- *Reasoning and Reading* by Joanne Carlisle
  www.classicalacademicpress.com (Grade 5 and up)
- *The Art of Argument* by Classical Academic Press
  www.classicalacademicpress.com (Grade 7 and up)
- *The Argument Builder* by Classical Academic Press
  www.classicalacademicpress.com (Grade 7 and up)
- *Introductory Logic* by James B. Nance and Douglas Wilson
  www.christianbook.com (Grade 7 and up)
- *Intermediate Logic* by James B. Nance and Douglas Wilson
  www.christianbook.com (Grade 8 and up)
- *The Fallacy Detective* by Nathaniel and Hans Bluedorn
  www.christianbook.com (Grade 7 and up)
- *The Thinking Toolbox* by Nathaniel and Hans Bluedorn
  www.christianbook.com (Grade 7 and up)

Books and courses by the Critical Thinking Company
- All of these are available at www.criticalthinking.com.
- *James Madison Critical Thinking Course*
- *Mind Benders*
- *Dr. Funster's*
- *Building Thinking Skills*
- *Critical Thinking Coloring Books*
- *Red Herring Mysteries*
- *Memory Challenge!*

Rhetoric—Critical Thinking Articulated

Rhetoric is a word that many people associate with lies, boring speeches, and ancient philosophers. All these things might perhaps resemble an aspect of this subject, but they are a distorted representation of it.

Rhetoric is simply 'the art of using language effectively and persuasively'. Logic is the art of reasoning well. Rhetoric is the oral continuation of logic.

There are curricula to help teach this subject, but like so many others, this subject can be taught by first using your composition, and next through public speaking practice.

You can start teaching rhetoric as soon as your child starts writing compositions. The first three canons or rhetoric are invention, arrangement, and style. These are all part of composing a paragraph or essay.

The fourth and fifth canons are memory and delivery, both important parts of public speaking. And once we've arrived at these two canons, it's time to introduce the three rules, or 'proofs', which are *ethos, pathos,* and *logos.*

When speaking in front of an audience, the first, and most important thing that happens is the connection between speaker and audience. Is the speaker proving to be a trustworthy source on the chosen topic? Does the speaker prove to be authentic and honest? This is called ethos, and you might recognize that this is related to the word 'ethics', which refers to the study of moral judgments.

Secondly, how well is the speaker connecting with the audience on an emotional level? Does the speaker capture the audience, or is she boring and stale? Does she communicate the topic in a way that seems relevant to the audience? This is called pathos. Gifted speakers are able to use the same speech for various audiences, adjusting their style to make it relevant for each audience.

Finally, there is logos. This refers to the content and reasons that the speaker uses to convince his audience. How well does the speaker connect her reasons to the point she is making? Do these reasons seem relevant, and is the speaker following the laws of logic?

How Even a Short Exposure to Rhetoric Matters

If the only lesson our students learn from rhetoric is to listen critically and 'dissect' speeches, ads, and Internet or magazine articles into ethos, pathos, and logos, you have succeeded as a teacher. Here is why.

You might think that the content is the most important part of the speech. But if you study a bit of history and think about some of your own experiences, you should see that that is not the case.

Have you ever watched a video or a live presentation about a product you didn't know existed, but now feel like you need it. Then you bought it and now it sits on the shelf or in the closet, unused? That has happened to me several times.

Now, let's think about a different scenario: This same product was presented in a way that didn't matter, so I easily ignored it and moved on. Same content, different effect on the audience.

Content matters, but the rest of the presentation matters more. Tyrants have succeeded and convinced entire nations that their ideas (content) are good and beneficial even though the opposite was true.

Our kids should learn to separate a bad speech from a good speaker, and vice versa. This is far more important than making speeches, although learning to make speeches helps.

You Don't Have to Use a Curriculum

If you'd rather not use a curriculum, then you can memorize speeches and poetry and practice speaking. Practice articulating and connecting with an audience. Practice imitating successful speakers, their gestures, tone of voice, style of speech. And practice various topics, serious ones, and silly ones. Having fun in the process is half the battle.

Elementary School Age
- *Writing and Rhetoric* by Classical Academic Press
  www.classicalacademicpress.com

High School
- *Rhetoric of Love* by Veritas Press
  www.veritaspress.com
- *Rhetoric Alive* by Classical Academic Press
  www.clasicalacademicpress.com
- *Rhetoric Companion* by Douglas Wilson www.amazon.com
- *Classical Rhetoric through Structure and Style* by IEW
  www.iew.com

No Curriculum

- Students read aloud excerpts from favorite stories with varying accents, moods, and voices.
- Students recite or read famous speeches and poetry.
- Students practice telling the same story from viewpoint of different characters.
- Watch speeches and ads and analyze them using the five canons of rhetoric and ethos, pathos, and logos.
- Students memorize famous speeches.

  Re-enact a scene from a movie or play.

14

Enrichment Studies

These are the subjects that every parent who dreams of home-schooling their child wants to teach, but sometimes these are the first ones to be scratched because they don't seem as important as math or science. The solution is to put them all into one category, line them up in a certain order (loop schedule) and spend fifteen to thirty minutes each day teaching what's next in line.

Combine Your Students

Enrichment studies is a list of content-based subjects that lend themselves to teaching by combining all your students if you have multiple kids. The older the student is, the more advanced the conversations and content of the lessons should be, but the process for each age group is similar.

The Enrichment Studies Binder

All these subjects are easier to keep track of if you have a plan. Because there are so many topics within this subject, it's a good idea to prepare a binder for each child with all the information you need, so that you have everything ready to go whenever you get to it.

The teacher's binder will contain the schedule and all the printed sheets with song lyrics, poems, memory work, blank maps for geography, and everything else. Each of your children will have their own, so you will have to decide whether you want to pre-load everything into it at the beginning of the school year, or whether you like to hand out the papers as you get to them.

Their binder might get very thick, so if you gradually hand out the papers, it won't be as heavy and thick until later in the school year. You can then take some papers out if it becomes too unmanageable.

Since this binder will contain every subject in your enrichment studies, you will probably somewhat skip around because you won't be doing every single subject every day. If you put dividers between each individual subject, you can find them quickly when you're looking for something specific.

Loop Schedule for Enrichment Studies

Part of creating your Enrichment Studies schedule is to create an order of topics. A loop schedule is very helpful for this because you can address the frequency in which you want to get to each.

To create a loop schedule, you put the topics in a specific order and work your way through it. If you run out of time, start at that point next time. It becomes a loop by finishing the list and then starting at the top again.

If you want to teach a topic more frequently, simply list it every fourth slot or so. That way you automatically return to this topic more frequently, even if you slow down on some days. For an example of a loop schedule, check out the chapter about your daily schedule.

This can be part of your morning routine. You can also do it in the middle of your day or finish the day off with these subjects. Keep in mind that if you put it at the end of the day, you may not get to it.

A solution could be to put it at the beginning of the day on some days, and in the middle or at the end of the day on others. That can give you a nice balance of subjects and, and a change of pace.

Geography

Who's ready to go on an expedition to a Far East country with Marco Polo? Or who wants to explore the arctic regions with Roald Amundson? How about actually visiting one of the sites where Lewis and Clark landed? Most kids would eagerly raise their hands and shout, 'Me! Me! I want to go!'

FOCUS ON EXCITING STORIES

Geography has a lot of potential to be exciting, but at the same time, many school curricula have turned this adventurous topic into dry, boring material.

Just following in the footsteps of famous explorers, we get a better understanding of our planet. Instead, many curricula turn geography into a subject of memorizing capitals, GDPs, crops, economic development, and raw materials.

We should ask ourselves once again what the goal and purpose of studying this subject is. Are we simply studying it, so we are able to rattle off a few facts to other people or to know the answers to questions on achievement tests?

I am sure that most of us agree that the goal is to gain a deeper understanding of the different places on our planet and the people that live there. That includes not only modern times, but also centuries and millennia ago when explorers traveled the world.

EXCITING AND OUTLANDISH STORIES FROM AROUND THE WORLD

There are innumerable, exciting adventure stories to be told about cultures and places long gone, which still have an influence on our modern culture. The more outlandish the stories, the more attention and interest will be created.

One of my kids' favorite lasting memories is comparing toilets of the world. They are pictured in the book *Material World* by Peter Menzel and Charles. C. Mann.

GEOGRAPHY RESOURCES FOR TODDLERS AND PRESCHOOLERS

For the littlest explorers among us, I had a selection of toys, puzzles, and games that teach basic geographic concepts, and that are entertaining to play with while I was reading aloud. Depending on the maturity of your toddler or preschooler, you can give her a map to color, just like the older siblings.

If your toddler is your oldest child, just playing with a few toys such as an inflatable globe, USA and world puzzles, and perhaps listening to songs about states and capitals will be fun and educational.

At this early age it's about basic exposure and having fun playing. Here are some ideas:

- Various educational toys www.timberdoodle.com
- *Leap Frog Magic Adventures Globe* www.amazon.com
- *IPlay iLearn* World Map Wooden Floor Puzzle www.amazon.com
- *Hug-a-Planet* soft planet cushion globe www.amazon.com

- *Jumbo Floor Puzzle of USA*, 50 States www.amazon.com
  From Melissa and Doug, available at
  www.melissaanddoug.com and www.amazon.com
- *Melissa and Doug* World Jumbo Jigsaw Puzzle
- *Melissa and Doug* Poke-a-Dot: All around Sunny Farm
- *Melissa and Doug* Poke-a-Dot: All around Our Town
- *Mellissa and Doug* On the Farm Cloth Book
- *Melissa and Doug* Book and Puzzle Playset-On the Farm
- *Melissa and Doug* Book and Puzzle Playset: In the Jungle
- *Melissa and Doug* Lace and Trace Farm

Design Your Own Curriculum

As with science, this subject lends itself to creating your own curriculum if you would like to save some money. Preparing ahead of time with the topics you would like to study avoids jumping around aimlessly.

STEPS TO MAKING YOUR OWN CURRICULUM

Step One: Choose a Continent or Region

Step Two: Find out who lives there (people, animals)

Step Three: Choose an animal and learn more about it.

Step Four: Learn about the people and their homes, ethnic food, clothing, language, and customs.

Step Five: Choose some topics that interest you about the region (such as government, mountains, rivers, legends, wars, other historic events, natural resources, language, or climate) and dig deeper.

Step Six: Find YouTube videos, request books at the library, download Google Earth, and prepare anything else you can think of so that the lesson will be smooth and uninterrupted by lack of materials you need.

Step Seven: Print out an unlabeled map. Each time you have a lesson, introduce one new 'label' such as rivers, cities, or mountain ranges. *Then,* have your student locate the ones they remember from last time. Add only one new 'label' per lesson; that way it does not get overwhelming.

The Lesson

I usually begin by pulling out an atlas or going to Google Earth on my laptop and studying the region of interest with my students. We sit next to each other and simply look at the map pointing out interesting features such as big cities, neighboring countries, and rivers.

Then I give my student a blank map, which I place in a clear sheet protector to save paper. My student uses a dry erase marker to label what she remembers which could be one thing, or five. You never know. Each lesson, I have her label what we have previously learned plus one more label. This could be cities, rivers, or mountains. Labeling should take around five minutes.

After finishing your map work, you can move on to reading a book and have your student narrate after each reading. This should not take longer than 10–15 minutes. I do not read the book every lesson. When we get to a place that lends itself to watching a video, we spend fifteen minutes or so doing that. This could be a video about an animal, plant, or of homes in different parts of the world.

Become a World Traveler

You can study geography from the viewpoint of a world traveler. Ask yourself or your student about a "dream destination" if they could pick any place in the world. You can help them by providing some options.

Check YouTube for a few videos, or type in your destination and see what kind of tourist attractions are recommended. Then, for the next lesson, check out books from the library about these tourist attractions, the people who live there, or explorers who have visited these places.

Surround Yourself with Maps

I love maps. Whenever I come across a good one, I find it difficult to pass it by. I have maps all around my house, especially in our school area. If you have the wall space, I highly recommend putting up maps of the world, of the United States, and all the other continents as you study them. Having visual reminders of the places in the world that you have studied, or would like to visit, is helpful for remembering what you have learned and can make for a great conversation starter.

Use a Curriculum

You do not have to come up with your own ideas. There are numerous curricula available that make this subject fun and easy to do. I have especially enjoyed curricula using the Charlotte Mason approach. My local library actually carries many of these. I have tried out several and will list them below.

Curriculum Choices

K–6

Traditional/Classical:

- Geography 1, 2, and 3 by Memoria Press
  www.memoriapress.com
- Legends and Leagues by Veritas Press
  www.veritaspress.com
- States and Capitals (US Geography) by Memoria Press
  www.memoriapress.com
- Daily Geography by Evan Moore
  www.evan-moor.com
- Skill Sharpeners Geography by Evan-Moor
  www.evanmoor.com, www.timberdoodle.com

Charlotte Mason

- *Visits to . . . Geography Series* by Sonya Schafer
  www.simplycm.com
  Each of the six books in this series explores a different continent/area. Use this in combination with the following books:

- *Material World* by Peter Menzel and Charles C. Mann
  www.simplycm.com

  Travel the world, and discover what an average family's belongings look like as they put them all in front of their house.

- *Hungry Planet* by Peter Menzel and Faith D'Aluisio
  www.simplycm.com Travel the world and find out what kind of food an average family eats in a week.

- *Letters from Egypt* by Mary L. Whatley www.simplycm.com
  A living book containing letters that Mary wrote when she moved to Egypt in 1879 to start a school. It's a very enjoyable read-aloud for all ages.

Unit Study

- Amanda Bennett's Unit Studieswww.unitstudy.com; search for 'geography'

Unschooling/Relaxed Homeschooling

- Legends and Leagues by Veritas Press www.veritaspress.com; search for 'geography'

More Curricula

- There is so much more available, if you are interested. Cathy Duffy reviews many more geography curricula. www.cathyduffyreviews.com

Extra Stuff (all are also available on Amazon)

- *Drawing Around the World* www.brookdalehouse.com They have some helpful and free teaching resources on their website.
- *Eat Your Way Around the World* by Jamie Aramini and Loree Pettit www.geomatters.com Cook up some yummy recipes from around the world.
- *Eat Your Way Around the USA* by Jamie Aramini and Loree Pettit www.geomatters.com Cook up some authentic recipes from each state.
- *Map Trek* by Terri Johnson www.masterbooks.com A large amount of maps from different historical time periods, a great companion for history.
- *The World—Reference Maps and Forms* by Evan-Moor www.amazon.com More maps for your student to fill in.
- *States and Capitals Songs* CD by Kim Mitzo Thompson www.amazon.com Pop this into your CD-player while you're driving, and your kids will memorize these songs in just weeks.
- States and Capitals Songs are on Spotify, either with subscription, or free with ads; search for states and capital songs, and you'll find many to listen to in a variety of music genres.
- *Mapology USA with Capitals* by Imagimake www.amazon.com A foam puzzle of the USA states, includes flags to place in he capital cities. This is great to work on during read aloud time.

- History Pockets—Explorers of North America by Evan-Moor www.amazon.com; a craft based history and geography supplement to your lesson plan.

Online/Phone App Games

- Seterra Map Quiz Games www.seterra.com (free)

Phone App: Stack the States and Stack the Countries. Go to the app store on your phone and check what's available.

Geography Books to Read (purchase or request at library)

- *Heroes of History Series* by Janet and Geoff Benge; check out famous people like Daniel Boone, Davy Crockett, Meriwether Lewis, or William Bradford.
- *Christian Heroes Then and Now* by Janet and Geoff Benge, great stories of Christian missionaries.

Movies

- The 1951 documentary *Kon Tiki—Thor Heyerdahl*. Rent or buy on Amazon. The incredible journey of a Scandinavian crew across the South Pacific. Viewer's discretion: at the end are several South Sea Island native girls who are not wearing tops. However, it's not until they get to their final destination. You can just skip around toward the end.
- *National Geographic* documentaries from around the world. Even if it's about animals, you still learn the geographic settings.
- *Once Upon a Time—Man* video series on You Tube has some great content.
- *Once Upon a Time—The Americas*, more videos about the Western hemisphere.
- Search for 'geography for kids' on YouTube and find more ideas.

ART AND MUSIC

Truth, Goodness, and Beauty

One of the purposes of educating children is to teach them to recognize truth, goodness, and beauty. These are abstract concepts, and difficult to describe. How do you explain why a picture, or a piece of music, is beautiful? If we immerse ourselves in beautiful music and art, we're teaching beauty by experiencing these concepts with our senses.

The methods of recognizing truth, goodness, and beauty are the same for every area of existence, but they are easily visible or audible in art and music. So, I'm placing art and music into the same category because they are related, and the reasons to study them are identical.

Kids are excellent at recognizing good and evil, wise and foolish. All you have to do is read *Pinocchio* to your kindergartener or first grader, and you will see what I mean. Kids are very vocal when it comes to distinguishing foolish versus wise and good versus evil.

How does this work with art? Most of the time, you can clearly identify a painting as good or bad if you see the theme and order it depicts. That also applies to art that has simple splashes on canvas.

If the artist had a revelation of 'sunset colors spilled together', there might be an argument to call it good and beautiful due to the fact that the order is created by the color choice. But if the artist just pours over the canvas a selection of paint because he felt like it, I'm not sure on what ground that would be considered good or beautiful. It just exists.

It's similar with music. There is a certain order and harmony that reflects truth, goodness, and beauty, again within certain parameters. Having a cat walk across a keyboard has no real meaning attached to it since (unless it is Mozart in cat form) it is pure coincidence what the order of notes is. However, if the composer uses knowledge and skill to put those notes together and create harmony (it might not necessarily be to our liking), it would be good and beautiful. Music Study trains us to be able to recognize this.

ART AND MUSIC IN CULTURE

In addition to equipping us with tools to recognize them as true, good, or beautiful, studying the artists, composers, pictures, songs, or big works of music along with their historic background is also very interesting for learning to understand our culture.

As long as there is a certain framework of cultural norms, art and music reflect this. If the framework changes, art and music reflect this change. This can be seen in the different art and music eras. To this day, many times the arts and music lead the way, and the culture follows.

There are several categories in which to study art and music: Picture Study, Artist Study, Drawing, Painting, Composer Study, Music Study (study of the music the composer wrote), Music Theory, Instrument Practice, for example.

Picture Study

Your student studies a picture for a few minutes, then tries to describe some of its notable features, interesting elements, and whatever he likes to talk about. You can play some calming music in the background while you are studying the picture. Before or after discussing the picture, you will read a selection from a biography of the artist. It should be from a living book and captivate the interest of you and your student.

Artist/Composer Study

This time is devoted to learning more about the lives of artists and composers. It can be done at the same time as the picture study by ready aloud from a picture book, biography, or any other living book. Or you can do it on separate days, it's up to you. Find out who the person was, what they enjoyed, where they lived, and what they were like.

Music Study

You will listen to a piece, or several pieces if you like, of music. Simply listen and enjoy. You can ask your student if there was anything remarkable that he noticed, or if he thought about specific things while listening. Some pieces of music tell stories, and he might have picked up on it. The idea is to train our kids to pay attention to detail, which takes practice.

Drawing/Painting

This is not a must to cover every week but should be done frequent enough to build skill. A great resource is books that have step-by-step instructions on how to draw something. You can also find YouTube tutorials.

Crayon or pencil and paper are enough at first. Then you can get some colored pencils. If you like to practice water coloring, the Crayola watercolor box is great. Get some extra thick paper for this and watch a youtube video on what to watch out for and get some inspiration.

There are websites where you can purchase a membership, and they have everything laid out for you. But this is not necessary. The idea is to practice putting on paper what we see. That includes working on certain perspectives, and shading.

Your student will become more observant by practicing drawing and painting. We did a term of weekly art, then we took the next term off, and so on. The art lessons lasted around two and a half hours, depending on what we did. Pencil drawing went faster, and oil pastels took the full two and a half hours.

Music Theory/Instrument Practice

I like to put these together because music theory is not very exciting unless you use it. The cheapest instrument you can buy is your voice. So, if you don't have access to a piano, flute, or other instrument, singing is a great alternative.

CURRICULUM CHOICES

Cathy Duffy has a list of free resources www.cathyduffy.com; search for Art and Music, then scroll to the bottom for free instrument lessons, and more.

Drawing/Painting

- Draw 50 Animals Series by Lee J. Ames; library or www.amazon.com
- Alisha Gratehouse's *Masterpiece Society* www.masterpiecesociety.com
  A complete visual art (not musical) curriculum. Instruction in drawing, painting, art history, art appreciation. Monthly or yearly subscription.
- Join Nana at *You Are an Artist*, visit www.chalkpastel.com. In easy-to-follow tutorials, Nana walks you through creating beautiful chalk pastel art. Check it out for some free lessons, or you can purchase themed sets of lessons. Visit YouTube for some free chalk pastel art lessons by searching for 'chalk pastel nana', you will find many video tutorials. YouTube will also suggest other videos, so you can check those out as well.

Listening:

Listen to classical music: Mozart, Beethoven, Bach, Handel, and others on You Tube or music app.

- *Classical Kids* CDs. Check these out at your library or order on Amazon.
- *Maestro Classics* CDs Check these out at your library or order on Amazon.

- SQUILT. Super Quiet Uninterrupted Listening Time gives wonderful content and lesson material for listening to classical music. www.squiltmusic.com
- *Welcome to the Symphony: A Musical Exploration of the Orchestra Using Beethoven's Symphony No. 5.* A well-designed book introducing the workings of an orchestra and everything you need to know about a symphony.
- Watch orchestras perform on YouTube: Mozart's *The Magic Flute*, or watch famous segments of operas such as *The Barber of Seville*, or *The Marriage of Figaro*. It helps to read what the storyline is before listening to the opera, so you may want to google a synopsis beforehand.
- *Peter and the Wolf* narrated by Leonard Bernstein, on CD or Spotify. Excellent explanation of the orchestra.
- The Choir of King's College, Cambridge has the most beautiful recording of Handel's *Messiah* and other pieces. You can listen to them on YouTube.
- *Meet the Orchestra* by Ann Hayes

Formal Music Instruction:
- Visit www.classicsforkids.com for music education lesson plans and information.
- *Theory Time* workbook series by Heather Rathnau, NCTM. Music Theory books www.amazon.com

Art Study
- *History of Art* by Veritas Press www.veritaspress.com Art history from the beginning. There is one flashcard with artwork and historical information per week for thirty-two weeks. Worksheets for review are in the book, but you can just buy the cards if you like.
- Picture Study Portfolios by Simply Charlotte Mason
- Masterpiece Society offers great resources for anything in the art study department. On the website, look for Art Appreciation and choose an artist to study. www.masterpiecesociety.com

Free resource
www.classicalcharlottemason.com, click on the picture study tab, and choose an artist. You will be able to download many paintings and print them out. You can find information

about the artist by doing a web search and voilà!, you have your picture/artist study. www.simplycm.com search for Art. These portfolios includes eight 8.5" x 11" UV-coated pictures of famous artists plus a teacher guide with a Charlotte Mason style read aloud biography of the artist.

Visit art museums and orchestras, if you live near one of these. If not, this could be a fun field trip.

Folk Song/Hymn Study

This is one of the easiest 'subjects' to do, thanks to YouTube and Spotify. There are lists of folk songs you can play and sing along with. Find the lyrics online, print them out, and put them in a binder.

Folk songs are history lessons in song. They tell of the roots of the culture, including the good, the bad, and the ugly. We should try our best to keep these songs alive as they are part of the fabric that makes up our culture.

Visit www.amblesideonline.com and select 'Folk Song' from the drop-down menu to find lists of recommended folk songs.

Poetry

Poetry is an easy subject to overlook. The reason not to skip it entirely is that it covers such an enormous span of human history. Homer wrote poetry, the books of Psalms and Proverbs are poetry, and many Greek and Roman writers wrote in meter, using many different literary devices. This continues all the way to today.

Poetry gives us a glimpse of how language works, the powers of carrying meaning on many different levels at the same time. Studying poetry gives our kids a broad perspective of language usage in a technical sense, while instilling the awareness to look beyond the words and into the deeper, hidden messages they convey.

You don't have to be a poetry buff yourself, but if you are, let your student discover some of these devices by himself. If you read a poem, you can ask if your student sees any patterns, either in meaning or in rhythm. Sometimes phrases are repeated, sometimes restated in different words. Sometimes there is only rhythm to the poem, and no other poetic device. Make it a "hunt for the rule."

Poetry lends itself to being memorized. Andrew Pudewa encourages memorizing poetry, explaining that reading poetry on a

┌── **Sidebar: Learning a Musical Instrument** ──┐

Making music is fun, at least for most kids, but there is also evidence that learning to make music benefits children in their emotional and social lives and their skill in language use. Children prone to autism or other problems may be helped to become more balanced personalities by becoming acquainted with classical music.

An interest in instrumental music can be pursued at various levels of seriousness, at a minimum just having a piano or guitar around and occasionally picking out a few chords. Here we'll look at the possibilities for more serious commitment, learning to play a musical instrument at a competent level. This requires regular lessons and daily practice.

We'll look at the violin, though most of what I say will be applicable to the viola, the cello, and the bass, and to a lesser extent to other, non-string instruments. Learning the violin is not something that can be picked up casually; you need to find a professional teacher, who can offer group as well as individual lessons. Many children take to the violin a lot more easily if they can learn in the company of other kids at the same stage of proficiency.

The teacher will have contacts with other organizations such as a local youth orchestra, and if your child makes good progress, she will be able to take part in orchestral performances, as well as chamber groups.

Children can begin violin at the age of three or four, though they can also start at any later age. Three-year-olds cannot be expected to pay attention to exposition of instrumental technique for more than a few minutes, if that, so violin teachers have evolved special teaching techniques to keep the lessons seeming like a fun game, and hold the student's attention.

Learning to play an instrument eventually involves picking up considerable knowledge of musical notation and theory, so it prepares the student for the pursuit of other branches of music, beyond the specific instrument. At the beginning, this 'theoretical' aspect is minimized.

In violin for children, there is a special 'triangular' relationship between parent, teacher, and child. The parent attends the lessons, knows what the child is being asked to do, and makes sure the child puts in time practicing every day. Sometimes the parent actually learns to play the instrument, along with the child or slightly ahead of the child, but this is not required. What is essential is that the parent understands what the child is being told by the teacher and is able to keep the child on track every day, in between lessons with the teacher.

It is impossible for any student to become proficient at a musical instrument without regular practice. Time, space, and toleration have to be set aside for the violin student to practice, making sounds which in the early stages will not have a polished quality. Young children begin violin with smaller sized instruments which don't have the resonance of full-sized violins,

It works very well if the first child begins to learn the violin, the second child follows a bit later, and so on. The second child is usually inspired to copy the progress of the first child, and the first child is pleased to be the object of emulation. Whether one child or all the children are learning the instrument, the home provides a good setting for mini-concerts in which the students can show off their developing skills.

Many families are committed to homeschooling and see the value of learning a musical instrument, but there is also the reverse effect: families with a strong commitment to musical performance find the school system, with its rigid hours, an annoying hindrance, and switch to homeschooling, in order to be more free to schedule lessons and public performances at flexible times.

FINDING A TEACHER

Your chosen violin teacher will have an impact on the child's life for some years to come, so it's worth going to some trouble to make an informed choice. You can use online resources, given below, to help you find a teacher in your area.

Your teacher will provide individual lessons and also group lessons, in which some of the teacher's students will learn together. Generally, young children learn better in groups. Often, there will be public performances of all the teacher's students at all levels, attended mainly by the families of the students, but open to anyone. You can arrange to attend these performances, observe what's going on, and talk to other parents. You will also be able to check on the teacher's record in teaching kids who later became established musicians.

THE SUZUKI METHOD

Most teachers will employ the Suzuki method, or some approximation of it, and will use Suzuki materials, such as graded sheet music. Suzuki has become a recognized standard, even though in many cases, the teacher does not follow Suzuki in all its details. The essential idea of Suzuki is that the child learns to play as she learned to talk, by listening and imitation. The lessons are made more fun by treating each stage as a little game, with the way to hold the violin and the bow, or some approximation to it, the first bow strokes, and singing along with the melodies, all carefully designed to fit the child's level of interest.

MIMI ZWEIG'S APPROACH

Mimi Zweig, at Indiana University, has achieved great success as a teacher of string instruments, most famously in teaching Joshua Bell, who became one of the greatest of contemporary violinists. Her approach is her own, but is compatible with many elements of Suzuki.

MUSIC AND ALL-ROUND DEVELOPMENT

Don Campbell's inspiring best-seller *The Mozart Effect* gave a boost to the idea that listening to classical music would improve IQ and other personal qualities. Campbell's book was later found to have made some unsupported and exaggerated claims, and is now widely viewed as debunked.

More recent scientific work has uncovered solid evidence for the mental and emotional benefits of music, and music therapy has emerged as an efficacious, evidence-based discipline within medicine and psychiatry.

For example, a recent study conducted by researchers at the University of Helsinki found that children exposed to classical music had better cognitive and language development compared to those who were not exposed. This study suggests that the structure and patterns found in classical music can help to improve spatial-temporal skills, which are important for problem-solving and decision-making, and can improve verbal memory and language skills. Listening to classical music can also help to reduce stress and anxiety and promote feelings of calm and relaxation.

MIMI ZWEIG STRING PEDAGOGY

Here you can find string teachers in your area, and much other free information about string teaching.

https://www.stringpedagogy.com

THE SUZUKI METHOD

Through the Suzuki Association of the Americas, you can find contact info for accredited Suzuki teachers in your area.

https://suzukiassociation.org

CIRCLING AROUND

A video about Mimi Zweig's Violin Virtuosi, with insights into youngsters learning violin.

https://www.youtube.com/watch?v=QM2f8YWdrjY

PRACTICING MUSICIAN

This site offers lessons for various instruments, with free sheet music and free video instruction.

https://practicingmusician.com

MEMORIA PRESS

Not specifically for instrumentalists, but offers useful materials on theory and music appreciation.

https://www.memoriapress.com

frequent basis introduces vocabulary to your student that might otherwise never be heard or spoken. Hearing the word used in certain contexts helps add vocabulary quickly to the active language usage. This can lead to some funny scenarios I will share in the next section which addresses memorization.

How to start a poetry lesson: If you have never done a poetry lesson before, grab a book with poems for children (a few are listed below), pick a poem you think is fun, and just start reading it. There are some hilarious poems out there, so you can choose one of those.

Poetry books

- *A Child's Book of Poems* by Gyo Fujikawa
- *Poetry for Young People* series, featuring a variety of poets (various authors)
- *The Random House Book of Poetry* by Jack Prelutsky
- *Where the Sidewalk Ends.* Poems and Drawings by Shel Silverstein
- Linguistic Development through Poetry Memorization by IEW www.iew.com

MEMORY

Speaking is using our memory. Without having memorized vocabulary, pronunciation, sentence and grammar rules, and a certain etiquette regarding what is okay or not okay to say in certain scenarios, we could not effectively use language to communicate. In other words, all our communication skills go back to memory work.

We don't think about this very much because it has become a part of us. Memory work accomplished two important goals: for one, it fills the brain with useful information that is on standby and ready to be used. But we should not underestimate the effect that memory work has on the brain in the long term.

I am no expert in brain function, but I think it is common sense to assume that the brain works like a muscle. The more it is exercised in certain areas, the easier a certain task becomes. Memory work trains the brain to have certain pieces of information ready to go.

Critics might call this a waste of time and argue that information can always be looked up. That is not wrong.

But the problem is that many times, we don't see connections and it won't even occur to us to look something up because we simply haven't considered the possibility. How can I ask a question that I can't think of asking?

Memorizing certain speeches, poems, scripture, rules, facts, are not a waste of time if they are wisely chosen and useful. Andrew Pudewa has given several talks on this topic and encourages parents to memorize passages with their kids to help with their language development because vocabulary is acquired, and new sentence patterns learned by memorizing complex speeches.

A great one to memorize is "Jabberwocky" by Lewis Carroll. Reciting this leads to some very funny moments. It is difficult not to try to re-enact this great poem as you recite it.

Spending just five minutes each day on memorizing something is not a lot of time, and gets the job done well. Start with funny poems (Like "Baby Ate a Microchip" by Neal Levin) or sayings from *Poor Richard's Almanac.* I incorporate scripture in my kids' memory work, so if you like that idea, choose some of your favorite scriptures and print them out.

Put the selected memory work into the Enrichment Studies binder so you can remember what you are working on.

Very young children

- Start out with your address and phone number.
- Pledge of Allegiance
- "Star Spangled Banner"
- If you're a Christian: The Lord's Prayer and the Apostle's Creed
- *Linguistic Development through Poetry Memorization* by IEW www.iew.com
- *Living Memory: A Classical Memory Work Com-panion* by Andrew A. Campbell; this book is ridiculously expensive on Amazon since it is out of print, but if you ever see it for $30 or less, it's worth having. This is a 452-page collection of memory worthy passages. Greek, Latin, Grammar, Shakespeare, Geography, Math, and much more. It's all there.
- *How to Teach Your Children Shakespeare* by Ken Ludwig www.amazon.com; full of great passages to print and memorize
- Memory Songs from CDs or Spotify; look for countries and capitals, US states and capitals, multiplication, division,

addition, subtraction, science facts, catechism, scripture memory, history timeline

- Classical Conversations memory songs
- Veritas Press History and Bible memory CDs

Nature Study

Unbeknownst to my kids, I was loading up my car with a picnic basket, hot tea in a thermos, coats, boots, hats, and gloves. "Who is ready to go on a hike?" I called once I was finished. Within one minute, everyone stood at attention, ready to go.

"If only the math lessons were this enticing," I thought to myself. Every negative attitude had vanished as we left for our favorite hiking trail. Once again, I was reminded of the importance of making time for hitting the outdoors.

BENEFITS OF NATURE STUDY

Nature Study is a subject that acts as an equalizing force in our busy lives. It is a subject that does not feel like school—at least it should not feel like school—and is therefore easily skipped. I have been guilty of that too many times myself. I tell myself that we still have to complete the math or writing lesson, and therefore cannot possibly go outside and do our nature study. Well, that is usually a mistake on my part.

Even just going outside for twenty minutes and spending time observing, or simply appreciating and enjoying nature, resets the brain and helps be more productive in all our other school subjects.

It teaches awareness of processes that cannot be learned by simply reading a textbook. Reading about birds and how they build their nests is not the same as watching it in action. Reading about trees in the spring, and how their leaves suddenly erupt, is not very impressive in a book, but in real life it is a miracle.

NATURE DEFICIT DISORDER

Maybe you have heard of the term "Nature Deficit Disorder." Richard Louv coined this phrase in his book *Last Child in the Woods,* in which he addresses a strong connection between the general well-being of children and the time they spend outdoors.

His observation is that, over the past decades, children are spending less and less time outside, which leads to increased ADHD diagnoses, general illness, depression, Vitamin D deficiency, and many other problems. Spending time outdoors increases brain function, metabolism, Vitamin D production, and general well-being, regardless of age.

This is where Nature Study comes in. What exactly is Nature Study? It is the intentional visit to the great outdoors with the purpose of learning to observe, appreciate, notice, connect, and enjoy what we encounter. When we are outside with a distracted mindset, is all too easy to miss the little cocoon, or singing bird, that are just outside our window.

Spending time outside frequently and doing Nature Study trains us and our children to pay attention and make sense of the world around us.

Truth, Goodness, and Beauty in Nature Study

One reason to do nature study is to recognize order and design when we see it. Death and decay are naturally repulsive to us unless we have never learned to recognize and value life and order.

Nature study gives us a grasp of what orderly design looks like. This in turn builds in us a framework so we can recognize order in other areas of life.

Why is it important to know these things? It is in nature that children can for the first time witness the complexity of creation. If you look around, everything you see has its place and its purpose. Observing the way that birds feed their young makes us ask questions such as 'How do they know to eat, and then regurgitate the worm before feeding it to the babies?' or 'How do they know how to build a nest before laying eggs?'

Spend time marveling at these things and figuring out an answer together with your child.

Masterly Inactivity

Charlotte Mason has a phrase, "masterly inactivity," which refers to activity that is not parent-guided but within safe and acceptable parameters. It is the "wise and purposeful letting alone" that Charlotte Mason advocated.

The child can seemingly be doing nothing important, but yet her brain is hard at work. In modern terminology it means that nothing is scheduled for the child to do except what she chooses to do, within a certain limit of course.

Much of this time can be spent outside, a time during which much growing up and maturing happens. Nature is an excellent teacher, and as our children grow in maturity, they can be trusted with more and more time alone outside.

BOREDOM

Finally, a quick word on boredom: boredom is a state of the brain that is extremely important for proper development. Much like sleep, boredom allows the brain to rest in a productive manner. If we do not allow our children to experience boredom, we are withholding a vital 'nutrient' from them.

Being bored and outdoors is an ideal combination. The child is allowed to learn how to find something to do without prompting by an adult, and this in turn, if repeated, leads to building neurological pathways that will be beneficial in the future. Boredom is a good thing.

How often and when do I do Nature Study?

Nature Study should be done at least once a week for an hour or two, depending on what you are doing during the lesson. If you drive somewhere to take a hike, plan on two hours, but if you are going into your back yard, an hour may be enough.

You can also build frequent breaks into your school day during some of which you can let your student play outside. Not every break has to be spent outdoors, but if you have nothing else planned, this can be your default.

I had Wednesday afternoon, starting at 12pm, reserved for our "Nature Day." Wednesdays we went on hikes, fishing, leaf walks, scavenger hunts for nature items, etc. Had I not reserved our Wednesday afternoons for Nature Study, it would not have happened. We went regardless of whether other subjects were finished or not. Sometimes the kids had work to do when we returned, but I tried to set up our Wednesday morning schoolwork so everyone could finish on time.

What about the weather?

Ahead of your Nature Study day, think of several possibilities for different weather conditions. Having a plan for Nature Study is for most of us the only way we will ever get to it, so prepare several ideas and whatever makes sense that day, do it.

You could have several stacks of index cards with nature study activities for rainy days, snowy days, hot and sunny days, or just plain normal days. Have one of your kids choose a random card and do what it says.

For ideas, you can visit any of the websites below, or google "nature study." There are several books I recommend which are helpful having on hand, but you can also join online groups and purchase a subscription to access some amazing content. I am listing some of those as well.

Resources I love:

- *Handbook of Nature Study* by Anna Botsford Comstock
- *Hours in the Out-of-Doors* by Karen Smith and Sonya Schafer
- *Nature Explorers* by Cindy West ourjourneywestward.com
- www.amblesideonline.com
- www.simplycm.com
- www.naturestudyhacking.com

Nature Journaling

Nature study lends itself to creating a journal of what you encounter on your walks. These can be detailed, or very basic. They can have words or pictures, or both. It is completely up to you and your students what you include.

It is not necessary to write in it every single time you go outside, though. I brought them, just in case, and my kids filled them in frequently. But sometimes they were so preoccupied with running through the leaves or trying to catch a fish or bug that it would have distracted them from the actual nature encounter.

Also, knowing that they are supposed to draw something every time almost made it drudgery. I usually sensed that ahead of time and did not have them fill it in just yet. During our next read-aloud session, or whenever they were bored, I asked them what they enjoyed about the last hiking trip and either write a sentence or draw something they saw. This had to be done from memory, but at least it made them think about it.

Every child responds differently to nature journaling, so watch your child closely and see how it is going. Does he need help with ideas? Is she too perfectionistic?

These can be impediments, but they are avoidable if you are prepared. If your child is not satisfied with his drawing, keep practicing until it looks to his liking. Perhaps you can print out a picture he can color in instead of drawing it himself.

You can combine art and nature study and study details about plant and animal features by drawing them.

> Alisha Gratehouse's www.masterpiecesociety.com has video instruction for art including nature journal art. She guides the viewer through drawing different kinds of plants and animals.

Another website is www.chalkpastel.com. There are wonderful art lesson videos, many of them nature art, all of them with chalk pastels. If you have a budding artist, this could be great fun.

There are different styles of nature journals. You can buy a pre-designed one, or you can just buy a simple sketch pad with thick paper that can be used for pencils, markers, or watercolors. I usually just buy each of my kids a sketch pad, box of colored pencils, markers, chalk pastels, watercolors, and brushes.

HAVE A BASKET

I already mentioned this a few times, but it is so helpful, it needs its own category: have a Nature Study basket ready to go. Fill it with items you will need, such as sunscreen, bug spray, water bottles, old cup for watercolors, watercolor set and brushes, pencils, sketch pad (thick paper), a few field guides, and some snacks, juice boxes, binoculars, towels, extra clothes. The day of our outing, I could just grab the basket and leave without having to scramble at the last minute.

- Note booking Pages www.notebookingpages.com
- Alisha Gratehouse www.masterpiecsociety.com
- Chalk Pastel Lessons www.chalkpastel.com
- More nature journal ideas: www.simplycm.com
  www.amblesideonline.com
  www.ourjourneywestward.com

Handicrafts

Do you have a child who loves to take things apart and figure out how they work? Learning how to take things apart, put them back together, and to create things with your hands is essential for developing proper motor skills. In the time of phones and tablets, working with your hands is becoming less of a focus and something few kids learn, whether in school or at home.

Younger kids can do simple projects using kits that can be purchased or prepared ahead of time. Crocheting, weaving, knitting scarves, hats, etc. are also good skills to learn, and they make great gifts. Older kids benefit from learning how to fix basic things around the house, or a leaking faucet. This is not something kids appreciate when they are young, but one day they will be very grateful when they can change out a faucet or toilet flush without having to call a plumber and pay a lot of money. Being able to fix basic things around the house is a very useful skill.

- Craft kits
- Video instruction DVDs by Simply Charlotte Mason www.simplycm.com
- YouTube tutorials

TYPING

There are many programs available that teach kids typing. Some are subscription-based, and some are free. Here are some that we have used:

- www.typinginstructorkids.com. This is game based and fun to use.
- www.typingclub.com. A free online typing program.
- www.typing.com. Another free online typing program.

LEARNING TO USE A WORD PROCESSING OR SPREADSHEET PROGRAM

Using a word processing or spreadsheet program is a skill that is not urgent, and completely depends on the interest of you and your child, but if you are interested in learning or having you child learn how to use a word processor, visit www.youtube.com and search for Microsoft Word Tutorial.

For learning how to use a spreadsheet program, visit www.youtube.com and search for Microsoft Excel for Dummies.

Basic coding skills

Some children are naturally interested in coding. Robotics and things like raspberry pi are fascinating hobbies to them. If you would like to encourage your student in this area, here are some ideas. Many of these are free and for beginner level and up.

- www.scratch.mit.edu
- www.codecombat.com (paid)
- www.code.org
- For going further in coding: www.w3schools.com
- www.codecademy.com

PE

This subject can be done in a lot of different ways. You can join a homeschool group that does PE together (I did that with my kids). You can also enroll your child in a team sport like soccer or basketball.

If you're a runner, you can let your child train to build up stamina every day to run a 5k. You could do swimming lessons, join a fitness club, or get your own equipment so you can do it at home. The options are numerous.

The main goal in PE is to create in our kids a desire to live a healthy and active life. Nutrition can be covered as part of PE. The best way to teach this is to be active ourselves. If our children watch us live a healthy lifestyle, they will get used to is and be more likely to continue it once they are on their own.

Masterbooks has several great online PE programs that my daughter used and enjoyed.

- PE Courses K–8 www.masterbooks.com
- High School: Strength and Conditioning www.masterbooks.com

You can also follow YouTube channels that offer fitness and workout programs. As long as you and your family move around frequently and make walking or running a habit, it will benefit the entire family, and your kids will likely continue this in their future lives.

Being Able to Take Dictation

Opinions on this skill vary. In the age of spell-checking software, why spend time writing what is being dictated? In my opinion, this is not an absolutely necessary subject, but should at least be sprinkled in a few times throughout the school year.

Being able to write what you hear with correct spelling and punctuation is sort of like learning good manners. It comes in handy, and people will respect you for it. And since parents are all about setting their kids up to be wholesome, respectable people, dictation can aid in accomplishing this.

Starting at a grade level in which the student is a confident writer as far as forming letters and words go, usually second or third grade, plan on five to ten minutes once every week or two. You can do more or less, but as long as it is done every now and then, it will serve its purpose.

Choose a passage from a favorite book, poem, or magazine. The younger the child, the shorter the passage should be. One sentence for a second grader might be a good start.

Read the sentence slowly and clearly one time. Then let the student write it. With longer passages, read each sentence slowly and clearly, then let the student write it, until it's finished.

Finally, choose your method of checking for mistakes. Either your student turns it in, and you go over it, mark it up, and have the student fix each mistake, or you can do it together by going over each word and punctuation mark.

This should not take long, but will be a great confidence builder, and when it comes to writing down notes during lectures in college, these short dictation sessions will have prepared the student for writing what he hears.

15

Learning and Teaching

"Mommy, why is the sky blue?" "Uuuhmm, son, because the molecules in the atmosphere scatter blue light more than other light." "What is that bug over there?" "I have no idea." "Why do birds like to eat worms?" Before I could even think about this question, my almost four-year old son continued, "Why is there a tree on that bridge?"

This was our typical conversation on any car ride. It took me a long time to figure out that I didn't always need to answer every question. He was simply observing the world around him, and asked every question that came to his mind. To him, the answers I provided were sometimes helpful, and sometimes he ignored them.

But it showed his curiosity about everything he saw, and at that age, he did not yet have a filter to prevent him from asking all his questions as they came to his mind. The amazing thing is that this curiosity and constant wonder is completely normal for that age group. It's what all healthy young children share in common.

Depending on their current level of development, this curiosity is the reason why parents and grandparents have to baby-proof the house, so that their little explorer won't choke on a small object or climb up the kitchen counter. Babies and toddlers are super sponges, perpetually going, only stopping in order to nap or eat, and then continue exploring. Curiosity causes babies and toddlers to taste, touch, bite, suck, or pull on anything in sight. It seems insatiable.

This curiosity is the reason that we must establish safety rules when walking in a busy street or when roasting marshmallows over a campfire. 'Why' and 'how' are favorite words for many three- and four-year-olds, even to the point of exasperation for the parent or caregiver. While this might be a trying phase, eventually most children do outgrow it.

Why? There are several reasons, but in my opinion, the most noteworthy one is that eventually the child learns that learning and curiosity are no longer enjoyable because learning loses relevancy.

Connecting Learning and Relevancy

Every learner needs a relevant reason to learn. Little kids find relevancy all around them. And then, usually, around age five, a child is sent off to kindergarten. Teachers now fill her mind with questions and facts that are supposedly more important than what she is curious about. Expert adults have figured out what each child should know at certain ages and how their curiosity can be guided in the setting of a large classroom, and this is what the school curriculum is designed after. The curiosity of the individual child is less and less encouraged, so over the years the child loses interest.

This is not necessarily the schoolteachers' fault—they usually labor diligently to facilitate a positive learning environment. But as the students get older and classes get less manageable, it's increasingly difficult to keep them engaged in meaningful and productive work.

By middle school and high school, the student has usually lost interest in learning because it is no longer seen as relevant. In classroom settings, many of the topics that must be learned are presented in terms that don't relate to anything the children find meaningful. Curiosity ceases when relevancy is missing.

How Can I Make a Topic Relevant?

So, one question that is very helpful to keep in the back of my mind when teaching my student is: How can I make this topic relevant to my student? This is not always easy or even possible. But we should try to connect every topic we teach need with a relevant reason for learning it.

My youngest daughter is not convinced that learning how to transform functions in Algebra 2 is relevant to someone who will not go into a math or engineering field. She didn't go for any of my 'Isn't-it-cool-to-be-able-to-do-this?' arguments. My only other answer was that if she is remotely interested in attending college, most degrees, STEM or not, require some level of math. And, sadly, functions are usually a big part of that. So, there is the connection to relevance. It's not a great one, but my daughter has accepted her lot in life and keeps at it.

Usually, however, relevance can be more practical and specific. Is there a topic your student enjoys which can be connected to the subject you are trying to make relevant? In composition, for example, could you write about a topic that he is already familiar with and enjoys thinking and reading about? In science, could you plan on spending some extra time on the 'fun stuff'? This will likely work as an incentive to get through the 'not-so-interesting' topics.

My goal in each of the chapters about various school subjects is to equip you with the foundational reasons to teach each of them. I don't know about you, but I need frequent reminders of why I'm teaching certain subjects, or I lose momentum.

One important thing I have noticed over the years is that many times, as long as I am motivated to learn the subject, my kids are more likely to follow. When I'm excited, my kids are curious why I'm excited. And the way to stay excited is to keep the subject relevant for myself.

SCHOOL WON'T ALWAYS BE FUN, BUT SHOULD ALWAYS BE RELEVANT

Students can be as different from each other as night and day. There are lessons and subjects that will appeal more to some students and less to others. This certainly keeps family life from getting boring. But it can lead to tricky situations when one student loves a subject, and the other does not.

My natural inclination is that I want my student to love every subject. That's not exactly realistic or even reasonable. I did not like every subject when I was a student, so why would my kids be any different?

Remember that not all learning will be fun and games. There will be hard work, and certain subjects will be on the 'my least favorite' list, yet they must still be learned. Maybe grammar is on the less-appealing subject list for your child, or perhaps mathematics.

Choosing the right teaching philosophy and materials for your family will help you with addressing how to teach a subject that your student or even you are not excited about. The philosophy will usually also help establish relevancy for each subject.

If a certain subject continuously bothers your student and becomes a distraction for her and everyone else in the family, it might be a good idea to re-assess the situation. Simply switching the time of day during which the subject is taught might do the trick. Perhaps a different person should be the teacher, or perhaps you could try a different approach to teaching this subject.

But here's another way to look at teaching 'that tedious sub-ject': Sometimes a school lesson teaches a life lesson, namely that not everything in life is fun and you have to do it anyway. Certain things must be done whether we like it or not. This 'explanation' can be overused, so we need to be careful about that. But every now and then it is appropriate.

The Early Years—Exploration Is Education

A good friend had her second son just a few weeks before my sec-ond son was born. As the babies grew up and became mobile, we had many playdates for the older brothers. It was usually a very chaotic scenario with two active toddlers and two emerging "destroying machines," in the words of their brothers.

One day, the older two boys were playing with legos, construct-ing various spaceships, and other flying machines, when one of them shouted, "Watch out! The babies are coming!" Immediately, two little heads, belonging to two eighteen-month-olds, popped around the corner, and the squealing began as the older boys tried to protect their precious creations.

Moms to the rescue! The sudden rise in noise caused my friend and me to check and see what was going on. We were just in time. The babies had not yet done any harm. Phew!

If you have toddlers, you are very familiar with this scenario. Babies and toddlers want to explore and see what is around the cor-ner and on top of the table. At that age, exploration is education.

Allowing them to have free range in a supervised environment is absolutely crucial for proper brain development. If you're inter-ested in learning more about the connection of mobility and brain development during the baby and toddler years, I will list some resources in the appendix.

Explore Nature

Outdoor exploration is equally as important as indoor exploration. When my kids were very young, I made an effort to take them into our backyard every day. Our yard was adjacent to the wood which was a dream come true for young kids. There is no better way to teach the beauty of nature than to experience it firsthand.

They had hours of playtime and did not want to come back inside. The time spent outside gave them much common sense about how the world and nature work. Trees have bark, leaves are green, insects can fly and creep.

Being outside has many other benefits, as well. It reduces stress levels, anxiety, and other mental health issues. Being in the sun increases vitamin D production which helps regulate your body's immune system, aids in calcium absorption, and plays a role in maintaining a healthy nervous system. This is why you feel refreshed and revived when you get back inside.

As our toddlers get older and enter school readiness, this encounter with nature should continue as part of school activities. The Charlotte Mason approach includes Nature Study as a subject that is done once or twice a week, usually outside. Doing Nature Study is a great way to keep in touch with nature on a weekly basis, even when the student is in middle school or high school.

READ BOOKS

To distract my toddlers from creating messes, I would many times pick them up, grab a stack of picture books, and start reading to them, talking about the pictures and moving from page to page at my toddler's pace. Sometime that was two page turns in a row, and sometimes we would go backward. They loved it. And I loved it.

Making time for reading is not always easy, especially if you're already exhausted from caring for your young child and doing house chores. It might not even feel like she's listening or getting anything out of this, so it's tempting to skip it. Try to have a place for books that is easy to grab when you need it and try your best to consistently expose your child to books.

COMBINING VARIETY AND REPETITION

"Read it again!" How could I say no to this request? My four-year old daughter absolutely loved reading the story of the Nutcracker Prince. She and I had the book memorized, and still she wanted me to read it . . . again and again. So, we started over.

She turned the pages to the beginning, and I started reading to her using the wrong words. "No, Mommy! That's not what it says!" she corrected me. "Read it again." Oh, well, I couldn't get away with it.

While it's important to read from a wide variety of books, repetition is necessary, as well. New books are always exciting, but most parents have experienced the toddler who has one or more absolute favorites that must be read again and again. These books feel like old friends and give a feeling of comfort and contentment to the toddler, and at times to the parents perhaps a feeling of—ahem—irritation?

Keep reading them. These well-known books reinforce familiar vocabulary and solidify sounds, words, sentence structure, language patterns, enunciation, poetic devices, and more. Take your child's lead in choosing from a selection of books that you have prepared, and then, have fun reading and re-reading. Even for just a few minutes each day. It adds up over time.

WHAT ABOUT TEACHING READING DURING THE EARLY YEARS?

Our culture projects certain expectations onto children, including reading skills. This can be contagious, and if we are not careful, we can push our kids too early toward a skill they are not yet ready for. On the other hand, some kids are indeed ready to learn letters and numbers at age three or four.

I remember being one of those kids myself who could not wait to learn to read. My mother tells me that as a three-and-a-half and four-year-old, I learned to read upside down from the school children in her day care, who were learning to read.

Apparently, I sat across from them and was so eager to read, that I just picked it up. I can remember a time in which I could not yet write but I can actually not remember a time in which I couldn't read.

None of my own kids followed the early reading pattern that I did. So, I was a bit worried. Okay, I was actually a lot worried. They all eventually learned to read, and I am not worried anymore. Now I worry about different things. Crazy, I know!

Some kids are just naturally more interested in reading than others. If you have an eager child, there is no reason to withhold it from him. If your child wants to learn letters, have fun with tracing and copying letters, or even making words.

It's all about not putting pressure on a young child but leaving room for natural exploration. Pinterest, or preschool activity books offer many ideas about fun activities, but then again, these ideas can lead down a rabbit hole that gets too entangled.

Do what you feel comfortable with and remember that your child will only be a child for a few years. Fill them with fun and enjoyable activities rather than formal lessons.

Shaving Cream Disaster

Speaking of fun activities, it helps to be prepared for the unexpected. When one of my sons was a preschooler, a friend of mine, who was a preschool teacher, recommended spreading shaving cream on the little kids' table, and having my son draw shapes, letters, etc. with his fingers. Excitedly, I went home to put this into action. What a fun activity!

What I did not expect was my son's reaction. He usually loved getting his fingers into dirt, picking up worms, insects, snakes, and grubs. So, you might understand my surprise when I showed him the "shaving cream game," and he absolutely refused to put his finger it. To make things worse, I tried to show him how harmless this cream is and put his finger in it. Bad idea. He had the biggest meltdown and actually wanted to take a bath after this traumatizing experience.

My solution, to make this appealing for my son, was to put a very thin layer of shaving cream into a Ziploc bag and close it, squeezing all the air out. He enjoyed using his homemade Magna Doodle, but not as much as I had hoped.

He was a very active little boy and less interested in letters than in bugs, snakes, and other creepy things in our back yard. So, instead of letters, he learned to count and write numbers very early on. I did not expect that either.

To my husband's dismay, both my daughters loved playing with shaving cream, so we had to take frequent trips to the store when he found that all his shaving cream was out. They loved using it in their bath time or at their little play table. I must say, it always smelled really nice in our house.

Book List Resources

- *Honey for a Child's Heart* by Gladys Hunt. An entire book about the best books you can read to your children ages birth to twelve.

- *Read Aloud Revival.* Sarah Mackenzie has a passion for reading aloud, and her website, blog, and podcast are full of amazing content from books lists to book clubs. www.readaloudrevival.com

- Sonlight Curriculum has some great suggestions regarding books for young children ages three and older. www.sonlight.com Dr. Hutton, Cincinnati Children's Hospital Pediatrician and researcher www.readaloud.org

- *My Book House.* A collection of great literature for all ages. It has been described as a liberal art education in one book collection.

- *The Fairy Books of Many Colors* by Andrew Lang are a collection of books featuring fairy tales from around the world. This is a great collection to own. Many of these are free or very cheap on Kindle. These are long fairy tales, but some children are ready to listen to them. If your child is not, read shorter books.

Activity Guides

- *Before Five in a Row* and *More Before Five in a Row* at www.fiveinarow.com
- *Preschool Kits from Timberdoodle* at *www.timberdoodle.com*

Starting Out—Kindergarten

School education, especially in the early years, is supposed to be filled with wonder and excitement, and as parents, we have the privilege to participate. Kids of that age are still naturally curious. If you foster this natural curiosity by allowing them the same free time they had as preschoolers, school will feel exciting, and not burdensome.

So, with the mindset of continuing what you have already been doing for the last five years, you and your student are probably getting excited to start this adventure.

At this point, your curriculum choice will have its greatest impact. If the daily lessons are short and meaningful, you've got a winner. This year will set your student, and also you as the teacher, up for the next school year.

Are you and your student looking forward to each day, or is one of you getting less and less excited? If it becomes drudgery, the lesson style may not be a good fit for your child or you.

Every child is different, and sometimes the same curriculum works for one child but not the sibling. Before ordering teaching material, download a free chapter and try it out on your student and yourself. Usually that gives you a pretty good idea if the teaching approach is a good fit.

Just like during the preschool years, the majority of the school day, and of the entire day really, should still be spent playing and exploring. Going outside should be a regular activity.

Gently, and depending on your child's disposition and eagerness to learn new skills, introduce additional activities, always keeping the lessons relatively short and the student engaged.

This early exposure to the learning routines setting will set the tone for the degree of enjoyment your student will experience in the future. While certain skills are important to learn, the priority is to be in tune with your students and adjust the content and pace of lessons to find your "sweet spot." The goal is to continue promoting a sense of curiosity in the student.

Here's a schedule that worked well for my kindergartener and first grader. I added in margin to allow plenty of time to move from one subject to another, cleaning up in between, and take short breaks.

Also, please remember that you can substitute the Bible slot, or any other subject, for your personal choices. I am sharing my schedules with you just the way I had them written down.

Kindergarten and First Grade Schedule with Margin					
Time/Day	Monday	Tuesday	Wednesday	Thursday	Friday
Morning:	Wake up / dress				
7:30-8:30	Breakfast				
	Take walk / Play outside				
8:30	Calendar	Calendar	Calendar	Calendar	Calendar
8:45	Bible	Bible	Bible	Bible	Bible
9	Read Aloud	Read Aloud	Read Aloud	Read Aloud	Read Aloud
9:20	Memory	Memory	Memory	Memory	Memory
9:30	Folk Song / Hymn	Folk Song / Hymn	Folk Song / Hymn	Folk Song / Hymn	Folk Song / Hymn
9:40-10	Math	Math	Math	Math	Math
10:10-10:30	Writing/ Phonics	Writing/ Phonics	Writing/ Phonics	Writing/ Phonics	Writing/ Phonics
10:35	Snack	Snack	Snack	Snack	Snack
10:40 10:55	Reading Practice	Reading Practice	Reading Practice	Reading Practice	Reading Practice
11-11:20	Science	History / Geography	Science	History / Geography	History / Geography
11:25	Fine Arts	Play Outside	Nature Study	Fine Arts	Play Outside

This is approximately a three-hour school day without fine arts, plus it already includes play and going outside. Twice a week, you would have up to four hours, including fine arts which is generally not perceived as 'school' by most kids.

This same schedule can be used for first and second grades as well. You might stretch the reading practice to fifteen minutes in first grade, and to twenty minutes in second grade. Plus, spelling will be added and take up five or ten extra minutes, so the school days of a first and second grader could be approximately three and a half hours without fine arts.

Elementary and Middle School

How do I know at what level to begin teaching?

If you're starting to homeschool an older student who has been going to school, you will have to figure out the understanding he has in each subject. To help you with this, most curriculum publishers have assessment tests to make it easier to find the right place to begin. Most of these are available online and have instructions to help you out.

You can also call a representative, and they will gladly assist you. I have talked with a large number of representatives of various homeschool publishers, and every one of them has always been courteous and helpful. Finding the academic level of the student is an important step in knowing where to start.

One critical issue to watch out for is putting too much emphasis on grade level. Grade levels are only relevant as broad guidelines. They help discern the order and complexity in which the subjects are introduced.

But parents, myself included, have this notion that if our child does not follow the prescribed rate of learning, something is wrong with either our student or us as parents and teachers. As mentioned above, it is best to aim for easier rather than harder. Speeding up is always an option.

The level you choose to start with should not be so difficult as to discourage your students, but it should not be so easy as to be offensive. I know, it sounds like one of those old southern recipes. Bake the biscuits not too hot and not too cold for just enough time so they are golden brown and fluffy. It's only by trial and error that we can figure this out.

Don't be afraid, and have your student take the placement tests. It is not at all a graded exercise, and there is no shame in being "below grade level." Starting out is the most difficult part, so you can make it easier for everyone if there is as little stress as possible. Then see where it leads, speed up or slow down as needed.

CURRICULUM IS A ROAD MAP, NOT A LAW

If you're starting out with an older child, say, a middle schooler, the pace depends on his confidence in each subject. The curriculum guide that you're using will help with the starting point, but sometimes, we need to adjust the speed of the curriculum to the ability of the student.

The curriculum guide and lesson plans will tell you exactly what to accomplish during each lesson. But what if your student is struggling with completing the assignment? This is where we need to remember that the curriculum is only our road map, not a law that has to be strictly followed. We get to decide the speed at which we travel.

You can slow it down, or you can speed it up, if your student is way ahead and has a good grasp on the concept. And the best part is that you get to do this for each individual subject. For example, the student could be way ahead in science and math and move a bit slower in language arts and reading. Adjust your speed as needed. In the long term it'll be a benefit to your student.

COMBINE YOUR STUDENTS

This concept of combining students did not occur to me the first year I had all my kids at home, and I tried to keep the fifth and seventh graders each on their own curriculum track, while keeping the first and ninth graders on their own separate track. It was exhausting, to be honest.

I eventually combined them for one or two very minor subjects (vocabulary and poetry), but everyone did their own history, geography, and literature. It was not until the last part of that year, or the early part of the next school year that I read about Morning Time, and how it transforms a homeschool family's life.

We started very small; a Bible chapter, a fun read-aloud, some memory work, and a song. Soon, this was the reason the kids wanted to start school each morning, and I added a few more topics. Latin and German, geography, composition.

You can call it Morning Basket, Morning Time, Circle Time, or even Symposium, and it can happen at any time during the day, not only mornings. Whatever you want to call it, it's bringing all your students together for certain subjects.

Use Your Lunch Break for Casual Book Conversations

During the middle- and high-school years, my kids appreciated having discussions around the lunch table or in a casual setting where food or hot chocolate was involved. This was a more relaxing setting and replicated a conversational setting rather than a school setting. Talking at the kitchen table gave us a lunch topic and led to some great conversations.

These conversations were very casual, and I tried hard not to turn this lunch break into school. My kids would make sure of that by calling me out, so I always knew whether I was in school mode or in break mode.

Finish before Lunch or after Lunch?

The Charlotte Mason Method allows students to be finished with their lessons by lunch and then spend their afternoons working on projects of their choice. There are guidelines and ideas within the Charlotte Mason approach as to what your student can do during these hours. It is more like an elective and won't feel like school, yet still plays an important role in your child's education. Some examples are reading, gardening, arts and craft, and instrument practice.

But a typical school day in, say, the classical or traditional approach, takes longer. The subjects are a bit longer, and the structure of the day is slightly different.

So, which is the better choice?

Both of them are good choices. It's a matter of preference. I love the idea of being finished by lunch time, but this usually never happened in my house because I did not strictly adhere to a Charlotte Mason education as far as subject content was concerned, especially in the high school years. As a result, my subjects tended to run a bit longer, and I needed to allow time for this.

For example, our daily high school science and math lessons were usually at least an hour and many times an hour and a half. My students enjoyed this and actually needed this time to complete their assignments. They were well prepared for college when the time came.

And since I also liked the classical approach in addition to the Charlotte Mason approach, I added Logic in seventh through ninth, and then Rhetoric in tenth through twelfth grades. Plus, Latin or Greek took us more than thirty minutes several times a week, so, all that added to the schedule.

Therefore, my kids were never done before lunch, but I do not think this is, by any means, the way everyone should do it. It was simply my preference.

But if this is your first time homeschooling, and you are starting with a highschooler, this may be a good schedule to start with.

The following two schedules are examples of how you could be either finished by lunch or closer to 2 pm. They will give you an idea of what a middle or high schooler could accomplish on a typical school day. I am including a broad margin for each lesson/ activity, so you can choose what fits your student best.

For the sake of efficiency, if you have multiple students, combine them for as many content-based subjects as you can. If you start at 8am, you can be finished by noon. But remember that does not mean that the afternoons are spent doing whatever. Check out Sonya Schafer's list of productive afternoons on her website www.simplyCM.com.

Time/Day	Monday	Tuesday	Wednesday	Thursday	Friday
Morning:	Wake up / dress				
7:00	Breakfast				
–7:45 am	Take walk / Play outside				
8 am Morning Time 1.5 hours	Read Aloud	Read Aloud	Read Aloud	Read Aloud	Read Aloud
	Enrichment Studies	Enrichment Studies	Enrichment Studies	Enrichment Studies	Enrichment Studies
	History	Memory	History	Memory	History
	Bible	Bible	Bible	Bible	Bible
	Snack	Snack	Snack	Snack	Snack
After snack 9:45-11	Math	Math	Math	Math	Math
	Language Arts	Language Arts	Language Arts	Language Arts	Language Arts
11 am- 12 pm	Science	Science	Nature Study	Science	PE
	Literature	Literature		Literature	

The following schedule finishes around 2:00 P.M. If you prefer to skip Logic, you can start a little later in the morning and still be done by 2:00 P.M.

Time/Day	Monday	Tuesday	Wednesday	Thursday	Friday
Morning: 7-7:45	Wake up / dress				
	Breakfast				
	Take walk / Play outside				
8-10 am Morning Time	Read Aloud	Read Aloud	Read Aloud	Read Aloud	Read Aloud
	Enrichment Study	Enrichment Study	Enrichment Study	Enrichment Study	Enrichment Study
	History	History	History	History	History
	Literature	Literature	Literature	Literature	Literature
	Bible	Bible	Bible	Bible	Bible
	Memory	Memory	Memory	Memory	Memory
	Snack	Snack	Snack	Snack	Snack
10:15-11:00	Math	Math	Math	Math	Mat
11:15-12:00	Language Arts	Language Arts	Language Arts	Language Arts	Language Arts
12:00-12:30	Lunch and Playtime				
12:30-1:30	Science	Science	Nature Study	Science	Extra Playtime or PE
	Literature	Literature		Literature	
1:30-2:00	Logic / Rhetoric	Logic / Rhetoric		Logic / Rhetoric	
2-2:30	Foreign Language	Foreign Language		Foreign Language	

High School

Middle and high school are very similar in their time distribution and teaching approach, so this outline will closely resemble that of the middle school outline. However, I am removing spelling from Language Arts and will be replacing Logic with Rhetoric starting either in the sophomore or junior year. I am also adding a slot for foreign language.

Time/Day	Monday	Tuesday	Wednesday	Thursday	Friday
Morning:	Wake up / dress				
7:30-	Breakfast				
	Take walk / Play outside				
8-10 am Morning Time	Read Aloud	Read Aloud	Read Aloud	Read Aloud	Read Aloud
	Enrichment Studies	Enrichment Studies	Enrichment Studies	Enrichment Studies	Enrichment Studies
	Social Studies	Social Studies	Social Studies	Social Studies	Social Studies
	Literature	Literature	Literature	Literature	Literature
	Bible	Bible	Bible	Bible	Bible
	Memory	Memory	Memory	Memory	Memory
	Snack	Snack	Snack	Snack	Snack
10:15-11:00	Math	Math	Math	Math	Math
11:15-12:00	Language Arts	Language Arts	Language Arts	Language Arts	Language Arts
12:00 12:30	Lunch and Playtime				
12:30-1:30	Science	Science	Nature Study	Science	Extra Playtime or PE
	Literature	Literature		Literature	
1:30-2:00	Logic / Rhetoric	Logic / Rhetoric		Logic / Rhetoric	Logic/ Rhetoric
2-2:30	Foreign Language	Foreign Language		Foreign Language	

Notice that I'm purposefully not replacing the fun read-aloud. This is what got my school day started on the right foot most days, so I tried not to ever touch it.

Of course, you can still use one of the previous schedules and be finished by lunch time.

You can also skip Logic and Rhetoric, and either be done sooner or do something else instead.

On a good day, we finished by 2:30 P.M. On a slower day, it was closer to 3:00 P.M. However, Wednesdays and Fridays were early-out and days for us and I planned fun afternoons.

This broke up our week into a variety of tempos. On Monday and Tuesday, everyone looked forward to Wednesday since it was an early-out day. Thursday usually went by quickly, and Friday was another early day. So, finishing between 2:30 and 3:00 P.M. was never a big deal to my kids.

Homeschool Slump

It was a gray, dreary day in mid-February. January had been long and cold, and where we live, spring weather does not usually arrive for two more months. The snow had been on the ground for four weeks now, and the fog made it uninviting to go outside. None of us, including me, was excited to begin our school day. We were hitting the mid-winter homeschool slump.

It happens every year. After the exciting fall and Christmas season, January comes around. And six weeks into the new year, the cold and dark feeling of winter catches up with us. I've come to expect this phenomenon and found a few things to do to help us through these approximately two weeks of feeling drudgery.

Be Prepared

This was a great time for field trips to the museum or aquarium. That took care of two days. Then, we had some favorite audiobooks that we enjoyed while knitting hats and scarves or fixing computers.

When only math and "writing from pictures" (IEW Unit 5, an all-time favorite for all my kids) were on the school schedule, plus the audiobook, and hot chocolate, the day suddenly seemed brighter.

We might even add in a few hands-on science experiments, cooking lesson, or a historical fiction read aloud.

By the end of February, things seem to brighten up a bit. Perhaps it's simply the name 'March' that makes all the difference. Regardless, I have come to anticipate these few weeks, and rather than taking a complete break which makes it difficult to begin school again, we simply take it slower and change our content and schedule for a few weeks.

Easy Plus One

A wonderful motto that Andrew Pudewa (IEW) uses is "Easy Plus One." This simply means, do what comes easy and add one new thing. That's it. Don't add two new things! And once this new thing has become easy (no matter how long it takes), add one more new thing.

This strategy works wonders and applies to all subjects. You'll notice that over the course of a few months or even just weeks, your student will be bored with the easy stuff. Now it's time to add one more new thing.

Observe your student so you can be ready when that moment occurs. The next thing to teach is whatever the curriculum material recommends.

Again, don't feel as if you're tightly bound to your teacher's guide or textbook. Let your knowledge of your child's abilities be your guide. The curriculum guide is the road map, and you are the driver and control the gas pedal.

If the material you are using is progressing too quickly and your student gets frustrated, you can slow down, repeat the lesson the next day, or, depending on the topic and subject, switch gears and go to a different chapter, revisiting the original topic in a month or so. Sometimes the human brain needs to ruminate and digest information.

Learning Spurts

Allowing a timeout and giving the brain a chance to process information and mature is a practice that is beneficial for everyone, but especially for children. You will have already noticed this: your child does not learn in a consistent and linear way. Learning, like growing, happens in spurts.

One of my daughters was learning to add and subtract fractions in fifth grade. This topic quickly rose to the top of her least-favorites list.

We played pizza fraction games, and how to add and subtract fractions by finding the common denominator. I scoured the internet for fun ideas about fractions and spent much time drawing examples for her to understand and enjoy.

She was so bored by it all; it seemed that it never really sank in. We moved through the lessons, but I was not sure how much progress was going on in her head, so I felt like a failure.

Finally, I decided to move on to the next topic for now and revisit adding and subtracting fractions when needed.

Looking back, I recognize that the curriculum was partly to blame. It was a curriculum using mastery approach, which I hadn't thought of at the time, and which meant that repetition was the basis of each lesson. She could have definitely used some variety by having a curriculum with a spiral approach.

In addition, the denominators were always large numbers, so finding a common denominator used up a lot of time and was more about practicing basic operations than understanding the principles behind the actual topic. So, we were both more than ready to move on to the next topic.

When she started Algebra 1 in seventh grade, fractions were a frequent encounter. But her brain had had a break from the dreaded common denominator, plus I had figured out that she is more of a spiral approach than mastery approach kind of girl. I wondered whether she would remember anything about it.

To my surprise, she remembered quite a lot, and she was able to work through the problems better than I expected. We stopped and reviewed when needed, but because her brain had had a break and was more mature now, she was able to get past the boredom of it much quicker.

By tenth grade, math was still not on her favorites list, but she had made great strides because she was finally able to see the purpose of these concepts. Whenever she needed a refresher, we stopped, reviewed, and then continued on. This learn-as-you-go method was very effective for her.

Plus, I had switched curricula several times over the years until I found one that worked for her very well. We ended up using Thinkwell Math, an online math curriculum that has short video lessons and immediate assignments.

As a result, she was able to do an online college level Calculus 1 class during her senior year in high school and very much enjoyed it. I could not believe it!

LEARNING SPURT VERSUS LEARNING WILL

Looking back, I realize that there were two parts to my daughter's learning experience: The first part was the kind of learning that happens when you tirelessly work through problem after problem, until it becomes second nature.

This is called "mastery learning" and is hard work. It is characterized by working though the same concept repeatedly, and after introducing a new concept, the old ones are reinforced by bringing them back repeatedly.

Indeed, this can be a very frustrating and discouraging task, but many times the frustration is short lived, the repetition does its job, and the concept sticks.

However, every now and then there may come a point at which the student becomes so bored and discouraged that, unless she sees a path forward, it becomes empty work.

This is where the second part of learning shows up: sheer will and determination. In my daughter's math case, this did not show up immediately, but only after a few years. She had finally set her mind on understanding this concept. She decided, and things moved forward.

A Most Valuable Life Lesson

Seeing her own determination in action was one of the most important lessons my daughter could learn while in my care. The math lessons were merely the means by which she realized that her determination matters, and that she is very capable of conquering any foreign concept if she makes up her mind to do so.

A crucial part of this lesson is allowing our kids to struggle and even fail in their school assignments, and then pick themselves back up. Personality definitely plays a big part in this. Some kids are naturally more at ease to recover after failure than others, but this is also a learned skill. The earlier our children are exposed to this mindset, the easier it becomes for them to do it.

As homeschooling parents it can be frustrating to realize that we cannot force our children to want to learn, but this is where we must learn to be patient with them and take the long view. Ask yourself, which lesson is important, the actual math lesson or the life lesson that comes along for the ride?

Then, as much as possible, enjoy the time you have with your child. Those school years fly by very quickly and they're over before we know it.

16

Your Homeschool Day

MORNINGS: WAKING UP

Which one describes your family right now?

A. PARENT: It's time to wake up.
   CHILD: Just five more minutes! Please!

B. CHILD: Mommy! What can I have for breakfast?
   PARENT: It's not even six o'clock yet. Go back to sleep.

In my experience, the morning wake-up 'mood' determines much of the rest of the morning attitude. Like adults, some kids are naturally early morning risers, and some kids are not. Many times, younger kids enjoy getting out of bed early, but as they enter puberty, they like to sleep longer. But then again, that's not necessarily true for all kids.

Also, there's a fine line between allowing kids to sleep in because they habitually go to bed too late, and between allowing for enough sleep. My goal was usually to allow for ten hours of sleep. That meant bedtime is around 9:00 P.M. and wake up time is around 7–7:30 A.M. That seemed to work out well over the years.

According to my sons, it's an unpleasant experience to be woken up by touching their feet. They both have vivid memories of dad coming into the bedroom, turning on the lights, and squeezing their feet. Not a good idea.

You can also teach your child the habit of waking up by himself with an alarm clock. This is definitely a good habit to instill.

CONSIDER YOUR OWN MORNING SPIRIT

Getting the day started on the right foot makes everything easier. When you set a time by which you want to start your school day, consider your personal preference. Regardless of whether or not you are a morning person, what kind of routine would help you get started with your day?

Consider the long haul. If you routinely have rough mornings with your kids or even just yourself, start closer to 9:00 or 9:30 A.M.

At the same time, if it works for your family to start at 8:00 A.M. or even 7:30 A.M., and you can see yourself seeing it through, that is what you should do.

For my family, getting transitioned from morning chores and breakfast to schoolwork tended to be the biggest hurdle. Usually, once we got going, the day took shape. So, I introduced "Morning Time," always starting out with a fun read-aloud.

All of a sudden, I was now usually the last one on the scene. My kids calling, "Mom, we're ready to read!" I chose books that I enjoyed as well, so it was a win-win.

Having a basic structure of our morning laid out helped me make the start of our day more pleasant for all of us.

THE GRUMPY SLEEPYHEAD

Now, let's talk about your children's morning attitude. Even with enough sleep, some kids are naturally more alert and cheerful in the morning than others. Your mornings have a huge impact on the course of your day. Managing morning expectations will set the stage for the atmosphere of your homeschool.

Sometimes, simply following a routine for a week or two will be enough to get used to the school day agenda. On the other hand, if you have a child that is routinely grumpy in the morning, build into your morning schedule a 'soft-start'.

Could it be a breakfast picnic on a blanket in the den while mom or dad reads a story, or everyone listens to an audiobook. Do keep in mind that some kids might go right back to sleep, so, reading-aloud might not be the best option first thing in the morning. Perhaps you could go on a scavenger hunt outside, looking for specific objects (leaves, flowers, rocks).

Do you have a project that needs to be worked on? Do you need firewood to be carried in? Morning chores, if done together, can be a way to get kids alert and awake.

FORTY-FIVE MINUTES

Let's say you spend forty-five minutes on morning activities which help get your day pointed in the right direction. These are forty-five minutes well spent. Trying to teach your child with a grumpy attitude will likely waste more than forty-five minutes of everyone's time. I am speaking from experience. It is extremely difficult to turn this ship named *Attitude* around once it has left the harbor.

Breakfast

Just a heads-up: homeschooled children like to eat. So, it greatly helped when I had a breakfast plan. Knowing what to expect each day as far as breakfast foods are concerned helped get the day started in the right direction, for children and adults alike.

What is the best breakfast routine that works for you? Eating as a family is awesome, but not necessarily an option for everyone. We ate breakfast together as a family for many years, but then we moved to a different state, and my husband had to go to work slightly earlier. So, we switched routines, and my husband and I started enjoying some quiet mornings with coffee while the kids were still asleep.

The kids ate breakfast around 7:45 A.M., and we started out school day by 8:00 or 8:15 A.M. Whatever works best for your family is what you should plan for. The path of least resistance is the path that you will be able to sustain in the long run.

Breakfast Ideas

Think about which breakfast foods are nourishing and keeping their bellies full long enough to get several hours of schoolwork done. Cereal is an easy choice, but my kids were hungry again an hour after breakfast. When I had cereal in the house, it was usually a whole grain version that metabolizes slower.

We usually enjoyed bagels with cream cheese, or toast with ham and cheese, and some slices of fruit. Anything high in fat and protein and not so high in sugar and other carbs is a good start to the school day and will keep the growing brain nourished. Eggs, bacon, sausage, oatmeal, waffles and fruit, yogurt (either sugar-free, or mix plain and flavored yogurt so you can determine the sugar content), bagels and cream cheese, or pancakes.

If you like to get fancy, you can cut up peppers, mushrooms, onions, tomatoes and other veggies, meat, and cheese for an omelet, a frittata, or breakfast burrito. Casseroles like quiches or frittatas last two or even three days, so that might be a good choice if your kids enjoy egg dishes. French toast casserole is also a yummy option if you reduce the amount of sugar and add fresh or frozen fruit instead of syrup (blueberries and peaches are delicious).

If you're not a casserole fan, you can cut some fruit on Sunday and store it in airtight containers or plastic bags to use each morning. Many fruits and veggies will be crisp and fresh for several days after you cut them. Some can be frozen and pulled out the evening before you plan on using them, and if you cook them or put them in oatmeal or frittata, it won't make a difference if they were frozen.

PREPARE AS MUCH AS YOU CAN

The idea is to use the time, when you are not rushed, to prepare for the time you will be rushed. The more food you can prepare ahead of time, the easier your mornings will be. If you like, you can buy frozen breakfast food, and have it on hand for the days when you don't have anything else ready.

Usually, those were the days I had my kids eat shredded wheat for breakfast. Having a backup breakfast is extremely helpful when you are behind, sick, or can't prepare breakfast for whatever reason.

MORNING CHORES/PERSONAL HYGIENE

After eating breakfast and before starting school, many families like to add some small chores to the schedule. These chores really need to be quick and easy because at this point in your day you want to keep things moving smoothly. Some ideas of morning chores would be to make beds, put your dish in the dishwasher, or feed the pet.

Also, brushing teeth, putting on deodorant, showering, all these can be added to this time. Having a firm morning routine including personal hygiene will set up your kids for habitual self-care when they are grown.

SNACKS

I learned quickly that when I was prepared for snack time, my kids were able to stay focused on the next item when hunger struck. They were less likely to rummage through the fridge and pull everything out to see what's in the very back.

So, as soon as breakfast was over, and if I hadn't already done so, I started cutting up some fruit, cheese, or veggies for a mid-morning snack. I found it helpful to prepare five days' worth of certain snacks (cheese cubes, grapes, crackers and salami, etc.) on Sunday evening or Monday morning. These keep well in small bags or containers.

But I wasn't always able to get that done ahead of time, so I built it into my morning plan for the following week.

Go Outside

Depending on your energy level or climate/weather, mornings can be a great time to take a short walk. Morning walks are extremely beneficial. The brain wakes up and is refreshed. Your whole body fills with energy and vigor. Starting your school day with this fresh feeling in your face, and the amount of oxygen that entered your bloodstream keeps your brain going longer than when you stay inside.

A MORNING SONG

I found one of my favorite ideas to get started on school in the morning on Pam Barnhill's website. She has wonderful resources when it comes to planning your school day. One of her suggestions is to play one or more songs and tell your students that by the end of the music, everyone should be ready for school to begin.

A different way to use this strategy is to make a play list and play it to help your child wake up and get ready for breakfast or during the morning chores (making bed, brushing teeth, putting their dish away, and so on).

LUNCH

It's time to eat . . . again. This is one of the most noticeable feats when you start homeschooling. It seems as if people are always hungry. Just like with breakfast, life is easier if you have a plan for lunch. It does not need to be fancy, or even cooked on the stove. Just have a few things ready to go.

Just some ideas:

For PBJ Sandwiches: bread, peanut butter, jelly
For other sandwiches: bread, mayonnaise, mustard, ham, cheese, lettuce, tomatoes
Pasta and sauce, fruit, and veggies
Macaroni and cheese, fruit, and veggies
Rice bowls with fried veggies, avocado, black beans, corn, salad dressing
Salad kits, add your own chicken or shrimp.
Chicken nuggets, fruit, and veggies

Having the ingredients ready for these meals is half the battle. Most of these do not take long to make. If you make a simple list of ten meals, you have two weeks' worth of lunches. The weekend before, get the ingredients, and pull them out that morning. If you have them ready to go, that will give you peace of mind.

School Time—A Day in My Homeschool

8:00 a.m.

"Mom, we are ready to read!"

"Okay, I'm coming! Have you all finished your morning jobs?"

"Yes!"

This happened frequently, so I knew we had a good routine down. Starting our day on this positive note was the most important ingredient that made our homeschool a success.

We started our exciting book by Douglas Bond, called *Duncan's War*, and after finishing a chapter, we moved on to Bible reading, memory work, and singing a few hymns. This usually took about forty-five minutes and concluded our Morning Time.

For this year, however, I had decided that we will combine all four students in geography, Latin, history, composition, and a ten-minute enrichment study session per day. This extended our Morning Time to two and a half hours. I did this in the one-room-schoolhouse style when needed.

In composition (around 30–45 min), the second grader would only be required to write a few sentences while the tenth grader wrote a few paragraphs. When the second grader was finished, she moved on to spelling or copy work, both easily done by herself in the same room with us.

Geography (10 min) was a combined effort of locating countries, cities, rivers, mountains, etc. and reading about life in these countries.

History (30 min) consisted of reading aloud biographies and discussing questions the students had and making a timeline of events. In Latin (30 min), we memorized chants of endings, parsed verbs, translated sentences, and memorized vocabulary. All this with a second grader, a fifth grader, a seventh grader and a tenth grader.

Around 10:30 a.m.

Snack Time, play outside.

Around 11:00 a.m.

It's time for Math. I had the oldest kids start by themselves and helped the youngest one to get going. Next, I moved to the next oldest until I made it to the oldest. Sometimes I needed to help an older child who was stuck, but usually we worked that out quickly.

We used two different, video-based math programs at the time. Thinkwell and Math without Borders. Both allowed the students to be somewhat independent of me.

Around 12:00 p.m.
Lunch time

Around 12:30 p.m.
Science, for the older kids. They were independently reading their books while I did Language Arts with the younger kids: Time for spelling, phonics (if needed), and reading practice for the youngest.

Around 1:30 p.m.
The youngest is done. The second youngest reads her chosen book independently. The older two read for Omnibus (literature class) and get ready for discussion with me.

Around 2:30–3:00 p.m.
If time allows, we complete a lesson in Logic with the two older kids.

Wednesday Nature Day
On Wednesdays, however, we cut Morning Time short, only focusing on read aloud, Bible composition and memory. We then moved on to math, and that was it for our sit-down school subjects because today was our Nature Day.

After finishing our morning subjects and packing everything and everyone into the car, it was now almost lunch time. So, I either packed lunch, or we stopped at the store and got some wraps.

We had our favorite spots at various local sate parks, or simply went into the backyard. I usually prepared a few activities that I had found online (see section on Nature Study). Many times we brought our kayak, swim clothes, and hiking boots. After doing our activity, we enjoyed swimming in the lake or taking a hike.

Afternoons
Our afternoons were spent doing a variety of activities. When my kids were younger than ten years old, they simply played, helped with odd jobs like cleaning out the car, vacuuming the house, or raking leaves in the fall. There was always work to do. Sometimes I paid them, sometimes I did not.

There were also music lessons, sports activities, Trail Life, American Heritage Girls, Wednesday Night Church events. Throughout the years, we joined new activities and left old ones, mainly due to our move.

As they entered their teenage years, both my sons were highly interested in earning money. My oldest son walked dogs for several neighbors, and eventually started running a lawn mowing and yard work business which turned into snow blowing in the winter.

His younger brother helped when he wasn't too busy with his own business, which was (and still is) fixing and upgrading computers for friends and family.

As my daughters entered the 'responsible teen age years', they started babysitting and working as instructors at a martial arts school. Both also had a job at a local store where they cleaned the shopping area. Our afternoons were usually productive and not boring.

Homeschooling has definitely allowed my kids to do things they would otherwise not have had the time to do.

Work and Life

If you have kids in their early-to-mid-teen years, be on the lookout for opportunities for them to work and get experience in areas that can earn them some money or that have the potential to enrich special interests they have.

If they play an instrument, can they play or someone? Can they babysit? Can they help someone with a project? Can they help neighbors with yardwork or snow removal? There are so many ideas. With your child, make an ongoing list and keep brainstorming.

Many of the things they can do as young teens will give them a solid foundation of a good work ethic. Doing jobs for others instead of just mom and dad is valuable in learning to receive feedback. Allowing our teens to work for money is a real motivator for them to work and then think about what to do with their money.

There is no better real-life economics lesson than that of a job that pays money. Learning to think about money related issues is one of the best ways to prepare our kids for life as responsible adults.

As homeschooling moms and dads, we get to choose how our children spend their time. We should use this to our children's advantage and set them up so they can learn real life lessons that are far more effective than mere lessons from a textbook.

17

Planning, Schedules, Strategies

Our morning was going smoothly. We'd finished our combined subjects which I call Morning Time, and it was time to let everyone take a break and have a quick snack before settling into their individual school assignments. I used that time to take a look at the daily flowchart.

I was using a flowchart instead of a detailed schedule because we were never exactly on time. And having specific times assigned for each subject always made us 'late', which stressed me out.

So, I had put the most important three subjects in the morning with a set starting time but no further time restrictions. Then, I used a timer in thirty, forty-five-, or sixty-minute increments to keep us roughly on track. It worked great.

But that particular morning was a bit tricky. For one, I had a grumpy child to deal with who really did not want to do start on math that morning. And then we tried to find the missing math book. Before I knew it, thirty minutes had gone by, and my blood pressure was rising. All of this was affecting the other kids, so our smooth morning very quickly turned into chaos.

How do you recover from a situation like that? I was not new to homeschooling, so I was very familiar with this scenario. But it still catches me off guard every time it arises. This is the very reason I had switched a detailed schedule for a flowchart.

After an unsuccessful search for the missing math book, I had the grumpy child start with science instead of math, which helped with attitude adjustment. Eventually, I found the book, and after finishing her science assignment, she continued with math. It wasn't the greatest morning, but we recovered and were able to get back into our routine.

Two Ingredients—A Plan and Consistency

THE PLAN

If there is one practical thing I have learned over the last decade of homeschooling, it is the concept of decision fatigue. Constant decision making is exhausting. Planning for your school year and preparing a schedule for your school day is necessary so you know exactly what to do next and don't lose momentum halfway through the day.

Here's the thing: Had I not had a written plan for that morning I was just telling you about, I would not have been able to simply switch subjects around. It didn't matter whether it was a flow chart or detailed timetable, it was a written plan that helped me stay on track without making decisions on what to do in that subject that day.

Schedules, plans, outlines, flowcharts, whatever you want to call it, come in all sorts of varieties, from a simple list of activities with no specific times, to a detailed breakdown of your day, in five, ten, or fifteen-minute increments.

You might even use a mixture of them for different parts of your day. For example, you could have a timetable for mornings, if that is a weak point, and then loosen up and have only a list of assignments going for the rest of the school day with no exact starting times. Be creative and let your schedule be your servant, not the other way around.

If you're new to homeschooling, you can experiment with a few ideas before you find your sweet spot. I love the idea of a detailed schedule with start and finishing times. But after I used one for several years, I realized that it was too exhausting for me. My planning style is more on the relaxed side. So, I switched to a flow chart with all the same subjects, but instead of specific times, it says 'morning', or 'after lunch'. Problem solved.

CONSISTENCY

The second ingredient is consistency. It doesn't matter whether you follow a detailed schedule or a basic flowchart. Being consistent means things get done on a regular basis, and everyone knows what's expected.

It's hard to maintain consistency if your daily plan does not reflect your natural inclinations and interests. So, plan your day in a way that you are not tempted to throw in the towel by 11:00 A.M. Set yourself up for success.

Getting Ready: Planning your School Year

Plan on spending about fifteen or twenty minutes to make decisions about your school year. For this planning session you will need a few items.

1. Your personal calendar (phone or otherwise),
2. A printed one-page school year calendar page. These are available as a free download at www.pambarnhill.com. Search for 'free homeschool planning mini kit',
3. One or more pens, of different colors if you like.

To get started, follow these directions.

1. Pick the first day of school and circle it.
2. Next, check whether there is a certain requirement of schooldays in your state.
3. If there is no such requirement, choose a number between hundred-sixty, and hundred-eighty, which are common numbers of days in a school year.
4. If you're planning to teach five days a week, divide the number of school days you chose by five. (Planning on teaching four days a week? Simply divide by four.)

   This will give you the number of weeks you will be teaching. If you chose hundred-sixty days, that would make thirty-two weeks. Hundred-eighty days give you thirty-six weeks.
5. Check your personal calendar to see when you want to take a vacation and cross out those weeks. How many weeks are left?
6. Decide how long your terms will be. You can take a one-week break after every term, or you can take longer breaks less frequently if you are planning on traveling for longer periods of time and would rather not take school materials with you. Cross out your weeks of break.
7. Count at least one week for sick days or unexpected circumstances, and cross these out sometime in February or March. If you don't use them up, you can finish your school year early.
8. How many days are left after crossing out the breaks? Try to have between hundred-sixty and hundred-eighty days left over.

9. Plan on one field trip each month. Mark a day each month with a different color or shape, but still count them as school days.

10. All done!

Transfer the important dates (like first day of school, field trips, breaks) to your personal calendar. Share them with your spouse or other family members and friends so they know what's going on.

Your Daily Schedule

SAMPLE SCHEDULE FOR QUICK STARTERS

Before jumping into detailed planning, I will give you several sample schedules to choose from so you can get started without much delay. One is more of a flow chart, and the other a more detailed schedule with assigned times.

A Broad Flowchart, Linked to Snack and Lunch, School Starts Around 9 A.M.

Time/Day	Monday	Tuesday	Wednesday	Thursday	Friday
Morning:	Wake up / dress				
8-8:45 am	Breakfast				
	Take walk / Play outside				
Morning Time (.1.5 hours)	Read Aloud	Read Aloud	Read Aloud	Read Aloud	Read Aloud
	Enrichment Studies	Enrichment Studies	Enrichment Studies	Enrichment Studies	Enrichment Studies
	History	Foreign Language	History	Foreign Language	History
	Bible	Bible	Bible	Bible	Bible
	Memory	Memory	Foreign Language	Memory	Foreign Language
	Snack	Snack	Snack	Snack	Snack
After Snack and 10 min Cleanup	Math	Math	Math	Math	Math
	Language Arts	Language Arts	Language Arts	Language Arts	Language Arts
After Lunch and Playtime	Science	Science	Nature Study	Science	Extra Playtime or PE
	Elective	Elective		Elective	

A Time-specific Schedule, School Starts Around 8:30 A.M.

Time/Day	Monday	Tuesday	Wednesday	Thursday	Friday
Morning:	Wake up / dress				
7:30- 8:15	Breakfast				
	Take walk / Play outside				
8:30- 10 am Morning Time	Read Aloud	Read Aloud	Read Aloud	Read Aloud	Read Aloud
	Enrichment Studies	Enrichment Studies	Enrichment Studies	Enrichment Studies	Enrichment Studies
	History	Foreign Language	History	Foreign Language	History
	Bible	Bible	Bible	Bible	Bible
	Memory	Memory	Foreign Language	Memory	Foreign Language
	Snack	Snack	Snack	Snack	Snack
10:15- 11:15	Math	Math	Math	Math	Math
11:30-12	Language Arts	Language Arts	Language Arts	Language Arts	Language Arts
12-12:45	Lunch and Playtime				
12:45- 1:30	Science	Science	Nature Study	Science	Extra Playtime or PE
1:30-2	Elective	Elective		Elective	

I used both of these schedules successfully at different times in my homeschool. Choose one and adjust it to your specific needs. Over the course of the school year, evaluate what works for you and what doesn't. Make adjustments as you go.

SAMPLE SCHEDULE FOR QUICK STARTERS

To create a schedule, you have a few different options. One idea is to write every subject down on an index card, creating one card for each time you want to put in in your schedule. For example, if you want to teach math every day, you will write math on five index cards.

Skill-based subjects should be covered each day while several content-based subjects only need to be taught one, two, or three times per week. You now need a large surface area (floor or table) to arrange these cards in columns, one for each school day.

As for unit studies, the schedule is usually built unto the unit study itself, so you can create a 'Unit Study' index card and block off the appropriate time for it. When you're done with your layout, take a photo with your phone and *voilà!*, you have it saved and can now clean up your mess.

MAKE A SCHEDULE USING A SPREADSHEET

This is my go-to system for creating schedules. You need less space, but you need to be somewhat familiar with a spreadsheet program. Personally, this is my favorite way of seeing how much we can realistically fit into one school day.

Big reminder, though: Leave margin. I find it very easy to fill every minute with school subjects. This quickly becomes over-whelming, so I need to remember to add extra time for clean-up, interruptions, short breaks, longer than expected lessons, and other unavoidable delays.

At this point, your teaching philosophy will have a major impact on the order and length of subject lessons. My family has used a mixture of Classical Christian and Charlotte Mason, so my schedules reflect this by allowing for short lessons and a large variety of subjects typical for these philosophies.

Block and Loop Schedules

One of my favorite go-to bloggers/podcasters when it comes to schedule and organization topics is Pam Barnhill. She has a wealth of information about ideas for every kind of homeschool scenario, especially in the area of organizing and scheduling your homeschool.

Pam shares two ideas that change up the traditional way of making a schedule: A block schedule and a loop schedule. Traditionally, you would take the subjects and list them in a column in each time slot. But the block and loop schedules each have a different purpose.

A *block schedule* blocks out a chunk of time for certain subjects that are well suited to teach together, or one subject that needs some extra time to get done. Depending on your family's interests, the possibilities are endless.

Let's look at science, for example. You can block off two hours three times a week for science lessons and experiments. Perhaps you can get more done in three days per week for an extended period of time than in five days per week with shorter lessons.

On the other hand, you may prefer a literature block, perhaps every day, or four times a week during which you read and discuss books. This can include history, or all your read-alouds across various subject areas.

Another idea is moving all your arts, or hands-on subjects like science experiments and projects into a block once a week. That way you can plan on having supplies ready once a week and work on your projects or experiments during that time.

A block schedule is a good fit for subjects that pair well with other subjects. Not every subject needs to be in a block, just a few that you think are a good match and will make it easier for you to have a natural flow from one subject to another.

One thing to keep in mind as far as combining, or pairing, subjects is this: be aware of how much and which side of the brain is being worked. I would hesitate to pair a difficult math lesson with math drills and logic or balancing chemical equations. It is more effective to pair a subject such as math with a subject that is hands on, or reading aloud, or any other activity that requires a different part of the brain.

If you remember Charlotte Mason's principles, this was the main determining factor of the order of subjects in her schedule. You don't want to fatigue your student's brain; you just want to stretch it.

A *loop schedule* is a great way to schedule subjects that generally don't take very long, but because there are so many of them, it's difficult to get to them all in your school day. Let's say I really want to do enrichment studies, but I have them spread out over the day, so I get to the ones in the early part of the day, but the later part of the day is hectic and I rarely finish the entire daily schedule I had planned.

Enter the loop schedule: For enrichment studies, every one of the topics goes on the loop, and you work your way through it. This could be four, five, or six topics such as art, composer study, certain read aloud books, or whatever you like.

You will set a timer for, say, forty-five minutes, preferably earlier in the day, and stop when the time is up. The next time you have enrichment studies, you pick up where you left off. If poetry is next on the loop, for instance, and you didn't get to it, you pick it up again tomorrow and start with poetry.

You can emphasize certain topics by adding them to the loop more frequently. Here's an example.

ENRICHMENT STUDIES LOOP WITH EMPHASIS ON POETRY AND MEMORIZATION

- Poetry: read poem (5 min)
- Memory: work on memorizing your selection (5–7 min)
- Folk Song: sing song (3–5 min)
- Geography: lesson (15–20 min)
- Poetry: read poem (5 min)
- Memory: work on memorizing (5–7 min)
- Artist Study: study you chosen artist (10 min)
- Nature Study: Go outside (30 min –2 hours or longer)
- Poetry; read poem (5 min)
- Memory: work on memorization (5–7 min)
- Geography: lesson (15–20 min)
- Shakespeare: read or watch play (20–30 min)
- Hand Craft: work on project (20 min)

Start over from the beginning.

As you can see, poetry and memory show up more frequently than other topics. If you spend 30–40 minutes per day on enrichment studies, you will cover a lot of ground. Plus, if you skip a day or can't finish a lesson, pick up where you left off the next time you return to it. If you stick with the order, poetry and memory will be covered more frequently than anything else.

This is simply an illustration, so you can come up with your own loop schedule as you see fit. You can change your loop from term to term to incorporate different topics, or you can keep it the same all year long.

USING A COMBINATION OF LOOP SCHEDULES AND BLOCK SCHEDULES

As you may have figured out, you can use both, loop and block schedules, in your day. Certain subjects are a better fit for one or the other at certain times in your homeschool.

Composition might lend itself to pairing with grammar, spelling, vocabulary, or literature to create a block. But you can also choose a different pairing each day, since you do not have to do spelling or grammar every day, but all as part of composition. You can create a mini-loop inside a block.

If you do unit studies, these can take up one or even two blocks depending on the age and level of material that is being covered.

Finally, not all subjects have to go into a block or loop, just the ones that make sense for your particular desire and family dynamics. Many subjects can just be stand-alones. Composition is an example. You can just do a composition lesson, give your student thirty minutes to work on an essay, and then move to a different subject.

SCHEDULE TERMS

There are several term lengths, ranging anywhere from six-week terms to twelve-week terms. That means you can custom design the subjects, schedule, and outside activities.

Skill-based subjects should be taught continuously throughout the year, but content-based subjects can be switched out every so often, which means they are not taught every term. Many schools switch history and geography, or science and social studies. Homeschoolers can do the same. Just make sure you have a plan, so you get done what you set out to get done.

OOPS, I FORGOT

Several years ago, I realized after six weeks of school that I had completely forgotten to include science in my student's schedule. I kept wondering why it felt as if something was missing. Well, something was indeed missing. It was not the end of the world but caught me off-guard. I had completely forgotten to even order the science curriculum.

That mistake led me to making spreadsheets of all my kid's subjects and curriculum. The following year I simply opened the last year's spread sheet, updated it, and saved it under a new name. After the six weeks of not doing science, I realized that we were spending that extra time (unbeknownst to us) on history and literature, so it was not lost time. The following term I simply added science and continued for the rest of the school year.

When you schedule your schooldays into terms, you will see just how much you can get done by the end of each term. It allows you to focus on weak areas if needed without feeling like you've lost the entire school year. Plus, you can take breaks at the end of each term, so it's a nice incentive for everyone.

DAILY ASSIGNMENTS

Clip Board, Spiral Notebook, Online

Over the years, I have given my students their assignments in every possible variation. I love changing things up, and my kids enjoy the variety. The point is to have all their assignments written specifically and clearly so my kids can quickly grasp what is required of them.

You don't need to spend a lot of money to be on top of your kids' school schedules. The simple spiral notebooks or any kind of wide-ruled notebook that's on sale will do. If you have a master list of every subject you want to cover each day, plus the lesson plans for those subjects, filling in the next day's work by hand is a five-to-ten-minute job per child.

Just make sure you have everything you need available in one place, so you don't have to go looking for it when you need it. That happened to me more than once, and it is very frustrating. I like to use different colors per subject and put a square beside each individual assignment so it can be checked off, because my kids like checking off boxes.

These notebooks were written by me but given to my kids in the morning and returned to me frequently during the day when I wanted to get a feel for what has been accomplished. I used this method during different terms and switched back and forth between online and handwritten daily planners for my kids.

I have also enjoyed using Homeschool Planet, an online assignment generator, for scheduling and printing out assigned subjects and giving each of my students an "assignment check list" every morning. These individual pages needed to be put on a clip board so they wouldn't get lost.

One of the features Homeschool Planet offers is that you can create an account for each of your students which they can view and check off their assignments online. So, I didn't necessarily have to print out the assignment pages, but my student can view them on their laptop or phone.

If you like to print out your own spreadsheet or Word document each day or handwrite the schedule on single pages, you can put these in a clip board, as well. These assignment sheets should have their own clip boards with no other pages on that same clip board. That way it won't accidentally end up in a stack of worksheets which you may have put in a different clipboard to be completed.

CLEAR AND SPECIFIC INSTRUCTIONS

When it's time to give my students individual assignments, I try to make sure they're written out explicitly and in detail. Giving page numbers and specific problem sets, for example, is more understandable than simply assigning 'Lesson 8'.

Some of my kids preferred a detailed schedule with times and specific order, while others would rather that I give them only the assignments and let them decide for themselves in which order they will complete them. The common denominator was that they all wanted clear instructions of the assignment.

It's even better if you help them get started on the problems or on the reading portion, and then allow them to continue independently as they are able. That way they have overcome the momentum of 'starting the assignment', which is many times the hardest part.

Observe your child to decide how independent he can be and still get the assignments done. Time management is a learned skill, and it takes years to become good at it.

ENCOURAGE YOUR STUDENTS TO HAVE THEIR OWN PLANNERS

I believe firmly that students benefit from having their own planner so they can track and examine their own progress. Ultimately, our goal is to teach our kids to be independent, responsible individuals who don't constantly need our guidance and supervision. Imagine having them fill in their own planners and doing what the planner instructs.

Obviously, this behavior does not happen overnight, but it does happen over the course of years. If you like the idea of filling in planners, you can let him have his own, and for that school year, train him to fill it out every day or every week, depending on your planning style.

Plan on doing this task together for the whole year, but if your student wants to do it without your help, you can either teach him where in the curriculum guide to find the assignments for each lesson, or you can let him copy of your own planner.

Personally, I was not consistent enough to train my kids in this task. I usually printed out the assignments for my kids on a one-page daily planner. They all wanted to have each specific subject listed with the individual assignments, even when we were doing it together as a family. That way they were able to check it off and see whether they were on track.

But whether or not kids fill in their own planners, the important part is whether they follow the assignments. Using personal planners or simple daily planning pages is a great way to teach independence and responsibility. This is one of the skills that helped my kids stay ahead during their college years.

Your Homeschool Planner

Homeschool teachers need to have a plan to stay ahead of their kids. It does not need to include every minute detail but needs to be clear enough so you know what you will do next during any given moment of you homeschool day.

Some parents like to use planners, and some do not. If you are in the 'I-love-a-planner' camp, there are some great options for you.

If you're a bit apprehensive about the whole planning thing, that's okay. There are a few ideas to help you. For one, don't spend money on any planner—yet. Perhaps you'll find one later, but for now, check out the free versions and see if you find a good design that appeals to you.

Having a clear-cut template that you can use to plan the basic course of your day is probably enough for the beginning. In addition, for each student, have one page with a list of subjects and curriculum so you can quickly find what you are looking for. That will do for a while.

As you continue homeschooling, pay attention to where your weak spots are during the day. If planning in more detail would help the situation, you will know what to do: plan in more detail. In my experience, each of my students needed a separate list of individual assignments so they had a good idea of what lay ahead. It helped me, as well. I looked at it when I wasn't sure what's next.

You do not have to have a professional planner to be a successful homeschool parent. You can use a spiral notebook if you like. Both are great, as long as they get the job done.

If you are interested in planners, here are some choices. If you are looking for a free option, check out the bottom of this list.

Online

All of these offer a free thirty-day trial. In order to try out different online planners, I usually started several free trials of various planners in June and used them to plan our summer. Since I had several trials going on at the same time, I was able to compare and contrast which worked best for me.

My personal favorite has been Homeschool Planet, but all of these are user friendly and effective in planning your homeschool year. You pay a yearly or monthly fee.

- Homeschool Planet at www.homeschoolplanet.com (this has been my favorite ever)
- Well Planned Gal at www.wellplannedgal.com
- Homeschool Panda www.homeschoolpanda.com
- Lesson Trek www.lessontrek.com

If you prefer paper calendars, there are several that I recommend.

- Well Planned Day at www.wellplannedgal.com
- The Ultimate Homeschool Planner by Debra Bell (yellow edition) www.amazon.com
- Any kind of calendar with weekly and daily sections
- Any notebook

Print Your Own

Some of these are free, and some cost money. Depending on your budget, see what fits your needs. For many years I used free downloads and a notebook.

- www.notebookingpages.com, find planner pages in the top bar
- www.pambarnhill.com, search for 'homeschool planner', or just 'planner' (free)
- www.freedomhomeschooling.com, a website containing a wealth of free homeschool re-sources from various other sites, including planner and calendar pages. Scroll down and search for 'planner' in the search bar. You may have to subscribe to some of the websites to gain access.

What subjects can you assign one student while you teach a different student?

It helps to know the kind of subject or activity each of your students are able to accomplish with minimal help. You can have everyone work on math at the same time which I have usually done. I let one of my students work on some review problems that I know she can do on her own while I introduce a new concept to another student.

Then I go back and forth for about an hour. This is one hour of math for myself, but as for my students, I may have assigned one of them a new subject depending on her age. For my family, that worked well, but you can try overlapping math for one student with a different, self-led subject of another student. That will give you time to only focus on math with one student.

If you prefer not to teach math to everyone at the same time, you can assign a reading passage, spelling practice, and perhaps a memory passage to the other students. You start instruction with your youngest since the older kids are usually able to work independently for longer periods of time. Simply, work your way from youngest to oldest child.

Some Things to Consider

What part of the day is the most or least interrupted?

Interruptions are unpredictable, so we need a way to deal with them because they will arise.

Toddlers usually have that gift of interrupting what you thought would be an easy task, which is okay, as long as we expect it and are prepared for it. There may be times when you know it's useless to even try to have your toddler entertain himself, but there may be times during which you can train him to sit quietly for a few minutes and play with a special toy that only comes out during a certain part of the day.

What about the phone? If it rings during your school hours, what will your strategy be to stay focused on school while still allowing for flexibility in the case of actually being needed by a neighbor, friend, or family member? Will your phone distract you by simply sitting on the table and making you want to check email, the weather, or social media?

What about the doorbell? How will you answer the door during school hours? Fortunately, the days where you had to hide your homeschooled kids during school hours are over, and neighbors usually don't turn homeschooling families in any longer. But your kids should probably still not answer the door during the day.

But how easily will you be caught up in a conversation with someone who just wants to talk? Be ready with a polite answer to let them know that you cannot talk right now.

Can you think of other interruptions you can prepare for ahead of time?

NAPTIME

Naptimes should be reflected in your schedule. If your child's naptime is unpredictable, there are two options.

1. Create a routine, so naptime becomes more predictable, or

2. Work around the naptime and have a flexible plan.

If your toddler has a napping schedule, or at least you know approximately how long he usually naps, this will be your valuable one-on-one time with one or two of your school aged students. If naptime is unpredictable, have specific one-on-one subjects ready to go and drop everything else you are doing as soon as baby is asleep and start working with your older children.

Your daily schedule should reflect a certain subject, or maybe two, that you teach during naptime. So, whenever the nap occurs, these subjects will be a priority.

SCHEDULING SCHOOL WITH SPECIAL NEEDS CHILDREN

I have the privilege of helping care for a precious, little eight-year-old girl with severe, non-verbal autism. It is really amazing how her energetic little body responds to various activities. At home, she loves playdough and puzzles and can sit for an hour or more when she has these items available.

But when it's time to drive in the car, she loves her special toy bag which always stays in the car. It has noisy toys, a toy laptop, and a few favorite board books. As soon as she gets in the car, she straps herself on and digs through the bag. It took me several weeks to figure these things out, but now, I am ready, and it saves me lots of stressful moments.

I find it very helpful to have a list of ideas on hand so when things are chaotic, I don't have to think about strategies but can focus on the child. Also, especially in the case of caring for one or more children on the spectrum, I really need to give myself extra margin in my schedule, so I don't constantly feel behind.

Schedule All Appointments on a Designated Weekday

What about doctor's or dentist appointments? Some families schedule all their outside appointments (doctor, dentist, and other) on a certain day of the week, say Thursday. That way, they know that Thursdays usually have the most interruptions, and they can plan on that.

Sometimes you can bring schoolbooks along, and sometimes that is just too complicated. In that case, don't worry about it and do something else instead. Audiobooks, or special, educational games may be fun on those days.

Have a List of Easy-Take-Alongs

The day before our away-day, I packed a bag with activities and assignments that can be easily accomplished on the go. This usually included Kumon math workbooks, spelling or copy work (if there's a good place to sit and write), and reading assignments for science, history, or literature.

While we were driving, we listened to audiobooks, or had conversations about the books we were reading together, or even individually.

One of my youngest daughter's favorite geography apps on my phone was 'Stack the States' and 'Stack the Countries'. These could be done in a waiting area, or while you are spending time in the car perhaps waiting while a sibling is in a music lesson or sport practice. My daughter became quite good at geography by playing these two games.

How Do I make Sure My Family Doesn't Become Isolated?

This is one of the reasons many parents are nervous about homeschooling. That's definitely a concern, but easily remedied with a few intentional choices.

Here is a list of things I do to help me stay grounded and not live in a bubble:

1. I intentionally plan to have my family involved in the community.
2. I sign my kids up for music, art, or other lessons with other teachers.
3. We join a homeschool group or co-op.
4. We join an outdoor adventure organization.
5. We participate in field trips and other activities with other homeschoolers.

18

Organizing Your School

In addition to a schedule, several other things helped me combat decision fatigue. For one, with several young children in the house and constant clean-up work I needed to make it easy on myself to put school supplies in a place where I could always find them, specifically, schoolbooks.

I also found it very helpful to have designated places for completed and not-yet completed worksheets. And finally, having a plan for getting started each morning saved many schooldays from disaster.

It took me a few years to figure out what that looks like for my homeschool, but by trial and error I figured out a pretty good system that works for my family. There is an abundance of blogs and other online resources available, so I won't even attempt to cover every possible option, but I will share a few things I have learned so you have a place to start.

You can go from there and see what works for you. I list some resources that I have found helpful at the end of this chapter.

Here is a list of the top three lessons I have learned. Adapt this to your personal need as you wish.

Everything has a place
I can't even recall how many times I had to interrupt the school day because of the 'missing book'. We went searching high and low, and finally, I had my student work on a different assignment so I could find the book. Being in this situation is frustrating and can easily derail the day if this happens frequently, or if you feel that this subject you are now putting on the backburner is an important one.

Here's what worked for our family. I put two tall bookshelves in our school area, and each student 'owned' one or two racks, depending on how many subjects that require books they had (not all subjects require books, and some require more books than others).

When the school day started, the materials would be on the designated place in the shelf, and at the end of the lesson the materials were returned to their place on the shelf. That did not happen 100% of the time, but it drastically reduced the times that we were looking for missing books, or other materials (protractors, rulers, workbooks, calculators).

The way I had my students organize their shelf rack was by stacking all math-related items together, notebook on the bottom, textbook on top. I had them lay the books flat, and not stand them upright. That way they were easy to grab and easy to return.

My children were not the only ones misplacing their books, so I applied the same rule to my teacher guides and books that I was using throughout the school year, except that I put my books on the shelf upright, not laying down. I needed a large shelf for all my homeschool books, teacher guides, and at first, I kept all materials I owned on the same shelf, regardless of whether I needed them that year or not. But it quickly became too cluttered, and I decided to put materials from past years, or future years, on a different shelf in a different room of the house, or even in the attic. This visually decluttered and newly organized shelf was a refreshment to my eyes and lifted my spirits.

During the elementary school years, I bought for my students smaller shelves that have little square cubbies with specially designed boxes that slide in and out. These were helpful for little odds and ends, such as math manipulatives, games, Legos, and Dr. Suess books.

As my kids got older, these cubbies would hold much of their note pads, books, and other materials. However, I noticed that as my students got older, their textbook grew larger in size and did not quite fit into these little cubbies. That is when I switched to larger bookshelves.

If you're on a tight budget, check facebook marketplace, amazon marketplace, garage sales, or goodwill for shelves. Any shelf is better than none, if it helps you keep school materials in order. The dollar store has plastic bins to place odds and ends, such as calculators, rulers, and supplies for projects.

Provide a place for completed and future work

Another thing I quickly realized was that my students completed some work every day. Where would I store it so I could easily find it if needed, like at the end of the school year when I want to show a sample of work (portfolio) to a teacher to fulfill my state's requirements?

Sometimes I needed to look at it during the school year for reference. Also, my kids sometimes enjoyed looking at completed work from a few months ago. Regardless of why I needed to look back at it, I realized that without a proper place to store it, chaos would ensue.

Ideally, I needed to create a place for each student to put it themselves, so I didn't have to worry about it. A system that worked well for me is several office trays. I used a stack of office trays for each of my students, so there was room for worksheets, essays, or any other completed work for each subject.

Another idea is to use file folders that are labeled, and each student knows to put their work into the correct folder. Each semester or trimester I sifted through these papers and picked out what should be kept, and what could be thrown out. Not every single math sheet has to be saved, and not every single spelling sheet needs to be held on to. Just choose the most important ones such as quizzes, tests, or the ones with special meaning.

I also needed to provide a space to store future worksheets. Usually, I printed out six or eight weeks of material ahead of time, and again, used office trays for each subject and for each student. You can definitely use file folders in boxes, if you're short on space since trays do take up a lot of room.

Personally, I preferred trays despite the room they took up because it was easier to access the papers. And I am all about making it easy for myself. That's one less thing to dig through. But again, not everyone has ample space, so a box with file folders is a great option.

3. *Don't run out of school supplies that you frequently use*

That includes paper, glue, pens and pencils, markers, favorite snacks, favorite drinks, wipes, paper towels, dry erase markers, sharpies, play dough, crayons, watercolors, stickers, batteries, etc. I recommend that you have a list on your fridge or somewhere visible, and whenever you run low, write it in your phone app or whatever you use as a shopping list and get it next time you go to the store. And don't forget yourself: Office supplies, printer paper, ink, and pens.

ORGANIZING IN A SMALL LIVING SPACE

Homeschooling takes up space, but there are some great ideas out there to utilize small spaces very effectively. Earlier, I mentioned that when my family was in the process of moving, and our house needed to look picture perfect for the showings, I used bins for each of my kids' school supplies. This worked very well, and everyone got used to this system quickly.

I bought one 30 qt. clear plastic storage tote for each of my children, and several smaller ones depending on what else needed to be stowed. The clear plastic allows you to see what is in the bottom of the box, and having a few smaller bins means that markers, glue sticks, pencils, and pens won't get lost in the big box.

You can use stickers to mark each bin, or you can use a permanent marker to write names on them. At the end of the school day every student cleans up their school supplies and puts them back in the bin.

Perhaps, instead of buying plastic bins, you already have boxes, or even an ottoman or other furniture that has storage space in it. Whatever you already have is what you should start out with. See if it fulfills your needs, and if it does, stick with it. It is your home and your homeschool, so use what you already have.

PROTECT SCHOOLWORK FROM STICKY BABY FINGERS

It's worth mentioning that, if you have babies or toddlers, and certain school supplies are stored in a place they can reach, that can lead to problems. It is very sad when a baby sibling chews on a school assignment or project. So, make sure that your little one can't get to the school supplies.

NOT ENOUGH WALL SPACE FOR POSTERS

If you have little wall space, but would like to display posters, charts, and maps, you can buy several big cardboard trifolds at the Dollar Tree or Walmart, and tape or glue everything to these 'walls'.

I've used this system several times, and glued multiplication charts, weather charts, maps, Latin conjugations and declensions, clocks, and whatever else you would like to hang up, but can't.

It helps children to remember information when they are surrounded by it, so during the school day you can set these 'walls' up, and at the end you can store them behind a couch or in a closet.

COMBINE YOUR STUDENTS

Another way to save space is to work extra hard on combining your students in the content-based subjects. That way, you only need one set of these books which will cover every grade. You can use your living room or den to do these subjects, and when your students are ready for their skill-based subjects, each student gets the assignment on a clip board or lap desk, and either moves to a different room, or stays in the same room. It all depends on how well they can concentrate when other people are nearby or talking.

DESK SOLUTION FOR SMALL LIVING SPACES

Using clip boards or lap desks eliminates the need for a big desk. You can avoid having them laying around by stowing them in the school bins at the end of the school day.

HAVE A SHELF WITH BOOKS

Even in a small living space, the most important school item that should be invested in is a shelf for books. It doesn't even need to be a big one. And you can simply fill this shelf with library books, but as long as you have books available, your child will look at them and read them.

If you spend time reading aloud, the books on that shelf will become even more accessible, because your child will be more likely to take a book and read it if he sees you do it. Whether you have a large house or a small one, or whether your homeschool budget is low or high, as long as you read aloud to your kids, these become irrelevant factors.

Statistically, reading aloud bridges every socio-economic difference, and having a bookshelf full of a large variety of books is the first and most important step any parent can take toward raising a kid who can read well, speak well, think well, and write well.

CREATE A SPACE FOR YOURSELF

Even if it is a little box and a lap desk, prepare a place where you can plan, store your materials, and have easy access. The easier the access, the more likely you will use it.

What do you enjoy during your planning sessions? A candle? A soda? A cup of tea? Have these things ready, or in the case of the tea, as ready as possible. Buy tea that you only use during planning sessions. Have a candle and matches together (making sure little fingers cannot reach it).

Your Front Door

Print out the advice sheets from HSLDA and have these sitting at your front door in case CPS or a social worker ever show up. It is good to be prepared for this scenario, even if the chances are extremely low.

19

Household Chores

First Some Bad News, then Some Good News

So, you've spent all this this time thinking and planning, reading and researching for your homeschool, only to realize at some point that your household chores are still around. They haven't vanished. And here's the bad news: actually, homeschooling makes completing your household chores more difficult and seemingly unmanageable. Having more bodies at home creates more messes, more dishes, and somehow less time to clean them all up.

That's the bad news. The good news is that there are many different ideas to choose from in order to make these chores manageable and integrate them into your school day. This is one of the reasons that homeschooled kids are usually ready and able to move out to college or a new job and take care of themselves very well.

Chores—Yes or No?

Should kids help with chores, or should they not? While probably most of us agree that the common-sense answer is a resounding 'yes', why is this so? And if indeed our children should have chores, to what extent, and how often?

As I watched my son, and later on my other children, participate in doing chores, I realized the importance of this part of family life. All people want to do things that are significant. If we look back and realize that our work served no purpose, we are dissatisfied and feel frustrated. Why? Because we are created to have significance.

We have the desire to prove it to ourselves and fill our lives with productive work that accomplishes a goal with purpose and worth. Remember the day when you worked really hard, perhaps cleaning out a closet, or planting a garden? Maybe you were finally able to fix something, or you finished reading a book. Whatever it was that you finished, go back, and recall the satisfaction you felt when you were done with the task.

As parents, we have the privilege to allow our children to experience this feeling of accomplishment. The chemical processes that happen in the brain after a job is finished are crucial to developing a habit of working hard. Unfortunately, living in the Western world of indulgence and instant gratification makes it increasingly difficult to instill any kind of work ethic into our children.

Nonetheless, assigning chores to your children creates the right environment to accomplish this task. A productive work atmosphere in which every family member has a meaningful task creates a healthy family culture and molds children into adults who know that hard work pays off.

Daily Chores

Certain tasks must be done daily and are highly important for the normal function of life like dishes and laundry. Assigning children daily chores is a way parents can show love to their children. There may be whining and complaining, but all this is part of training our children so that one day they will be adults who get the job done despite not feeling like it.

Be ready with a response when there is whining and complaining and be consistent. My husband and I usually reminded our kids of Philippians 2:14: "Do all things without complaining and disputing." Whatever response you choose, be consistent with it and insist that the chore (within reason) is completed in an acceptable and timely fashion.

Adjust your expectations and try to give positive feedback if the job is not finished by praising the effort and reminding him that there is still more to do. This is what Charlotte Mason calls "Habit training." It is hard work but becomes easier as you develop a routine. Your kids will thank you one day that you took the time to love them enough to have them create a strong work ethic and healthy habits.

HAVE A PLAN

The most important part of managing your household chores is, once again, to have a plan. If you're like me, you might love planning, only to throw out your plan after a while and come up with a different one. I love changes in schedule and plans. I usually like to change things up each school term, which is anywhere from every six to nine weeks.

If one of my plans works well, I will re-use it at a later time, and if not, I abandon it completely. But perhaps you like creating your plan and sticking with it because you thrive on long-term routine. Regardless of your planning preferences, you need a plan for getting those chores done.

Here is a master list of possible chores, some logistical questions, and then a sample chart to get them done. I used a spreadsheet program to create these, and when I print them out for myself, I like to add colors and graphics to make them easy to read.

The sample chart is one that I used with my four kids, so there are four columns. You may add yourself and your spouse to the list, or anyone else living in your household. I am leaving some blank spaces for you to fill in what you can think of for your family. Once created, print out your sheet, put it in a sleeve protector, and post it on the fridge or another visible place in your house.

MASTER LIST

Kitchen Work	General House Work
Empty the dishwasher	Laundry (collect, wash, fold, put up)
Set the table	Deep Clean (how often, which rooms?)
Wipe kitchen counters	Make beds (every morning?)
Mopping kitchen floor	Tidy up own room
Clean up messes from meal preparation	

One more thing: the more children you have, the more help you will have. But you also have more dishes, more kitchen cleaning, and more work in general. So, you can assign one chore to more than one kid. It all sort of evens out in the end once you have your system going.

Miscellaneous Chores	**Fun Chores**
Feed pets	Bake cookies
Walk the dog	Prepare a special dessert
Water plants	Make pancakes for the family
Get the mail	
Wash the car	
Organize closet or bookshelf	
Help unload groceries from car	
Get wood for the fireplace	

SAMPLE CHART FOR THE WEEK OF JANUARY 3–9

Child 1	**Child 2**	**Child 3**	**Child 4**
Make bed in morning	Make bed in morning	Make bed in morning	Make bed in morning
Set table (every meal)	Clear table (every meal)	Load / empty dishwasher (every meal)	Help prepare meals
Take out trash on Monday nights	Vacuum playroom Friday afternoon	Feed and play with the dogs	Wipe kitchen counters
End of day tidy up	End of day tidy up	End of day tidy up	End of day tidy up

I had daily tasks for them that included personal hygiene. This chart serves as a reminder of these things, and I printed the same list out four times, only changing the child's name on it. I had my kids decorate these with stickers, or whatever they wanted to do, and posted them on the bathroom mirror or in a visible spot in the hallway or bedroom.

CHILD

Morning Tasks:	Evening Tasks:
Breakfast	Shower
Brush Teeth	Pajamas
Morning Devotion	Brush Teeth
Bring dirty clothes to the utility room basket	Bedtime

WHAT TIME IS CHORE TIME?

Now that you have a chart and have assigned each child a chore, how and when do these get done? You need to decide what time of day the chore makes sense to do and how to incorporate them into your day, so that you're not wasting time trying to figure out what to do next.

Some chores are done in the morning, some in the afternoon, some on the weekend, and some at mealtimes. So, you will have to decide what time works for you.

My Family Chores

My family is not 100 percent efficient, and I'm not the best drill sergeant, but on most days, most chores and tasks got done. I could have probably done a better job inspecting finished jobs (you've probably heard, "inspect what you expect"). Sometimes I simply did not have the energy to do that, which probably created some confusion, and my children learned that they could get away with a job badly done when mom is too tired.

But in general, my kids did their chores well enough to call it done. And the important long-term goal is consistency, not so much perfectionism. If you have a child who consistently struggles with getting the chore done, do it with her for a while. Then slowly make it a challenge: "Let's see how much you can do by yourself." Or "Let's see if you can beat the timer. I'll set it for two minutes." Timers are extremely useful motivators. If winning is the objective, count me in!

Start with longer time allowance for the chore, then slowly raise the bar, and expect her to get the job done in the time you think she is capable of. This is hard work and requires a lot of patience on your part.

INCENTIVES FOR MYSELF

Without consistent practice the chores will not turn out better, instead the frustration level will increase for both you and your kids. Give yourself an incentive. I told myself that if I am patient and fulfill my own desired behavior (i.e., expectation of my own behavior toward the kids) I will pour myself a cup of coffee with my favorite special creamer that is only for these occasions. You can have your favorite cookies or chocolate on hand for just these occasions. I love incentives for myself!

CHORE HUSTLE

Having a chore assignment for each child is the basis of my cleaning system. I added all the chores that needed to be completed, and I assigned each of my children one or two chores he could handle. If everyone worked for fifteen minutes each morning before or after breakfast, we all felt very accomplished.

Again, having a plan makes this fifteen minute "chore-hustle" efficient. Add up the time it takes to complete what you would like to get done in the morning, including breakfast, and perhaps a short walk. Add that time to your children's wake-up time, and this will be when school starts. You could also do it backwards. Subtract the time it takes to complete these things from the time you want to start school. This gives you the time at which your children should wake up.

AFTERNOON CHORES

I found it helpful to have another "fifteen-minute chore hustle" at the end of our school day. This consisted primarily in straightening up little messes so that the house looked decent when dad got home from work. This is a good time to make sure all schoolbooks and other supplies are in their rightful place, so you know where to find them for the next lesson.

"One Thing for Mom"

One chore I had for my kids was the "do one thing for Mom" chore which meant they each had to do one thing I specifically asked each one of my children to do. I used this type of chore only about two or three times a month, but they were usually significant. Cleaning out the minivan, collecting trash from around the house, cleaning up the playroom, washing mom's or dad's car, or when we were expecting guests, helping with preparations.

Incentives for The Kids

The reward for these chores would be something like milk and cookies, or a special teatime. We had teatime on many days, so this had to be a special tea with special pastries. If it was something yummy, and I announced it ahead of time, everyone was highly motivated to get the job done. We played some fun music while we were working, which made the time go by much quicker.

We tried to listen to audiobooks, but that lost its appeal quickly because of moving through the house, and not being able to hear, or because of loud noises such as vacuuming etc. Plus, I am tempted to sit down and devote my time to listening rather than working, so I have not done that very often. Loud music seemed the best choice for us.

Yard Work

If at all possible, plant a garden at some point as part of your homeschool. It doesn't even have to be every year, but enough so that your kids get to experience it. Knowing where fruits and vegetables come from, and how they grow, is an important piece of learning and should be part of everyone's education.

The biggest reason to include yard work is to connect kids with nature and have them experience how to care for it. If you remember the importance of Nature Study, and how it can combat Nature Deficit Disorder, here is a concrete way to teach this subject.

Depending on how long the job takes, yard work can be integrated into your school day during nature study a few times a week. If the job takes longer, like cutting grass for instance, you could use your afternoons when the "sitting down" part of your day is finished; or you could do yard work on weekends.

Yardwork as Exercise and Reset Button

Cutting the grass with a push mower (self-propelled or not) could also be counted as PE, if your yard is large enough to break a sweat. The main point is to do it with some frequency, so your kids learn what to expect and how to get the job done. This kind of physical labor is not only healthy for the body but also improves the emotional well-being and stress level of your child.

Working outside is like a reset button that helps re-adjust attitudes or frustration and allows you to work through issues in a quicker way than most other activities. In addition, it teaches valuable lessons about lawn care which might seem trivial at first, but actually leads to a valuable learning experience.

Raking leaves in the fall and shoveling snow in winter is also great exercise. I made sure to send my kids outside whenever possible to let them do these kinds of chores. After getting them started and working alongside for a while, I would go back inside and prepare hot chocolate or cold lemonade for them to enjoy when they finished. That was usually a good incentive for them to keep going and get the job done without delay. You will be able to decide what kind of work your child is ready for, and how much supervision they need.

Planning a Garden

If you're planning on planting a flower or vegetable garden, you can have your students care for certain jobs like planting, weeding, or watering. This would be done during your nature study time. It does not take very long, and you don't even have to do it every day, maybe two or three times a week, depending on where you live and what plants you are growing.

There were times when I didn't really feel like bothering with a garden, so I purchased planters and let my kids choose flowers to create their own flower gardens. We decorated the front patio with these beautiful creations, where my kids could easily access them to care for them.

If you live in an apartment, or don't have a yard, you can simply put a small table by a window and use several flowerpots to plant anything from herbs to flowers. This is a fun little project and will be a great learning experience for the whole family.

Make It a Subject and Put It on the Schedule

Using yard work as content for either P.E. or Nature Study is an effective way to get it into your schedule. Usually, the biggest problem for me with some of the things I want to do in my homeschool is to find the time to do them. I can't remember how many times I've wanted to do things like "go on a nature walk" or "spend time watching birds," only to forget it by the end of the day, and never get to it.

Just like any other subject, put yard work on your schedule during a certain time of day, make a specific list of things that you would like to get done, and when the time comes, head outside. It helps to have a basket of items such as gloves, sunscreen, bug spray, sunglasses, water bottles, etc. by the door, so you do not have to be delayed by searching for these items.

In my experience, the best and most successful activities are the ones that are meaningful and have a real purpose. Kids don't really see the immediate purpose of math or writing, so they tend to challenge why they have to do it. Growing food or flowers, or simply cleaning the yard is self-explanatory.

Caring for plants is necessary if we want to have a plentiful harvest. Or if you want to play in the back yard, having really long grass or lots of leaves invites unpleasant critters, or makes it slippery in wet weather. Plus, having a pile of leaves is a worthy goal in and of itself.

RAINY DAYS

Sometimes the weather does not cooperate. I do encourage you to go outside even in wind, rain, snow, or sleet. But some yard-work can be unsafe or useless under these conditions. What can you do instead?

You could still go outside, just with a different purpose. Finding earth worms, jumping in puddles, or dancing in the rain could be reasons to go outside.

Or you could stay inside and take this time to research some farm work, like how corn is planted and harvested, or how cows are milked. You could use this time to copy off a flower or leaf from a nature guide. Perhaps you could switch some subjects around because the weather will be nicer in a few hours. Whatever works for you that day, have a backup plan in mind in case of a change of plans.

INCENTIVES: YES OR NO?

Incentives are a real-life connection of work to results. Without incentives, no work would ever be done by anyone. We work for pay, or for a good outcome, for praise, or for good grades. If utilized as a special reward for a job well done, and not as a threat, incentives can create a positive work environment.

In other words, incentives are a good thing, even for getting yard work done. Perhaps you can bake some brownies, cookies, or have tea, or cocoa? Or could you simply read aloud a special book?

Four Steps to Success

Adding yard work to your school schedule takes some preparation, so here are four steps to make it a success:

1. **Add it to your schedule with specific tasks for each person.**
2. **Prepare the necessary equipment beforehand.**
3. **Have a backup plan in case outdoor yardwork is rained or snowed out.**
4. **Plan an incentive and have it ready.**

20

What I Would Do Differently if I Could Do It All Over

1. COMBINE MY STUDENTS SOONER

In my early homeschooling years, I tried to keep my older three kids, who had been in a school setting, on their own track of education. All my energy was spent by the time evening came around, and then I still had to check all their work and plan for the next day in case they made a lot of mistakes and had to re-do the lesson.

It took me several years to fully realize that there are better ways to do this. But being in the trenches, I did not have time to re-evaluate very much because I was constantly pushing ahead with each individual student and subject.

Combining my students for history, literature, composition, foreign language, and all the enrichments studies left only math and science for individual subjects. As my kids got older, they were also able to choose a subject which they could complete on their own with some supervision.

2. SEPARATING MY ROLES—PARENT VERSUS TEACHER

I have always found it challenging to separate my role as a teacher from my role as a mother, and it is a constant battle between me and myself. My kids have learned to hold me accountable, and yes, it has led to frustration and strife. I usually have to eat humble pie and apologize. So, I can't emphasize enough how important it is to first be a mom (or dad) and then a teacher.

It's tempting to look at my kids and turn all their actions into school grades. Worse yet, it's easy to turn their failures into my failures. I have gone down that rabbit hole too many times, and usually my husband digs me back out.

Ultimately, our kids will have to choose to take on what we teach them. So, if you need to, put that as a reminder in a place where you will frequently see it. Education is just a process, nothing more, nothing less. The final product is not up to us parents, but up to our kids and, in my worldview, up to God.

3. SEPARATING SCHOOL FROM HOME

"Mom, I don't want to feel like I live at school." My daughter had a point there. Our family room space had stacks of books, clipboards with schedules and assignments, and everything else that reminds you of school. I had gotten used to it, but my daughter did not appreciate it.

Are your kids constantly reminded of school when they go about their leisure time? This is a bit tricky, because many rooms in the house are more lived in and perhaps associated with school than if your kids left the house each day for school and returned in the afternoon for homework.

Here are a few strategies:

If you have a big enough house, turn one room into the school room, and when you're done, your kids can physically leave.

But if the size of your house does not allow for this, another way to accomplish this is by setting up your school space in a way that it can easily be turned into a play space or living space.

I turned our living room into a school room by using a system of shelves and bins that held all our supplies. I decorated the shelf tops with 'living room' décor, and when everything was put away, the room did not look much like a school room, but like a living room. It's pleasant now for anyone to hang out in that room.

When we were in the process of selling our house, I always had to be ready for a showing. So, I purchased clear plastic storage bins with lids. Each of my children put all their school supplies into their bin, books and all. When the realtor came to show the house, I moved the bins into the bedroom closets, and the school supplies were out of sight.

4. ALLOW MY KIDS TO TEACH EACH OTHER MORE

Having an older sibling help out a younger sibling is a precious thing. I sort of knew that, but when I saw it in action, I really understood it. So, I tried to incorporate that into our schedule more often, but many times I felt like we needed to keep moving ahead with our subjects and something had to give.

Yes, it is slower to give the kids time to work things out among themselves. And yes, there were arguments at times, but for the most part, this time was sibling bonding time, plus the older kid reinforced their own knowledge of the matter while the younger sibling had a chance to look at it from a peer perspective rather than "mom-teacher again" perspective.

When kids explain what they have learned to others it makes it stick much more than studying for a test ever could. So, if you are on the fence about letting kids teach kids every now then because it takes too much time (as I once thought), think of it as study time for a test. That would be a wise investment of time.

5. HAVE MORE CONFIDENCE IN MY KIDS

I knew my kids' strengths and weaknesses. Unfortunately, it's all too easy to get hung up on the weaknesses and think that they will not be prepared for adulthood.

But my children grew up, and now I am standing on the other side of it. Having been homeschooled, they all have a good understanding of real life outside of school. They all had jobs as teens and learned certain skills like paying taxes and turning in their hours.

They all learned responsibilities that come with living in a family, and they all understand real-life challenges because they were out in the real world interacting and working with people.

I wish someone had told me early on that these skills outweigh academic disciplines by a long shot.

21

Homeschooling the Reluctant Teen

Homeschooling a reluctant teen is not an easy feat. If you have been homeschooling all along, and your teen is starting to resent it and wants to go to a school, there are two options. You can either grant the wish, or you can change your homeschool strategy.

By changing the strategy, I mean you completely abandon what you have been doing and transform your approach.

Teens respond very well to clear expectations and a paying job. Choose your bare minimum subjects and allow your teen to pursue a hobby he enjoys and get a job in the afternoons. Check your state's laws on child labor.

Encourage your teen to start a business. This is where the hobby comes in. Is there something she really likes to do that can earn some money? Teaching our kids that money doesn't grow on trees and that people have to work to earn a living is possibly the most important lesson they will ever learn.

If your teen's reluctance is simply due to needing friends and feeling lonely at home, perhaps you can join one or more homeschool groups. Could she possibly take a class at a community college? Could she learn an instrument and start playing in a community orchestra or band? Perhaps there is a theater group that he could join?

The New-to-Homeschool Teen

It's always difficult to start something new after you have been doing it a certain way for a long time. Homeschooling a teen after he has been in school is no different. Obviously, your desire to homeschool means that you see a need for change. But since you're not dealing with a kindergartener but a teen, his opinion in this matter influences the path forward a great deal.

Ideally, there is a mutual understanding of the reason behind your decision to homeschool, but many times it's not possible to be on the same page. Your relationship with your child will greatly impact how you should proceed.

And while in your care, your child depends on your decision-making, so I want to encourage you to create a plan of action specifically geared toward building the relationship with your child and making school secondary. Once there is mutual respect, understanding, and trust, the academic subjects will automatically follow.

Rewards, Yes or No?

I am a supporter of rewards. There are some limits in my opinion, but overall, I like the idea of rewarding hard work. This includes schoolwork. Some people argue that education in itself is a reward. While that is certainly true, it is equally unrealistic.

Many of the things I learned in elementary and high school were not rewarding to me at the time. And telling me that education is a reward in itself was no motivator for me.

If you're doing a job and getting paid for it, you will be motivated to do it right. School work is very similar to this. I am not arguing that we should pay our kids every day for doing their schoolwork, but perhaps we can cut a deal that they get a certain reward at the end of the week for making an effort to do their best. This could be money, or it could be a dinner at her favorite restaurant, or going to the movies.

The Angry Teen

And then there's the teen who is angry with you for even suggesting such a thing as homeschooling. This will require your full attention to relationship building. It's impossible to achieve anything academically unless your relationship is right.

Before the school year starts, can you research homeschool groups so she can meet new friends? Perhaps you know of another family which is already homeschooling, and you can plan a get-together.

You could also spend the first month on outings and field trips. It's usually a big hit when your child realizes that most of her friends are sitting in the classroom while she gets to visit fun places.

Homeschooling a child who is in extreme opposition to being homeschooled requires patience, resolve, and faith. If you have an underlying conviction that this is the right choice for your family, be prepared to spend a lot of energy to get going and keep going. But you'll be rewarded with easier times in the future.

Your motivation and conviction for homeschooling will affect the lengths through which you are willing to go. Think of it like a sprint to build up momentum. It's hard work initially, but it will pay off in the long run.

CREATE A TRANSITION SEMESTER

If your student has an extreme reluctance to be homeschooled, one strategy is to create a transition semester or even year, depending on which grade your student is in, the severity of the reluctance, and, of course, the legal requirements in your state.

Always keeping the long view in mind, think about the focal point of this time, which should revolve around building up the relationship and trust between you and your child.

Some families, if the budget allows it, have gone on an extended trip and used this time to educate their child by firsthand experience of different places. This could be different state parks, enjoying and studying nature, or different countries, experiencing different cultures and languages.

Taking a semester or year off from your 'normal' school experience is by no means less of an education; it just has a different focal point.

Spend lots of time with her and be the person you want her to resemble. Our children watch everything we do and hold us to a high standard. If we ourselves don't do what we tell them to do, we had better learn to be humble, apologize, and try again. Being vulnerable as parents is a great start to an improved relationship with our kids.

Read Aloud with Your Teen

One of the most powerful family-building activities out there is reading aloud to your child. From what I have seen and experienced, the homeschool families with the closest family relationships are those who read together.

It doesn't matter what time of day you do it. But the connection it creates between you and your child, and if you have multiple children, between siblings, is irreplaceable.

If you're new to reading aloud, choose a book that he enjoys. Going to the library may or may not be a good idea because there are so many books on display that do not have good quality content, and yet their cover might look tempting.

Start out with ten minutes, if that is all that works at this point. But don't be surprised if he asks for more. During the relationship-building phase, my advice is to keep going as long as you like. Your voice might give out after a while, so get some tea, or say, 'We'll continue this tomorrow, same time, same place'.

Many times, the book is too good to put down. He might ask you whether he can keep reading to himself because he is really into this book, so you have two choices: say yes, but remind him that you will continue reading where you left off, so he'll have to listen to it again. Or say no and give him a different book to read at this point.

You might take some time and read the first chapter of the new book aloud (after drinking some tea) to get him interested enough to continue.

BABY STEPS

When you're just starting out to homeschool, you should plan on taking baby steps. Day by day, week by week. It is not a race. Think of growing a garden. Too much water or too much fertilizer will ruin the crop. But a little bit at a time, and there will be much growth. Once you have built up a relationship in which learning can take place, ease into it and slowly increase your daily workload. At one point you may be surprised how quickly a day can go by.

Initially, to get this momentum going you can have a daily after-school incentive for your student, such as Mondays: ice cream, Tuesdays: watch an educational show, Wednesday: dinner outside, Thursday: stay up reading book at night, Friday: movie night with pizza, Saturday: games.

JUST-BECAUSE-YOU-CAN DAYS

One of my favorite podcasters, Sarah Mackenzie, recommends adding the Just-Because-You-Can Days into your schedule simply, well, because you can. You are homeschooling to be able to do what you like to do. That includes outings that you do just because you can whenever you want.

You can announce them beforehand so your kids look forward to them, or you can make them a surprise, and the morning of that day let everyone know about it. Sarah advises adding one of these days every month or two, depending on what makes most sense for you. I have done this with my own kids, and it was always a big hit. Remember that building relationships is just as important as doing math and science. So, plan on these days even if you have a big blow-up with your kids that morning. Sometimes those are the best days to get away from home and enjoy different scenery.

You Can't Do This Alone

Finally, with a reluctant teen in the house, life can be tough, and you need support. Your spouse, a friend or family member, anyone who knows you, your family, and your situation, and is in agreement with you. So, find a few people that can lend an ear or a helping hand. They will be a great source of encouragement as you pursue this adventure with your teen.

22

Knowing Your Worldview

We must look at the lens through which we see the world, as well as the world we see, and that the lens itself shapes how we interpret the world.

—STEPHEN COVEY

Successful people have a clear sense of purpose and direction. Regardless of where this sense of purpose comes from, without it, they would not be able to function and be driven to high achievements.

Guiding our kids toward this sense of purpose and direction is not only a key aspect of homeschooling but of raising kids in general. This is not taught as a subject, but through the overarching message we convey as we interact with our children.

How is this achieved? To start with, I need to take a look at my basic view of the world around me. After that, I can figure out how my family and each family member fits into my "worldview." With this as my foundation, I can guide my child toward finding his purpose and direction.

Worldview

My worldview is the filter I use to make sense of everything around me (the world). It is the set of standards and values I have that help me judge between right and wrong, good and evil, truth and falsehood.

Webster's dictionary defines it as "a cause, principle, or system of beliefs held to with ardor and faith." Every subject we teach to our children is part of a worldview.

A Lesson from the Cheshire Cat

Perhaps you remember the scene from the movie Alice in Wonderland in which Alice is trying to figure out her way. She met a cat who was sitting in a tree and asked, "What road do I take?" The cat answered with the question, "Where do you want to go?" "I don't know," Alice said. "Then," said the cat, "it really doesn't matter, does it?"

Alice doesn't know which way to go and is presented with a choice. Since she does not know where she is going, any road will do. It is the same with my worldview. It will direct my choices and give me a path forward. If I don't know which worldview I have, any choice will do. But in the end, will I agree with myself?

Everyone Has a Worldview

How would you answer questions like 'Why is stealing wrong?' or 'Why is it bad to cheat on a test?' The answers reflect your worldview. We may have to think about this for a while, but most of us will have one or more reasons for why stealing and cheating are wrong. Your reasons may be different from mine, but nevertheless, they are rooted in your beliefs about right and wrong.

We have all been confronted with issues that challenge our sense of justice, and our instinctive response to the issue gives us insight into parts of our worldview. Everyone has a worldview because everyone has a sense of justice.

How is this related to Homeschooling?

When I started homeschooling my eighth grader, our conversations about books or historical events included many ethical topics. I noticed that I had not thought some of the implications of my worldview all the way through, and I got stumped a few times.

I needed to have an opinion of why I thought a certain character in the story was acting justly. I needed to have an opinion about the rights and wrongs of historical events, of mistakes that could have been avoided, and how I know these were indeed mistakes.

It would have taken me a long time to figure out good answers to some of these questions, so this is where my curriculum came in handy. So, when I chose my homeschool curriculum, it was important that I chose one that agreed with my worldview.

The two main worldview categories are the secular worldview and the religious worldview. Within each of these categories you will find sub-categories that define nuances.

Some parents would like to leave the choice of values up to their children. While this may sound like a good plan right now, there are problems with this approach which I will address later in this chapter.

Tennis Match Analogy

A simple way of thinking about your worldview is by comparing it to a tennis match. The world of tennis is your worldview. It is not soccer or football (other worldviews). You love tennis, and you know and respect all the rules. You are sitting in your seat watching the Wimbledon final, and everything is going great so far. Your favorite player is ahead, and the game is nearing the end. You know all the rules, and you and everyone else in the audience respects them.

Imagine that the ball hits the ground out of bounds, and because you were distracted for a split second, you did not see it. What now? You can ask other people what they saw, or you can watch a replay from different cameras. However, you did not see it for yourself but are relying on other people's (or cameras) accounts.

Does that mean the ball is not out? Who gets the points? And who even says that anyone should get points? Can we just say everyone wins and we go home?

Obviously, this is not an acceptable solution, and you want to know the truth, even if it means the ball was out. There are rules which the players and the audience accept. As long as everyone accepts the rules and the decisions that the umpire makes, things go well.

Why Do We Need Game Rules?

But here's the reason that there are rules in the first place: defining the game's purpose, the desire to win, disagreement between players.

First, we need to define the game (worldview) and its purpose. There are several overarching purposes: recreation, fitness, competition, for instance. But specifically, the purpose of tennis is spelled out by the definition or the game.

When playing tennis, we observe tennis rules and not soccer or basketball rules. Playing tennis means that there is no goal or basket. It has a different pace and a different purpose.

But it doesn't end there. Players have encountered specific circumstances. The ball is on the line. Does that mean it's in or out? Or what if a player is thirsty and simply leaves the game to get a drink? Is that forfeiting the game? Rules for special circumstances need to be agreed upon.

Finally, the desire to win will cause each player to see things from a point of his own advantage. We need a third party to help assess reality and aid in just decision making.

In our lives, we need rules for making decisions between good and bad, or right or wrong. Where do these rules originate? Where does our value system originate? It comes directly from our worldview.

What are some examples of worldviews?

There are several different worldview options. Some examples are atheism, naturalism, humanism, agnosticism, pantheism, dualism, deism, and monotheism. Each of these are based on a set of assumptions that are taken in faith when it comes to the implications they have for the meaning of life, an after-life, right and wrong, good and evil, and reality itself.

Sidenote: I am ignoring the worldview that adheres to the belief that we cannot be sure of anything because it is a contradiction. The statement, "I am not sure of anything," includes itself. A statement is something I am sure of, so I am really saying, "I am sure that I am not sure."

Each of the above-mentioned worldviews fits into one of two categories: secular (human centered) and religious (non-human centered). Atheism, naturalism, humanism, and agnosticism are human centered. Humans come up with the rules, and humans can modify them based on individual or majority opinion.

Pantheism, dualism, deism, and monotheism are all centered around one or more god-figures. The rules are generally not thought of as man-made, and there is usually a special time set apart for worship. Due to the fact that the rules are not man-made, they are usually more stable and difficult to change than the man-made ones.

The Basic Question

The most basic question to answer in my thinking about my worldview is "Why do I, or anything I do or don't do matter?" This will lead us to consider the origin of our sense of purpose. If I can answer that question, I am ahead of the game.

Unfortunately, science does not answer the basic questions of 'Why do I, or why does anything I do, matter?' and 'What is my purpose?' This is where science and philosophy meet.

Science is observable; philosophy interprets science. Both of them put together give me my worldview. With the help of science, I can observe that I exist, but I cannot know why I exist. The reason for my existence is determined by my worldview.

Worldview and Morality

This sense of purpose will determine the rules of morality. If nothing I do matters, then morality does not matter. If morality only matters to some people but not others, there will be constant conflict between these two worldviews which will be the backdrop of society, which is what we are seeing in this country and in the world today.

So, instructing our kids in the area of worldview and morality will equip them with purpose and direction to succeed in life. So many children today grow up without a set of moral standards and purpose that it shows in the increased violence and suicide rates. As homeschooling parents, we have the privilege to ensure that our children are equipped with morality and purpose.

IF I DON'T, SOMEONE ELSE WILL

Regardless of who or what is at the center of my worldview, I am imparting my way of seeing the world to my children. If I don't, someone else will, because everyone has a worldview. If my kids are in public or private school, they will be subject to the worldview of the curriculum and the teacher. Every aspect of learning is subject to a worldview. Each worldview has its own set of standards and excludes other worldviews which means that there is no such thing as neutrality.

IT DETERMINES HOW AND WHY I HOMESCHOOL

My worldview determines the reasons for my decision to homeschool, and it will guide me toward picking my teaching materials. My worldview will by default permeate how and what I teach my children.

My family has chosen the Christian worldview because in it we have found how to explain our world. In my opinion, it answers the basic questions on life better than other worldviews. People are born sinners, which explains why we need laws. People want to get away with bad things, so we need police.

In addition, every person has a purpose because everyone was created in God's image. That is why life has value. These are just a few Christian basics.

A Word about Faith

The word 'faith' induces in some people a feeling of 'unintelligence' or 'irrationality'. The funny thing is that we all have everyday scenarios in which we use faith. We fully expect certain things to work without understanding what they are or why they are reliable. Here are some examples: Next time you drive across an intersection on green, notice your blood pressure. How worried are you to get t-boned? You probably look for traffic, but you don't panic or are scared for your life. We have faith that people obey traffic rules.

I Want My Kids to Choose for Themselves

What if I want to let my kids choose their own worldview? The problem with this is that my kids have no basis for choosing. The only way to teach this skill is by teaching them a worldview.

Our world today has many conflicting worldviews to offer, and all of them are inundating our kids from every direction (social media, movies, Internet, magazines, other people).

The loudest one will win, so it's not really a choice but intentionally pushed on them by someone else. Whose agenda should we enforce in our homeschool, ours or the loudest one out there?

Worldview Leads to Morality

My worldview determines my set of values, my decision making in matters of right and wrong, true and false, good and evil. This is called morality. Almost 75 percent of parents homeschool to provide moral instruction to their children. Morality remains important to parents.

Thomas Jefferson was of the conviction that the central document from which the schools teach morality should be the Bible. He realized that this country needed a cohesive moral standard. Whether every student was a born-again Christian was beside the point.

Several hundred years later we find that this central document is no longer acceptable for education in public schools, and a multitude of clashing worldviews are inundating the classroom.

The latest worldview is that there is no worldview, which—hopefully you agree with me on this—is not a possibility. Or perhaps I should say, the latest worldview is all worldviews rolled into one, which is equally impossible.

MEN HAVE FORGOTTEN GOD, THAT'S WHY ALL THIS
HAS HAPPENED

Aleksandr Solzhenitsyn, a prolific Russian writer, critic, and
Nobel Prize recipient, had enormous impact on the way the western world viewed Communism and the impact it has on society.
One of his books, *One Day in the Life on Ivan Denisovich*, published in 1962, is worth reading aloud to your high schooler.

On May 10th 1983, Solzhenitsyn was awarded the Templeton
Prize for Progress in Religion in London, England. The following
excerpt is from his acceptance speech:

> More than half a century ago, while I was still a child, I recall hearing
> a number of older people offer the following explanation for the great
> disasters that had befallen Russia: "Men have forgotten God; that's
> why all this has happened."
>
> Since then, I have spent well-nigh fifty years working on the his-
> tory of our Revolution; in the process I have read hundreds of books,
> collected hundreds of personal testimonies, and have already con-
> tributed eight volumes of my own toward the effort of clearing away
> the rubble left by that upheaval. But if I were asked today to formu-
> late as concisely as possible the main cause of the ruinous Revolution
> that swallowed up some sixty million of our people, I could not put it
> more accurately than to repeat: "Men have forgotten God; that's why
> all this has happened."

So, now that I have told you all these things, your brain may be
buzzing, and you are wondering what to do.

How to Do Morality and Worldview Instruction

Many authors who write about personal and professional improvement recommend finding time in your day to read from your
creed, plus from another classic book of wisdom that has with-
stood the test of time. The goal is to reflect on our worldview by
challenging it with different ideas and other views so we ourselves
can emerge stronger.

If you're a Christian, there are many publishers who have created materials to teach your children about their Christian faith
and biblical history. If you are not a Christian, be intentional about
teaching your creed, but I still recommend you read from the
Bible regularly.

There are many ideas how to accomplish this with your children in your homeschool. Here are a few suggestions to get you started. Feel free to adapt them to your need:

1. If you eat breakfast, lunch, or dinner as a family, add this to your table talk' topics. For many years, my husband read to our family a variety of books. Usually old ones. Stories of missionaries in different countries around the world, or about someone who lived in the early days of this nation. It usually took five to ten minutes, and our discussions lasted a few more minutes. The time increased as the kids got older. Our children remember this time as special because there were certain inside jokes about different books, and they were challenged in their thinking, even at 6:45 A.M.

2. Instead of reading during mealtimes, you can do this during the period of school in which you combine your children for certain subjects. After moving to another state, our family mealtimes changed for various reasons. The best time to have these discussions now was during our Morning Time (which is the name I chose for our combined studies).

3. Snack time is another good option because children are motivated to sit still and eat. You can get ten or fifteen minutes of reading and discussion before everyone goes back to their schoolwork. It does not have to be a very lengthy discussion. As long as you do it most days, it will accumulate and be very effective in the long term.

4. Driving in the car is one of the best times you can have conversations with your kids. Audiobooks are the perfect way to spend the driving time, and when you're ready to talk, you know where to find your kids. It usually helped my kids to think about things other than poking their little sibling next to them. At least for a little while.

5. It can be part of the bedtime routine. You can gather your kids and have your reading time and conversations after dinner and after everyone has gotten ready for bed. For many families, this is a great option because it's a meaningful way to bring the day to a close and stay connected, especially if everyone is going in different directions throughout the day. It can be tricky to keep everyone focused because kids can become very curious and inquisitive right around bedtime, which might delay your evening plans. However, if you start

early enough in the evening, it can be a great routine, and I know many families who enjoy this special time together.

Curriculum and Book Recommendations:

Since my family adheres to a Christian worldview, the curricula and books I have personally used have strictly Christian content. I will list my favorites. If you adhere to a non-Christian worldview, you can take a look at the Christian curricula to get an idea of the basic structure and content of worldview instruction. Then do a google search and see what you can find to use for your family.

- *The Consequences of Ideas* by R.C. Sproul This is an easy-to-read book discussing common philosophical ideas and their consequences in society and our own lives.

- *The Universe next Door* by James W. Sire. This book breaks down common worldviews and their implications.

- *Worldview Guides* by Logos Press www.logospressonline.com These guides help the teacher having discussions about literary works and worldview. There are thirty-nine guides available, each covering important topics from a classic work of literature.

- *Worldviews in Conflict* by Kevin Swanson www.masterbooks.com This is a comprehensive curriculum which guides the teacher through teaching literature through worldview discussions. The reading selections are included in the book, so it is an all-in-one curriculum.

- Worldview Academy Events www.worldview.org. This website contains information about worldview conference events and has a bookstore link.

- Summit Ministries www.summit.org offers classes, conferences, and curriculum for children and adults to strengthen their worldview.

APOLOGETICS: NEXT LEVEL WORLDVIEW (FOR CHRISTIAN FAMILIES)

The next level of worldview training for a Christian is called Apologetics, which simply means "being able to explain the faith" in a matter of fact, logical manner. Many Christian families raise their children in the church, only to see them leave their faith during the high school or college years. One of the problems is that during the formative years, their faith was not explained well to them so that any argument that sounds intellectual will cause them to question their beliefs. If parents discuss difficult topics with their children starting at a young age (elementary school), the kids will not be surprised by some of the questions our culture asks. I will list a few of my favorite books and other resources I have used for my family.

- A Blueprint for Thinking by R.C. Sproul (Ligonier Ministries) www.ligonier.org. This six-session video mini course covers the basics of how to think. A study guide is available.

- *Defending Your Faith* by R.C. Sproul (Ligonier Ministries) www.ligonier.orYou can read the book, or you can watch over thirty video lectures, each of them about twenty minutes long, in which Sproul explains step by step strategies and philosophies to help defend the Christian faith in the face of the world's most popular philosophies.

- *By This Standard* by Greg Bahnsen.
  In this book, the late Bahnsen explains the necessity of a Christian worldview to gain objective morality. This is not an easy read in my mind (as in, sit down and relax while reading) but gives a deep insight into biblical morality. Well, deep insight at least for an amateur like myself. Compared to his other books, this is one of his 'easy-reads'.

- *How Do We Know the Bible Is True?* (Two volumes available) by Ken Ham and Bodie Hodge. This easy-to-read book lists commonly asked questions about biblical facts and truths and answers them with the most up-to-date information.

- *Demolishing Supposed Bible Contradictions* (two volumes available) by Ken Ham. This easy-to-read book deals with the most common questions people have about seeming contradictions in the Bible.

23

Why Are Public Schools in Trouble?

Why do things look so bleak in the realm of public education in the United States? There are many deep issues here, and I will merely scratch the surface.

> The philosophy of the schoolroom in one generation will be the philosophy of government in the next.
>
> —ABRAHAM LINCOLN

> Education is a weapon whose effects depend on who holds it in his hands and at whom it is aimed.
>
> —JOSEPH STALIN

> Whoever controls the youth, controls the future.
>
> —ADOLF HITLER

All three of these men were powerful leaders, the latter two extremist revolutionaries and dictators who left their mark on the countries they once ruled. They vehemently disagreed with each other on most political issues, but what was crystal clear to all of them was the significance of who educates the kids. Each of them saw the classroom as a battleground for the future. They disagreed on most other things but agreed on this one.

How did we arrive at a point at which we believe that the responsibility of educating our children rests with a gigantic governmental institution? When presented with this fact on the first day of school, we resist the urge to keep our kids home (most moms have this sick feeling in the pit in their stomach when they drop their child off for the first time).

Year after year, parents rest more and more trust and responsi-bility on the teachers to raise their children. Each year, new kinder-garteners enter this realm, and it's perfectly 'normal'. What I want to highlight is the submissive behavior and mentality of our culture to do things without question: 'Everyone is doing it and it has always been done this way'. Or, 'Experts say this is the best way'. History has shown that these are not good reasons.

Two Problems with the US Education System

The topic of 'government-led' education brings out intense emo-tions in some, while others have not even thought about it. I am advocating that parents actively participate in the education process of their children. By that, I mean actively choosing who teaches your children and what is being taught to them.

The freedom of speech, press, and religion all play a part in this ability to choose. Assuring families the right to decide how to edu-cate and what they teach to their children was one of the funda-mental concepts on which this country was founded.

The US school system was designed with this concept in mind. It was to operate through a school board whose members are elected by the citizens. It's a well thought out system that allows parents to participate in their children's education by choosing representatives who make all educational decisions with the con-stituents in mind.

This ingenious way of balancing the right to make educational choices while encouraging the responsibility to be engaged worked well. But as time went on, two major problems arose: structure and content.

The Structure

While the same basic system is still at work today, the sheer size of it, plus poor voter turn-out, make it extremely difficult to continue to be effective.

Do you remember the last time you voted for your local school board? When looking at the list of school board candidates, did you recognize all of the names, knew them in person, what their values are, and how they will represent you and your child? I find it difficult to even know who most people are that are running for any local office, not just the school board. The ballot has hundreds of names on it.

The sad truth is that "locally elected school board members compose the largest group of elected officials in the country and yet the National School Boards Association (NSBA) estimates that voter turnout is often just 5 or 10 percent for these elections" (Carnegie Corporation of New York).

And if you think about it, low voter turn-out means that every vote counts even more. For example, if people with extremist political and social agendas, who might not even have kids themselves, vote, and their vote is one in only a few others, it carries more weight.

Another problem is that many board members are uncontested. They don't even have to campaign; they just get elected without having to ask for votes since there are not enough people running for this office.

And the cherry on top is that according to a 2014 Gallup Poll, 56 percent of Americans believe that local school boards should have the greatest influence on what is taught in public schools, rather than state or federal government. However, the voter turnout says otherwise. There is a big discrepancy between saying and doing.

This is not good news. The system has become so large, so political, and so impersonal, that its original purpose is no longer operative. Sadly, too many Americans are taking their rights for granted and don't think about their responsibility to vote anymore.

The drifts in the classroom today reflect the viewpoints of the few voters from several years ago when they elected board members. Changes do not happen overnight, so I don't think the political and sexual content that's taught in the classrooms today is going to disappear anytime soon. For many parents, this alone is enough reason to homeschool their kids.

The Content

The original structure of the school system was not designed for use on such a massive scale, and the consequence is a system that cannot think beyond its own walls. This problem is more about the content. By that I mean the people, methods, philosophies and curricula that are used to educate our children. I experienced this firsthand when I checked out school for my son.

A few months before my son's fifth birthday, I started looking at a few different schools that were available. I had three kids by now, and I was not so sure any more about sending my son to the local public school.

I was getting cold feet, like so many moms, who are sad to let their baby leave the house for such a long period of time. So, I spent several weeks visiting three public and three private schools, and meeting with their principals and teachers.

Because I was very curious about what was being taught, I asked specific questions about the curriculum they used. I really wanted to know what exactly was being taught in each subject in the early grades.

While the private school principals told me all there is to know about their curriculum, the public-school visits were less informative. I finally decided only to inquire about kindergarten curriculum.

When I realized that I was not going to get a clear answer, things started getting awkward and I started to dislike the atmosphere I was sensing. One of the principals introduced me to other staff saying that "This mom thinks she has a school choice." It was infuriating.

In the end, we chose a private school because I loved the curriculum and atmosphere at one private school I visited.

Schools Are Continuously Behind the Times

There's an abundance of evidence that the way to teach reading is phonics. Phonics means teaching kids the sounds of the letters, so that the kids can then decode the words they read. Attempting to get children started in reading without phonics ensures that most kids will have serious difficulty reading.

Yet many teachers in public schools, for some reason, have often resisted this clear message and clung to ineffective teaching methods such as 'whole language'.

What caught my attention last Christmas was the toy department at Walmart. What method do toy companies who make educational 'learning to read' toys employ? Phonics! Leap Frog, Vtech, and countless other toys use this method to teach reading. Toy companies understand what the latest research shows. Why are schools behind the times? They are difficult to change due to the size of the institution and the bureaucratic system.

Perhaps we should put toy companies in charge of public education.

What Is It about Age Five?

As I was school-shopping for my son, I started to wonder what exactly it was about the age of four or five that made me all nervous and self-conscious about who should be teaching my own child. I wasn't feeling that way a year before, and I didn't know exactly why I felt this way now. I just did.

I came to the conclusion that it is engrained in our culture. Most cultures, eastern or western, have this notion that child education is best accomplished outside the home. It certainly is easier and less stressful for the parents in the short term, but usually ends with the state's over-regulation as we see today.

What about Private Schools?

Private schools are not necessarily exempt from any of the problems that public schools experience. You will have to be the decider on whether the private school you are thinking about has problems with worldview, safety, curriculum, quality of teaching, or some other aspect. All the same rules apply.

The only difference is that, in my experience, private schools are run more like a business in which the customer matters, so the school is usually accommodating and forthcoming with information.

Origins of the US School System

It all started in early nineteenth century Prussia (at the time, modern-day northern Germany). Napoleon marched across Europe, leaving destruction and chaos in his wake. The Prussian king decided that an education reform would bring normalcy and unity back to his empire. Wilhelm von Humboldt, diplomat, philosopher, and pioneer when it came to educational reform, was put in charge.

Among many new concepts, Humboldt's vision was to introduce a generous liberal arts education with the classical languages, Greek and Latin, as the foundation. The students were also to receive instruction in math, science, history, and other liberal arts subjects, and one of the long-term goals was to teach children to think for themselves.

This education was to be for all children, regardless of their economic background. All young children were to attend elementary school. Then they would continue with higher academics in a high school called gymnasium which was divided into middle school and high school. Kids could graduate from middle school and attend a vocational school continue, get their 'Abitur', which is a high-school degree equivalent to a college entrance exam, and attend university. Humboldt wanted children and young adults to be as educated as they possibly could be.

Education up until that point had been mainly in the hands of church clergy or other individuals who had no previous training in teaching. Humboldt instituted teacher training so that the quality of instruction across the schools increased remarkably.

This new system was initially helpful for the general population. But before long, a major hiccup occurred. The whole reason this compulsory system was introduced in the first place was political. Prussia was being ravaged by Napoleon. Humboldt to the rescue!

Initially, his education reforms were successfully introduced. But after Napoleon's big defeat at Waterloo, the momentum in Prussian education changed. Several of Humboldt's reforms were reversed, and a new direction in the field of education emerged.

Napoleon's march across Europe had left major scars on Prussian territory. The solution was to create a new goal to promote unity in Prussia: nationalism. This is where the hiccup occurred. While some of Humboldt's curriculum content remained in place (like learning Greek and Latin in gymnasiums), much of it now focused on teaching nationalism, submission to Prussian policies, and basic facts so Prussian kids could enter the work force.

You may already recognize the slight inconsistency here. Humboldt's curriculum was aimed at creating well-rounded, free-thinking citizens. Yet, the new and revised curriculum was now more focused on teaching obedience and submission while still somewhat adhering to Humboldt's philosophies.

So, there was a bit of contradiction in the classroom because free-thinking individuals may or may not be obedient or submissive. And, depending on where in Prussia you lived, the amount of "free-thinking" content of the curriculum ranged from completely absent, to somewhat present, and anything in between.

A dangerous pattern began to emerge: The state started to assume the role of the parents. Historically, this scenario has never had a good ending.

What Happened to Prussia after the Education Reforms?

The idea of free and equal education was a big hit in Prussia. The strategy of teaching nationalism worked, and we all know the outcome: Prussia conquered several surrounding areas, annexed them, and became a European superpower known as the Deutsche Reich. However, two main questions emerge: at what cost? And what happened as a result?

What was the price? Parents abdicated their responsibility of being in charge of their children's education and handed it over to the state, no questions asked. To be clear, there is nothing wrong with hiring a teacher for your children. And again, the question is not whether children should go to school or not, but who chooses that teacher, and who chooses the teaching material.

As far as the consequences were concerned: Prussia's goal was to grow the kingdom. And to fight a war, you need people, preferably young people, willing and ready to serve. That's exactly what was created with this new compulsory school system.

Although the Prussian empire was eventually defeated, the education system remained in place. Hitler was able to use it to accomplish his goal of expanding Germany in the same manner as the Prussian king. He was able to do this with obedient young men and boys who strongly believed in his cause. Education is a powerful tool.

Influence on the US Education System

Throughout the last several centuries, there has always been a heavy exchange in the areas of philosophy and education between Europe and the United States. During the mid-1800s, the United States' education system experienced growth and change.

American statesman and educator from Massachusetts, Horace Mann, traveled to Europe and became infatuated with the Prussian school system, both as a structure, and as a tool for 'nation-building'. Upon his return to Massachusetts, Mann began lobbying for the establishment of the first public schools.

Mann's efforts were successful. Soon, the Prussian school system was adopted by several states in the US. One might argue that only the structure of the school system was adopted, and the content was not. But that is not exactly the case. As Mann refined his views, it became clear that one of his goals was to replace the role of parents with school instruction, just as in Prussia.

This eventually caught on. Over the next decades, public schools sprang up across the US, and parental responsibility to participate in the education of their children slowly began to decline. Home-education was proclaimed ineffective and was even discouraged despite the fact that several of the founding fathers of this nation were self-learned and home-educated.

So, if you look at the root of the public school system of the United States, it has never been very much in alignment with the principles on which this nation was founded. Personal choice and responsibility had always been built into the psyche of the American people. So, taking away the choice of education had a profound impact on future parent involvement. The more time passed, the less parents were involved.

In the late 1800s, home education or the one-room schoolhouse were still more normal on the frontier due to the circumstances of rural life. But the days were counted. Most one-room schoolhouses became history with the arrival of John Dewey's new ideas in the 1920s and 1930s of focusing the curriculum content on preparation for the workforce. Individualized instruction was replaced with same-age classrooms where everyone learned the same thing.

The biggest problem that public schools face nowadays is that cultural norms are re-written. Topics such as history, sexuality, purpose, responsibility, are being re-defined. The battle for this nation's future norms and worldview is taking place in the classrooms. But it is an almost invisible war that is being fought because it is taking place in the minds of our children.

Impact on Homeschooling

For over a century now, the United States has trained public officials to tell parents that they are not qualified to teach their children at home. It looks as if they were successful. During the 1900s, the number of homeschool families was very low.

But there's good news! Despite the regulations, there have always been courageous parents who decided to homeschool, which kept this movement alive. And over the last twenty years, many parents jumped on board because they either saw problems with the school system or simply wanted to take responsibility for their children's education. This led to a tremendous growth in the homeschool movement.

And since the pandemic, it has skyrocketed. Many families tried homeschooling and stuck with it even when schools opened up again because of how well things went. And that is a very exciting reality.

So, if you're planning on homeschooling, there has never been a better time to do this. Curriculum choices and state regulations are in your favor.

I hope all this lays a good foundation for your decision to homeschool. Personally, I find it very useful to know the history of the US public education system as it reminds me of why I am 'giving up' certain services that I am actually paying for.

Some families, like mine, choose an alternative option for education while other families opt to stick with the public school system. And since the law allows for various options, I find it very important that parents know and understand each of these choices so they can make the best decision for their family and children.

With this in mind, consider your options, learn as much about them as you can, keep a list of pros and cons, and mull over them for some time, if needed. Or go with your gut instinct and make a quick decision.

While I sincerely hope that you will choose to homeschool, I completely understand that circumstances and seasons in our lives influence our desires and choices. If you still have questions, which I am sure you will, I will list several great resources in the appendix that should help you find answers.

Always remember that the two most important aspects in the area of education are not the math test or research paper but teaching our children strong character and a deep curiosity. Every subject that was listed in this book should serve the purpose of developing these two qualities in our children.

Having a strong foundation in these areas will serve our kids well for the rest of their lives.

Enjoy every moment you spend with your family and each of your children.

I am cheering you on!

Some Useful Contacts

RESOURCES/ORGANIZATIONS

Focus on the Family
www.focusonthefamily.com
Institute for Excellence in Writing
www.iew.com
Homeschool Legal Defense Association
www.hslda.org
Trail Life, USA: Christian Outdoor Adventure Organization
for Boys **www.traillifeusa.com**
American Heritage Girls: Christian Leadership and
Character Development for Girls
www.amaricanheritagegirls.org
Kindermusik: Music Education through Play for Infants
through Age 7 **www.kindermusik.com**

BLOGS AND PODCASTS

Homeschool Encouragement

Homeschool Better Together with Pam Barnhill
https://community.pambarnhill.com
Called to Homeschool with Meg Thomas
https://called to home.com
Little by Little Homeschool with Leigh Nguyen
https://littleby littlehomeschool.com

Homeschool Made Simple with Carole Joy Seid
  https://homeschoolmadesimple.net

GENERAL PRODUCTIVITY, FAMILY, AND PARENTING
Laura Vanderkam
  www.LauraVanderkam.com
resources on productivity and parenting

FAMILY AND PARENTING
Focus on the Family with Jim Daly
  https://focusonthefamily.com
Focus on the Family Parenting Podcast
  https://podcasts.focusonthefamily.com/show/
  focus-on-parenting.podcast

CHARLOTTE MASON
Simply Charlotte Mason with Sonya Shafer
  https://simplycharlottemason.com
A Delectable Education: Spreading the Feast of the
  Chalotte Mason Method
  https://www.adelectableeducation.com
The New Mason Jar Podcast with Cindy Rollins
  https://thenewmasonjar.com/podcast
Charlotte Mason Volume 6 Read by Rachel O'Neill
  https://charlottemasonvolume6.wordpress.com

NATURE AND OUTDOORS
No Sweat Nature Study with Cindy West
  https://ourjourneywestward.com
Wild and Free with Ainsley Arment
  https://www.bewildandfree.org

LANGUAGE, LITERATURE, AND READING
The Arts of Language Podcast with Andrew Pudewa and
  Julie Walker
  https://iew.com/the-arts-of-language

Read Aloud Revival by Sarah Mackenzie
    https://readaloudrevival.com
The Literary Life Podcast with Angelina Stanford and
    Thomas Banks
    https://www.theliterarylife
BiblioFiles: A Center for Lit Podcast
    https://www.theunlikelyhomeschool.com

SPECIAL EDUCATION

Flamingo Feathers with Beth Corcoran
    https://www.listennotes/flamingo-feathers

Some Useful Books

*means highly recommended.

Adler, Mortimer J. 1972 [1940]. *How to Read a Book: The Classic Guide to Intelligent Reading.* Simon and Schuster.

Aesop. 1998. *The Complete Fables. Penguin.*

Alcott, Louisa May. 2016 [1871]. *Little Men.* Penguin.

———. 2019 [1896]. *Little Women.* Bantam.

Alexander, Lloyd. 2006. *The Book of Three: The Chronicles of Prydain Volume I.* Square Fish.

Allard, Harry. 1985 [1977]. *Miss Nelson Is Missing!* Clarion.

Anderson, C.W. 1992 [1936]. *Billy and Blaze.* Simon and Schuster.

Andreola, Karen. 1998. *A Charlotte Mason Companion: Personal Reflections on the Gentle Art of Learning.* Charlotte Mason Research and Supply.

Andrews, Adam, and Missy Andrews. 2004. *Teaching the Classics: A Socratic Method for Literary Education.* Institute for Excellence in Writing.

Augustine. 2018. *Confessions.* Modern Library.

Austen, Jane.1996 [1815]. *Emma.* Penguin.

———. 2002 [1813]. *Pride and Prejudice.* Penguin.

Bahnsen, Greg. 2020. *By This Standard: The Authority of God's Law Today.* Covenant Media.

Ballantyne, R.M. 2022 [1857]. *The Coral Island: A Tale of the Pacific Ocean.* Legare Street.

* Barnhill, Pam. 2018. *Better Together: Strengthen Your Family, Simplify Your Homeschool, and Savor the Subjects that Matter Most.* Spotted Dog.

Bauer, Susan Wise. 2015 [2003]. *The Well-Educated Mind: A Guide to the Classical Education You Never Had.* Norton.

* ———. 2016 [1999]. *The Well-Trained Mind: A Guide to Classical Education at Home.* Norton.

———. 2019 *Rethinking School: How to Take Charge of Your Child's Education.* Norton.

Baum, L. Frank. 2019 [1900]. *The Wonderful Wizard of Oz.* SeaWolf.

Birdsall, Jeanne. 2005. *The Penderwicks: A Summer Tale of Four Sisters, Two Rabbits, and a Very Interesting Boy.* Yearling.

Blackwood, Gary. 2000 [1998]. *The Shakespeare Stealer*. Puffin.

Brown, Marcia. 1997 [1947]. *Stone Soup*. Simon and Schuster.

Brown, Margaret Wise. 2007 [1947]. *Goodnight, Moon*. HarperCollins.

Bunyan, John. 2003 [1678]. *The Pilgrim's Progress*. Dover

Burnett, Frances Hodgson. 1988 [1911]. *The Secret Garden*. HarperCollins.

Byock, Jesse L., trans. 2000. *The Saga of the Volsungs*. Penguin.

Carle, Eric. 1967. *Brown Bear, Brown Bear, What Do You See?* Holt

———. 1994 [1969] *The Very Hungry Caterpillar*. Philomel.

Carroll, Lewis. 1993 [1865]. *Alice's Adventures in Wonderland*. Dover.

———. 2018 [1871]. *Through the Looking Glass, and what Alice Found There*. SeaWolf.

Chaucer, Geoffrey. 1976. *Canterbury Tales*. Bantam Dual Language.

Cervantes Saavedra, Miguel de. 2003. *Don Quixote*. Penguin.

* Clarkson, Sally. 2003. *The Mission of Motherhood: Touching Your Child's Heart for Eternity*. WaterBrook.

* ———. 2004. *The Ministry of Motherhood: Following Christ's Example in Reaching the Hearts of Our Children*. WaterBrook.

* Cleary, James. 2018. *Atomic Habits: An Easy and Proven Way to Build Good Habits and Break Bad Ones*. Avery.

Collodi, Carlo. 2011 [1883]. *The Adventures of Pinocchio*. Puffin.

Cooper, Elaine. 2004. *When Children Love to Learn: A Practical Application of Charlotte Mason's Philosophy for Today*. Crossway.

DeAngelis, Corey A. 2024. *The Parent Revolution: Rescuing Your Kids from the Radicals Ruining Our Schools*. Center Street.

Defoe, Daniel. 2023 [1719]. *Robinson Crusoe*. Sky.

DiCamillo, Kate. 2009. *Mercy Watson to the Rescue*. Candlewick.

Dickens, Charles. 2023 [1859]. *A Tale of Two Cities*. Viking.

Dumas, Alexandre. 1982. *The Three Musketeers*. Penguin.

Evers, Williamson M., ed.1998. *What's Gone Wrong in American Classrooms*. Hoover Institution Press.

Farris, Michael. 2006. *Constitutional Law for Enlightened Citizens*. Homeschool Legal Defense Association.

———. 2014. *Constitutional Literacy: Workbook to the 25-Part DVD Series*. Apologia Educational Ministries.

———. 2015. *History of Religious Liberty: From Tyndale to Madison*. Master Books.

Fernando, Rosie, ed. 2021. *Hippocratic Oath: An Illustrated Greek-English Reader's Edition*. GlossaHouse.

Flesch, Rudolf. 1986 [1955]. *Why Johnny Can't Read: And What You Can Do about It*. Morrow.

Foster, Genevieve. 1996 [1947]. *Augustus Caesar's World: A Story of Ideas and Events from B.C. 44 to 14 A.D.* Beautiful Feet.

Freeman, Don. 1968. *Corduroy*. Viking.

Fujikawa, Gyo. 2007. *A Child's Book of Poems*. Union Square Kids.

Glaser, Karina Yan. 2018. *The Vanderbeekers of 141st Street*. Houghton Mifflin.

* Gordon, Meghan Cox. 2020. *The Enchanted Hour: The Miraculous Power of Reading Aloud in the Age of Distraction*. Harper.

Green, Roger Lancelyn. 2010. *The Adventures of Robin Hood*. Puffin.
———. 2011. *Tales of Ancient Egypt*. Puffin.
* Hakim, Joy. 2007. *A History of US*. Ten volumes. Oxford University Press.
Hamilton, Alexander, James Madison, and John Jay. 2014. *The Federalist Papers*. Dover.
Hayek, F.A. 2001 [1944]. *The Road to Serfdom*. Routledge.
Henderson, Harold. 2006. *Let's Kill Dick and Jane: How the Open Court Publishing Company Fought the Culture of American Education*. St. Augustine's Press.
Herodotus. 2009. *The Landmark Herodotus: The Histories*. Anchor.
* Hicks, David V. 2024 [1999]. *Norms and Nobility: A Treatise on Education*. Rowman and Littlefield.
Hoban, Russell. 2008 [1964]. *Bread and Jam for Frances*. HarperCollins.
Hobar, Linda Lacour. 2019. *The Mystery of History*. Four volumes. Bright Ideas.
Hunt, Gladys. 1989. *Honey for a Child's Heart: The Imaginative Use of Books in Family Life*. Zondervan.
Hutton, John. 2016. *ADH-Me!* Blue Manatee.
Homer. 2006. *The Odyssey*. Penguin
Kerr, Judith. 2009 [1971]. *When Hitler Stole Pink Rabbit*. Puffin.
Kline, Morris. 1973. *Why Johnny Can't Add: The Failure of the New Math*. St. Martin's.
Lamb, Charles, and Mary Lamb. 1994. *Tales from Shakespeare*. Wordsworth.
Lang, Andrew. 2019. *The Blue Fairy Book: Fairy Books of Many Colors Volume I*. Racehorse.
Levison, Catherine. 2000. *A Charlotte Mason Education: A Homeschooling How-to Manual*. Champion.
Levitin, Daniel J. 2007 [2006]. *This Is Your Brain on Music: The Science of Human Obsession*. Plume.
Lewis, C.S. 2004 [1950]. *The Lion, the Witch, and the Wardrobe*. First volume in *The Chronicles of Narnia*. HarperCollins.
Lindsay, James. 2022. *The Marxification of Education: Paula Freire's Critical Marxism and the Theft of Education*. Lindsay.
Lobel, Arnold. 2020. *Frog and Toad Storybook Favorites*. HarperCollins.
Ludwig, Ken. 2014. *How to Teach Your Children Shakespeare*. Crown.
Macaulay, Jake, and Ricki Pepin. 2019. *Civics and the Constitution: An American View of Law, Liberty, and Government*. Master Books.
Macaulay, Susan Schaeffer. 2022. *For the Children's Sake: Foundations of Education for the Home and School*. Crossway.
* Mackenzie, Sarah. 2015. *Teaching from Rest: A Homeschooler's Guide to Unshakable Peace*. Classical Academic.
Marx, Karl H., and Friedrich Engels. 1987 [1848]. *The Communist Manifesto*. Pathfinder.
Mason, Charlotte. 2017. *A Philosophy of Education*. Living Book.
* ———. 2023 [1925]. *A Philosophy of Education Volume 6*. Many editions.
McClay, Wilfred M. 2020. *Land of Hope: An Invitation to the Great American Story*. Encounter.
McCloskey, Robert. 1976 [1948]. *Blueberries for Sal*. Viking.

McDonald, Kerry. 2019. *Unschooled: Raising Curious, Well-Educated Children Outside the Conventional Classroom*. Chicago Review.

McGraw, Eloise Jarvis. 1986. *The Golden Goblet*. Viking.

* McKeon, Greg. 2020. *Essentialism: The Disciplined Pursuit of Less*. Crown Currency.

Miller, Olive Beaupré, ed. 1951 [1920]. *My Book House, Volumes 1–12 and Parents' Guide*. United Educators.

Milne, A.A. 1996 [1926]. *The Complete Tales of Winnie-the-Pooh*. Dutton.

Milton, John. 2003. *Paradise Lost*. Penguin.

Minarik, Else Homelund. 2018. *Little Bear*. HarperCollins.

Montgomery, L.M. 2018 [1908]. *Anne of Green Gables*. Wordsworth.

Moody, Ralph. 1991 [1950]. *Little Britches: Father and I Were Ranchers*. Bison.

Nance, James B., and Douglas J. Wilson. 2006. *Introductory Logic: For Christian and Home Schools*. Canon.

———. 2014. *Intermediate Logic: Mastering Propositional Arguments*. Canon.

Nesbit, Edith. 2015 [1900]. *The Children's Shakespeare*. Leopold Classic.

Notgrass, Ray. 2016. *Exploring Economics* by Ray. Notgrass Company.

———. 2016. *Exploring Government*. Notgrass Company.

Orwell, George. 1993 [1945]. *Animal Farm*. Everyman's Library.

Osborne, Mary Pope. 1991. *American Tall Tales*. Knopf.

———. 1992. *Dinosaurs before Dark: Magic Treehouse No. 1*. Random House.

Peterson, Andrew. 2023 [2008]. *On the Edge of the Dark Sea of Darkness: The Wingfeather Saga Book I*. Random House.

Phillips, Wanda C. 2007. *Easy Grammar*. Easy Grammar Systems.

Piper, Watty. 2001 [1930]. *The Little Engine that Could*. Grosset and Dunlap.

Plutarch. 2010. *Lives of the Noble Grecians and Romans*. Benediction Classics.

Prelutsky, Jack. 1983. *The Random House Book of Poetry*. Random House.

Pudewa, Andrew. 2018. *However Imperfectly*. With DVD. Institute for Excellence in Writing.

Reimer, Luetta. 1994. *Mathematicians Are People Too: Stories from the Lives of Great Mathematicians*. Dale Seymour.

Rey, H.A. 1973. *Curious George*. Clarion.

Rylant, Cynthia. 1994. *Mr. Putter and Tabby Pour the Tea*. Clarion.

———. 1996. *Henry and Mudge: The First Book*. Simon Spotlight.

———. 2016. *Annie and Snowball Collector's Set!* Simon Spotlight.

———. 2019. *Poppleton: An Acorn Book (Poppleton 1)*. Simon Spotlight.

* Sayers, Dorothy L. 2017. *The Lost Tools of Learning: Symposium on Education*. CrossReach.

Seuss, Dr. 1957. *The Cat in the Hat*. Random House.

———. 1960. *Green Eggs and Ham*. Random House.

Sewell, Anna. 2018 [1877]. *Black Beauty*. Wordsworth.

* Schafer, Sonya. 2007. *Laying down the Rails: A Charlotte Mason Habits Handbook*. Simply Charlotte Mason.

———. 2008. *Planning Your Charlotte Mason Education*. Simply Charlotte Mason.

———. 2009. *Simply Charlotte Mason Presents the Early Years: A Charlotte Mason Preschool Handbook*. Simply Charlotte Mason.

Shakespeare, William. 2005. *The Oxford Shakespeare: The Complete Works.* Oxford University Press.

Shelley, Mary. 2006 [1818]. *Frankenstein: Or, the Modern Prometheus.* Penguin.

Silverstein, Shel. 2014. *Where the Sidewalk Ends: Poems and Drawings.* HarperCollins.

Slobodkina, Esphyr. 1987. *Caps for Sale: A Tale of a Peddler, Some Monkeys, and Their Monkey Business.* Harper Collins.

Smith, S.D. 2014. *The Green Ember.* Story Warren.

Sophocles. 2000. *The Three Theban Plays.* Penguin.

Speare, Elizabeth George. 1997. *The Bronze Bow.* Clarion.

Sproul, R.C. 1992. *A Blueprint for Thinking: Reforming the Christian Worldview.* Ligonier Ministries.

———. 1998. *Essential Truths of the Christian Faith.* Tyndale Elevate.

———. 2018. *Defending Your Faith: An Introduction to Apologetics.* Crossway.

Spyri, Johanna. 2024 [1922]. *Heidi.* Sky.

Stanley, Diane, and Peter Vennema. 1988. *Bard of Avon: The Story of William Shakespeare.* Morrow.

Steig, William. 2010. *Doctor De Soto.* Farrar, Straus, Giroux.

Stevenson, Robert Louis. 2003. *The Collected Poems of Robert Louis Stevenson.* Edinburgh University Press.

Sutcliff, Rosemary. 2005. *Black Ships Before Troy: The Story of the Iliad.* Laurel Leaf.

———. 2005. *The Wanderings of Odysseus: The Story of The Odyssey.* Laurel Leaf.

———. 2010. *The Eagle of the Ninth Chronicles.* Oxford University Press.

Swanson, Kevin. 2015. *Worldviews in Conflict.* Master Books.

Swift, Jonathan. 2010 [1726]. *Gulliver's Travels.* Ignatius.

Thinknetic. 2023. *How to Argue with Anyone: Expand the Boundaries of Your Thinking through Resolving Conflicts.* Thinknetic

Tolkien, J.R.R. 2012 [1937]. *The Hobbit: Or, There and Back Again.* Mariner.

———. *The Lord of the Rings: 50th Anniversary One-Volume Edition.* Mariner.

Tocqueville, Alexis de. 2003. *Democracy in America and Two Essays on America.* Penguin.

Turner, Juliette. 2012. *Our Constitution Rocks.* Zonderkidz.

* Vanderkam, Laura. 2020. *Tranquility by Tuesday: Nine Ways to Calm the Chaos and Make Time for What Matters.* Portfolio.

Warner, Gertrude Chandler. 1989. *Boxcar Children.* Random House.

Warren, Luke. 2021. *The Art of Debating: Seven Crucial Techniques of Influence and Persuasion—Essential for Millennials and Generation Z.* Warren.

Watson, Jean. 2014. *Corrie ten Boom: The Watchmaker's Daughter.* CF4 Kids.

Wilcox, Brad. 2024. *Get Married: Why Americans Must Defy the Elites, Forge Strong Families, and Save Civilization.* Broadside.

Wilder, Laura Ingalls. 2008 [1935]. *The Little House on the Prairie.* HarperCollins.

———. 2002. *Mystery of the Roman Ransom.* Clarion.

Wilson, Melanie. 2016. *Grammar Galaxy: Mission Manual.* Fun to Learn.

Winterfeld, Henry. 2002. *Detectives in Togas.* Clarion.

Winthrop, Elizabeth. 1994 [1985]. *The Castle in the Attic*. Yearling.
———. 1994 [1993]. *The Battle for the Castle*. Yearling.
Wright, Blanche Fisher. 2014 [1916]. *The Real Mother Goose*. Scholastic.
Wyss, Johann David. 2024. *The Swiss Family Robinson*. Sky.

Thanks

I want to thank my amazing husband who always cheered me on and encouraged me to continue to homeschool our children, even when I felt like quitting. Without his constant support, our homeschool journey wouldn't have lasted very long, and I would have never endeavored to write this book. I also want to thank my children James, Timothy, Emilie, and Alayna for their patience with me as their mom and teacher, and the enthusiasm with which they interacted with one another and made homeschool life new and adventurous every day. A big thank-you goes also to Blouke Carus who inspired me with his insatiable curiosity and passion for education. And of course, thank you to the Carus Books editor David Ramsay Steele for hanging in there with me. Finally, I want to thank and praise my God for His blessings and guidance as our family grew and learned together. Soli doe gloria!

Index